AFRICAN AMERICANS IN SPORT

contemporary themes

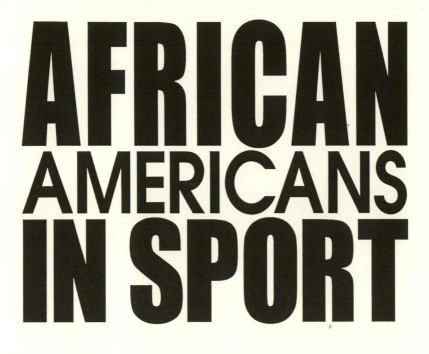

AFRICAN AMERICANS IN SPORT

edited by

Gary A. Sailes

Transaction Publishers
New Brunswick (U.S.A.) and London (U.K.)

Library of Congress Catalog Number: 98-10468
ISBN: 0-7658-0440-9
Printed in the United States of America

Library of Congress Cataloging-in-Publication Data

African Americans in sport : contemporary themes / edited by Gary A. Sailes.

    p. cm.
   ISBN 0-7658-0440-9 (pbk. : alk. paper)
   1. Afro-American athletes. 2. Afro-American athletes—Social conditions. 3. Sports—Social aspects—United States. I. Sailes, Gary Alan.
GV583.A56   1998
796'.089'96073—dc21   98-10468
                                  CIP

Contents

Sources

Ch. 1: Reprinted with permission from the editor of *Sociological Focus*. Harris, Othello, 1997, "The Role of Sport in the Black Community," *Sociological Focus*, 30:4, pp. 311–320.

Ch. 2: Book chapter reprinted by permission from Richard Majors, 1990, "Cool Pose: Black Masculinity & Sports" in *Sport, Men & Gender Order*, edited by Michael Messner and Don Sabo, (Champaign, IL: Human Kinetics), pp. 109–114.

Ch. 3: Sailes, Gary, 1997, "Betting Against the Odds: An Overview of Black Sports Participation," *Journal of African American Men*, 2:2/3, pp. 11–22.

Ch. 6: Reprinted with permission from the editor of *Sociological Focus*. Dufur, Mikaela, 1997, "Being Like Mike: Representations of Athletes in Advertising, 1985–1994," *Sociological Focus*, 30:4, pp. 345–356.

Ch. 7: Hunter, David, 1997, "Race and Athletic Performance: A Physiological Review," *Journal of African American Men*, 2:2/3, pp. 23–38.

Ch. 8: Harpalani, Vinay, 1997, "The Athletic Dominance of African Americans: Is There a Genetic Basis?" *Journal of African American Men*, 2:2/3, pp. 39–56.

Ch. 9: Sailes, Gary, 1996, "An Examination of Basketball Performance Orientations Among African American Males," *Journal of African American Men*, 1:4, pp. 37–46.

Ch. 10: Granted with permission from Nelson-Hall Publishers. Sailes, Gary, 1994, "The Case Against NCAA Proposition 48," in *The American Black Male* by Richard Majors and Jacob Gordon, (Eds.), Chicago: Nelson-Hall Publishers, pp. 94–104.

Ch. 11: Andrews, Vernon, 1997, "African American Player Codes on Celebration, Taunting and Sportsmanlike Conduct," *Journal of African American Men*, 2:2/3, pp. 57–92.

Ch. 12: From G. Sailes, 1998, "The African American Athlete: Social Myths and Stereotypes" in D.D. Brooks and R.C. Althouse, (Eds.), *Racism in College Athletics: The African American Athlete's Experience*. Morgantown, W.V.: Fitness Information Technology, Inc.

Ch. 13: Smith, Earl & Harrison, Keith, 1997, "Stacking in Major League Baseball," *Journal of African American Men*, 2:2/3, pp. 113–130.

Ch. 14: Brooks, D., Althouse, R., & Tucker, D., 1997, "African American Male Head Coaches: In the 'Red Zone,' But Can They Score?" *Journal of African American Men*, 2:2/3, pp. 93–112.

Ch. 15: Harris, Othello, 1997, "Race, Sport & Future Orientation" *Journal of African American Men*, 2:2/3, pp. 131–150.

Ch. 16: Book chapter reprinted with permission from the publisher. Sailes, Gary, 1996, "A Comparison of Professional Sports Career Aspirations Among College Athletes," *Academic Athletic Journal*, 11:2, pp. 20–28.

Introduction

The research on African American athletes generally focuses on negative and socially controversial themes, such as racism, prejudice, discrimination, and exploitation. Moreover, there is no shortage of studies
that contrast African American and Caucasian athletes on a number of
variables that support prevailing elitist stereotypes and which denigrate
African American athletes. For example, many comparative studies
focus on graduation rates, grade point averages, athletic performance,
physiology, and psychological attitudes. Those comparisons have consistently disclosed differences which generally were negative portrayals of the African American athlete. Few studies investigate the rich
diversity and sociocultural complexities that exist within the sports
subculture in the African American community. The assumption that
sport and sport participation have a single, relatively unchanging meaning among African Americans establishes a dangerous precedent leading to stereotypes that reproduce problematic forms of race relations in
sport and in American culture.

Research and analysis based on a one-dimensional conception of
African American sports experiences seriously distort the reality of those
experiences. It is crucial to develop a more comprehensive cultural
approach when investigating African American involvement in competitive sports. It cannot be argued that racism, prejudice, discrimination, and exploitation are inherent institutions in a society that is racially
and culturally diverse and they should be investigated. However, there
are also intrinsic cultural paradigms that are evident and which portray
a more informative and interesting narrative regarding African American athletes. Those cultural paradigms should be investigated just as
extensively as the prevailing line of inquiry. The purpose of this collection of articles is to immerse the reader into the complex and diverse
social worlds within which African American experiences give meaning to sport and how sports participation impacts their lives.

A major premise that permeates many of the current investigations
about race in sport is the assumption that, collectively, African Ameri-

cans view sport from the same perspective. This built-in bias ignores many interesting social and cultural differences which exist among African Americans, and African American athletes in particular. An investigation of the sociology of poverty and Afro-American studies literature clearly establishes that impoverished African Americans have distinct value orientations that shape their lives when compared to working-, middle-, and upper-class African Americans. This premise is the central theme in William Wilson's book *The Declining Significance of Race* and Andrew Hacker's book *Two Nations*. It appears plausible to surmise that with distinct socioeconomically based value systems, their sports socialization and value orientations about sport might also be distinct. However, the sport sociology literature offers no contrasts in the socialization or value orientations of African American athletes emanating from different socioeconomic backgrounds.

My current research strongly suggests that different sports value orientations and socialization patterns do exist among African American athletes from different socioeconomic backgrounds. For example, working-, middle-, and upper-class African American athletes had traditional values and backgrounds. They came from two-parent homes, had higher expectations regarding their chances of playing professional sport, and participated in a greater variety of high school sports than their less affluent counterparts. The more affluent African American athletes also had stronger educational skills demonstrated by higher grade point averages and standardized test scores coming out of high school, were less likely to be partial qualifiers regarding NCAA (National Collegiate Athletic Association) initial academic eligibility requirements, graduated from integrated high schools, and lived in either integrated or predominately black middle-class neighborhoods. There also appeared to be a distinction between the two groups that was apparent through dress, diction, personal mannerisms, and ability to adjust to and become entrenched in the predominantly white college campus environment. Surprisingly, less affluent African American athletes viewed college sports as an opportunity to obtain an education. Conversely, more affluent African American athletes viewed college sports as an opportunity to improve their skills and exposure to further their sport career at the professional level. It is widely believed that less affluent African American college athletes had the highest aspiration to play professional sport when in actuality, it was middle- and upper-class African American college athletes who do. Finally, the NCAA disclosed that the majority of African American athletes participating in college sports on athletic scholarships came from middle-class backgrounds and not from poverty stricken inner-city ghettoes as is widely believed.

Sport participation is very much a part of African American male socialization. However, sport has taken on particular importance in America's poorer African American neighborhoods. There exists a valued predisposition in many less affluent African American males to place an overemphasis on successful participation in organized sport. Many less affluent African American youth view sport as the only opportunity to social respect and material success, especially when doors to other opportunities appear to be closed. College recruiters routinely believe that the best athletes come from poorer families. It is felt they work harder because sport is their only shot out of poverty.

Sport organizations routinely use sports in poorer African American neighborhoods as a vehicle to keep kids out of trouble. Police Athletic Leagues, Midnight Basketball Leagues, Boys Clubs, Summer Sports Leagues, YMCAs, and other social organizations have traditionally used sport to attract African American youth to provide social, educational, and cultural opportunities and experiences. My program, the Indianapolis Sport and Education Consortium, is such an organization.

Distinct cultural norms have emerged in America's poorer black neighborhoods that establish "rites of passage" through sport for African American males. This cultural norm places an importance on sport participation because it leads to social acceptance, respect, and status. Consequently, fundamental norms regulate participation and become apparent in the athlete's attitude, behavior, dress, and sport participation patterns. In his book *The City Game*, author Peter Axthelm illustrates the unwritten norms and dress codes for basketball players competing at inner-city public parks. In his autobiography *A Guide to Basketball and Cool*, former New York Knicks All-Pro guard Walt Frazier clearly depicts the importance of image and style in inner-city basketball. For example, during pick-up basketball games at city gymnasiums or parks, college basketball players have more status than high school or non-school players. Wearing your school's practice jersey, keeping your basketball shoes clean, beating your man to the basket, and winning were also important status symbols.

In his book *Elevating the Game: Black Men and Basketball*, Nelson George illustrates how the game of basketball has changed since African Americans began to dominate it. The slowed down, passing and shooting oriented game of the past was replaced by speed, quickness, fancy moves, impressive dribbling, powerful dunks, trash talking, and chest bumping. Julius "Dr. J" Erving was quoted in an NBC special titled "The Black Athlete: Fact or Fiction" as saying, "Style counts for the black athlete!"

Being poor limits access to intercollegiate sports. In their book *The Case Against the SAT*, Trusheim and Crouse found that a relationship existed between family income and composite SAT scores. Specifically, SAT scores increased by 200 points with an increase of $18,000 in family income. When the NCAA imposed eligibility rules based on minimum scores on standardized tests (SAT=700 ACT=15), they also imposed institutional barriers against African American athletes coming from impoverished backgrounds. When the rule was enforced in 1986, African Americans averaged 706 on the SAT and 13.7 on the ACT according to the Educational Testing Service. In 1990, the NCAA reported that 91% of the basketball Proposition 48 casualties were African American and the number was approximately 65% for football. I wonder what percentage of those Proposition 48 casualties came from impoverished backgrounds? No one seems to know or care.

Being poor also limits one's access to individual sports. The United States Tennis Association reported recently that the average tennis family spends approximately $25,000 to $30,000 annually to maintain a junior tennis player's national ranking. A national ranking is necessary to win a scholarship to play tennis at a major college. This same figure remained constant in maintaining an athlete's involvement in national or international competition in swimming, diving, ice skating, and gymnastics. With the average salaries of African Americans at approximately $18,500, approximately half that of white Americans, it is no wonder they are absent from national competition in the individual sports. Most African American tennis champions rely on the philanthropy of the American Tennis Association and private donations to compete at the national level in tennis. Tennis greats Althea Gibson and Arthur Ashe relied heavily on the support of Dr. Walter Johnson and college scholarships to achieve their tennis success. Both of these champions went on to become top tennis players in the world, each reaching a ranking of #1. Professional tennis players Venus and Serena Williams were sponsored by Reebok during their early development. Sadly, the cost of competing at the top level in individual sports like golf and tennis prevent most African Americans from participation.

Because of their limited income, African Americans rely heavily on public facilities to recreate and to participate in organized sports. Limited financial resources restrict their involvement in individual sports that are taught almost exclusively at private clubs that require costly memberships and private lessons. Most public facilities offer inexpensive or free programs centered around team sports that are both popular and available to local residents. Consequently, African American participation in team sports programs is extensive at the high school, college, and professional levels. Socioeconomic status plays a significant role in the sport participation of less affluent African Americans by restricting their access to individual sports and channeling them into team sports.

These are just some examples of the complex diversity and sociocultural depth of the sport experiences of African American athletes. These types of experiences are found in the biographies of famous athletes but rarely in the scientific literature. I feel that the social class circumstances, families, peers, views of the world, the sense of possibility and the personal connection and commitment to the sport that exist in the African American community are worthy of scientific inquiry. Past research and analysis has ignored the heart of the sport experiences of African Americans. This book is designed to put the heart back into the discussion on the totality of the African American sports experience.

The reader will notice that this anthology did not include African American women. I do not apologize for my omission for the very reason that my research the past fifteen years focused exclusively on the sport socialization of African American males. I consider myself a scholar of African American Male studies, a line of scholarly inquiry established in 1991 by noted Afro-psychologist and author/scholar Richard Majors. My omission was intentional in that this book focused on my personal research interests, the African American male in sports. It was not the intent of my omission to diminish the importance, significance, or contributions of African American women to American sport. In fact, I respect and read with great interest scholarly works on African American women and encourage further interest and scholarly inquiry in that area of investigation.

What follows are essays from noted scholars who write about the different components of the experience of African American male athletes. These scholars were selected based on their notoriety and expertise in their specific academic areas. The essays contained in this anthology represent a collection of topics I feel give a diverse overview and summary representation of the issues which impact on the African

American athlete. In so far that media depictions of African American athletes are not factual representations, it is the intent of this collection of essays to give a more accurate representative and diverse portrayal of the experiences of African American athletes. This anthology is far from complete and is only the first of what I hope will be other anthologies. It is my intent to stimulate dialogue, discussion, and criticism.

I

African American
Culture and Sport

1

The Role of Sport in the Black Community

Othello Harris

> *"Athletics is to the Black community what technology is to the Japanese and what oil is to the Arabs. We're allowing that commodity to be exploited.... We really need to turn it around...if those schools cannot do for us what we need done, i.e., provide an education for the next generation, then we should be looking to steer clear of those institutions."*
> —Charles Farrell, Director, Rainbow Coalition for Fairness in Athletics

Farrell's quote, above, reveals what many believe about sport and the black community: that the athletic prowess of young black males is a precious commodity to the black community. No longer ignored by collegiate athletic programs, sports franchises, fans and the media, African Americans have come to define certain sports and/or sports positions. For example, the image one typically gets when listening to a sportscaster describe a game battle between a wide receiver and a cornerback is of black contenders engaged in a contest of skill. Black *is* the cornerback, receiver, basketball all-star, boxer and all-around athlete. The black athlete has arrived, conquered many challenges and displaced many whites on the playing field.

Therefore, sport, we are told by some, has opened its doors to African Americans, offering untold direct and indirect opportunities for social mobility.[1] Farrell, cited above, while acknowledging the exploitation that occurs in many college programs, appears to believe that college sport can and should provide a gateway to a better life for African Americans. He is like many observers, coaches and former players, at least in his belief about what sport could provide. Yet, others like Edwards (1973, 1979), Coakley (1994), Eitzen and Sage (1993), Curry and Jiobu (1984) and Leonard (1997) dismiss the idea that sport is an easy route to social mobility for African Americans. What is the role of sport in the black community?

To understand the meaning of sport to the black community this paper examines some of the crucial athletic events in American sport and their impact on the black community. It begins with Jack Johnson at the turn of the century.

A Black Champion

In 1908 Jack Johnson defeated Canadian Tommy Burns to become the first black heavyweight champion of the world. But Burns was a lightly regarded champion: He had won the title from the dull Marvin Hart, who occupied the title after Jim Jeffries retired and named Hart one of the contenders for his crown (Roberts, 1983). Johnson, perhaps realizing that there was little interest in boxing at the time, seized the opportunity to position himself for a match with the newly crowned champion. He followed Burns to England and Australia, seeking what he believed to be his rightful place in the sport of boxing—as holder of the most prestigious title in the sportsworld—the heavyweight champion.

Johnson was not the first African American to fight for the heavyweight title; that honor goes to Tom Molineaux, a former slave from Virginia who won his freedom as a result of defeating another slave in a match that earned his slave owner $100,000.00 (Harris, in press). Molineaux bolted from America to England where he would, eventually, meet the white heavyweight champion, Tom Cribb, in "the battle of the century" nearly 100 years before Johnson fought a white champion for the title. In a controversial match, Molineaux lost to Cribb.

Despite Molineaux's unsuccessful bid for the belt, the fact that he and a few other slaves received special privileges and were, in rare cases, manumitted undoubtedly led some to proclaim sport's ability to elevate the status of African Americans. However, Frederick Douglass, himself a former slave, proclaimed, boxing and wrestling, drinking and other merriments during holiday periods were the most effective means slaveholders had for keeping down insurrection" (quoted in Sammons, 1988, pp. 31–32). For him, sport was a means of social control used by planters, not a way to a better life for America's black population. Thus, even before Johnson and the black boxing champions who preceded him (e.g., Dixon, Walcott and Gans) took the stage, the discussion about the role of sport in the black community had begun.[2] Johnson's accomplishments would accelerate the debate. According to Sammons:

> Since prizefighting has been characterized by some as a true test of skill, courage, intelligence, and manhood, boxing champions have traditionally stood as symbols of national and racial superiority. Consequently, black challengers to white American champions have been perceived as threats to white and national superiority. (1988, p. 31)

Johnson as champion was, therefore, a threat to social order and whites' beliefs about their black brethren. His defeat of Burns so outraged some whites that they began to search for a "Great White Hope." When Great White Hope Tournaments yielded no suitable prospects for returning the crown to white America (Roberts, 1983), Jim Jeffries, the former champ who had retired undefeated, was coaxed out of retirement to "wipe the Golden smile" from Johnson's face (London, 1992). In a fight fraught with implications for social Darwinism and racial superiority, Johnson easily defeated the white hope, setting off nationwide celebrations in black America. The fight also resulted in riots across America, principally whites attacking African Americans (Gilmore, 1973, 1975).

More important to this paper are perceptions, then, about sport and the elevation of people physically similar to the new heavyweight champion. For he had knocked down an important wall of segregation; he had defeated notions of black athletic inferiority (at least as far as boxing was concerned); he had challenged the widely held belief that, amazing as it seems now, African Americans *lacked* the physical wherewithal to compete with whites.

This caused whites to anguish about Johnson's impact on the black community as well as what his accomplishment would mean to businesses that employed African Americans. At least one cotton-buying firm was concerned that there would be a shortage of field laborers after Jack Johnson won the heavyweight title because African Americans would, in large numbers, enter the field of boxing (Roberts, 1983). Of course, boxing could no more offer opportunities to the masses of African American males than other sports can now offer positions to the black populace. Nevertheless, there was concern about a shift in the employment and aspirations of black workers.

On the other hand, Booker T. Washington, while castigating Johnson for public behaviors that Washington found to be injurious to African Americans,[3] seemed also to be circumspect about sport's ability to uplift his people when he stated that "all men should be educated along mental and spiritual lines in connection with their physical education. A man with muscle minus brains is a useless creature" (quoted in Gilmore, 1973, p. 25). Washington did not view sport as the vehicle that would take African Americans from subordinate to equal status with whites. And some whites, threatened by the prospect of blacks challenging whites on their terms in physical feats, thought it wise to counsel blacks against both seeking equality (upward mobility) through sport and behaving like Johnson. For example, Mrs. James Crawford, vice-president of the California Women's Club, who declared herself a friend of the black race, offered that:

> the Negroes...are to some extent a childlike race, needing guidance, schooling and encouragement. We deny them this by encouraging them to believe that they have gained anything by having one of their race as a champion fighter. Race riots are inevitable, when we, a superior people, allow these people to be deluded and degraded by such false ideals. (Roberts, p. 112)

There were, during Johnson's reign, disparate beliefs about the role of sport in the black community. Interestingly, much of the opposition to any new found hope for prestige through sport for African Americans came from whites. This would change when new black superstars, more to their liking, took center stage.

Black Athletic Heroes to Americans

Unlike Jack Johnson, who was despised by whites, especially for his behavior towards them (i.e., he behaved as if he were whites' equal), Joe Louis and Jesse Owens were, to some extent, loved by many white Americans. And they should have been. They were both careful to follow whites' prescription for black behavior; that is, they were compliant and obsequious and showed the proper amount of deference in the presence of whites. But they also represented American might and superiority. Whereas Johnson was seen as a hero to some segments of black America, Louis and Owens became the first black athletic heroes to white America.

Owens was in the spotlight for a relatively short period of time. His claim to fame was his outstanding 4-gold-medal-performance at the

1936 Olympics, which was supposed to "check" Hitler's arrogance about his "master race." Louis's tenure was much longer, as he held the heavyweight title for 12 years. He, too, was catapulted to prominence and accepted by much of white America largely as a result of his encounter with Nazism. Even now, he is perhaps more renowned for his defeat of the German, Max Schmeling, than for winning the heavyweight title from James Braddock.

The effect of Louis's and Owens's accomplishments was to heighten the discussion about what sport had done, or could do, for African Americans. Sport, it was argued, might be the first rung on the social ladder for blacks. Louis and Owens were credited with opening doors for others in and apart from sport. If those who followed behaved like them, African Americans were told, sport and other institutions would be more accepting of black presence. For example, the Governor of Michigan took it upon himself to write Louis and proclaim:

> Destiny seems to have pointed you for a high rank in pugilism. Your ability to overpower others by skill and physical force is something of which you may be proud....You'll have world prominence and money. They will mean little, Joe, if you do not use them as God intended that gifts of Nature should be used....Your race, at times in the past, has been misrepresented by others who thought they had reached the heights....The qualities which may soon make you a world champion should call to the attention of people the world over, that the good in you can also be found in others of your race....So Joe, you may soon have on your strong hands the job of representative-at-large of your people. (quoted in Mead 1985, pp. 55–56)

Others, especially whites, from all sorts of occupations found it necessary to counsel Louis and Owens about the impact of their public behavior. They were groomed to favorably represent African Americans. Today, countless prominent African Americans such as John Thompson, Andrew Young, Vernon Jordan and Jesse Jackson often cite Louis's and/ or Owens's accomplishments for catalyzing their own achievement. Many felt their situations would improve or decline as a result of Owens's, or especially Louis's, performance. Maya Angelou wrote:

> If Joe lost we were back in slavery and beyond help. It would all be true, the accusations that we were lower types of human beings. Only a little higher than apes. True that we were stupid and ugly and lazy and dirty and, unlucky and worst of all, that God Himself hated us and ordained us to be hewers of wood and drawers of water, forever and ever, world without end. (1970)

It is ironic that Louis and Owens are both credited with opening the doors to sport and other institutions for African Americans, improving race relations (even black newspapers said Owens was "good for the race"), and demonstrating the path from rags to riches for blacks (through sport), yet neither retired with substantial wealth or income and both had trouble with the IRS. Both were success stories without the usual spoils of success. Still, they attained everlasting, if not universal, fame, heretofore unknown to African Americans. The message from their era seemed to be "look at what Joe and Jesse have done for race relations in America, and look at what sport has done for them" (and by extension, "Negroes"). Whites and African Americans, it seemed, felt that American society and, in particular, the sportsworld were more open to African Americans. Louis and Owens had paved the way for black athletes in other sports. Jackie Robinson would pick up where they left off.

Jackie Robinson: Breaking the Color Barrier in Team Sports

Joe Louis and Jesse Owens changed whiles' perceptions about black presence in individual sports, but professional (and most college) team sports remained segregated. Numerous reasons were given for this phenomenon, including that African Americans lacked the interest, talent and training to compete alongside whites. But the absence of black ballplayers in team sports had more to do with whiles' reluctance to socially interact with African Americans—or to rub elbows with blacks—than to any of the above reasons. It was feared that many whites—players, fans, managers, owners, etc.—would take offense at blacks acting as whites' peers in so public an institution as sport. Also, if blacks were included in sport, what would happen to whites' protected status in other areas?

Branch Rickey, the Brooklyn Dodger general manager who presided over baseball's desegregation, worried about whites' reaction to his plan to recruit black ballplayers. Rickey wanted to be very sure to recruit not necessarily the best black ballplayer but one who would be tough and courageous and able to allay white fears about the threatening nature of novel interracial interactions. During their first meeting Rickey said to Robinson:

> We can't fight our way through this, Robinson. We've got no army. There's virtually nobody on our side. No owners, no umpires, very few newspapermen. And I'm afraid that many fans will be hostile. We'll be in a tough position. We can win only if we can convince the world that I'm doing this because you're a great ballplayer and a fine gentleman. [Robinson asked] Mr. Rickey, are you looking for a Negro who is afraid to fight back? Rickey replied, I'm looking for a ballplayer with guts enough not to fight back. (quoted in Levine, 1989, pp. 131–132)

While Robinson was not the first African American to play on a professional sport team with and against whites, his accomplishment is, nonetheless, a significant one. He was the first African American to play in "professional baseball" (i.e., white major league baseball) in the twentieth century. Finally, African Americans had reintegrated the most sacred of American athletic institutions—baseball. Soon the belief in white athletic superiority would be crushed and replaced with a belief in African Americans' "natural athletic advantages." With this belief came a shift in the meaning of sport for the black community. More and more Americans believed that sports could be a way to improve African Americans' social status.

Sociologist Hubert Blalock offers an example. In an article which purports to describe how and why professional baseball is an occupation which is remarkably free of racial discrimination," Blalock asserted that:

> Historically, most American minorities have entered the labor force at or very near the bottom of the occupational ladder....each immigrant group was followed by more recent arrivals to take its place at the base of the pyramid....[but] the Negro has been exposed to a different situation in several important respects. (1962, p. 242)

After pointing out the problems faced by skin color and condescendingly commenting on the tendency for the Northern born Negro to be confused with the criminally-prone recent black immigrants from the south," Blalock argues his main point, which is that, unlike other white-collar occupations that African Americans find all but closed to them, "Professional baseball has provided Negroes with one of the relatively few avenues for escape from traditional blue-collar occupations" (1962, p. 242). Following Jackie Robinson's desegregation of baseball and the subsequent desegregation of professional football and basketball, many African Americans and whites, undoubtedly, believed the same.

The 1968 Olympic Protest Movement

For years the dominant theme concerning sport and the black community during the period preceding the proposed Olympic boycott was that sport had taken black men, and a few black women, out of the "ghettoes" and provided them with opportunities for social mobility. For example, George McCarty, athletic director at the University of Texas at El Paso (UTEP), proclaimed, "In general, the nigger athlete is a little hungrier, and we have been blessed with having some real out-standing ones. We think they've done a lot for us, and we think we've done a lot for them" (Olsen, 1968, p. 15). The evidence seemed clear to many: Joe Louis and Jesse Owens, Hank Aaron and Willie Mays, Althea Gibson and Wilma Rudolph and many others could be used to demon-strate sports' capacity to increase African Americans' social status.

However, some present and former black athletes repudiated this claim. Harry Edwards, who later organized the Olympic Project for Human Rights, argued that sport exploited African Americans. For example, African American collegiate athletes were denied the same housing, hotel and restaurant accommodations as their white team-mates; they were often demeaned by fans, coaches and teachers; and they were "stacked" into positions, leaving many spots on the roster open for white competition only. Edwards advised black collegiate athletes to become activists and to boycott the 1968 Olympics as a way to bargain for better treatment by the sports establishment. He stated that:

> once their athletic abilities are impaired by age or injury, only the ghetto beck-ons and they are doomed once again to that faceless, hopeless, ignominious existence they had supposedly forever left behind. At the end of their athletic career, black athletes do not become congressmen, as did Bob Mathias, the white former Olympic decathlon champion, or Wilmer Mizell, ex-Pittsburgh Pirate pitcher. Neither does the black athlete cash in on the thousands of dol-lars to be had from endorsements, either during his professional career or after he retires. (Edwards, 1969, p. xxvii)

Edwards led a movement during the late 1960s that demanded a change in the treatment of African Americans students, sometimes by disrupting collegiate football and basketball contests at campuses all across America. Some colleges were forced to cancel football games because of expected disturbances. This movement also signaled a change in black athletes' (and perhaps the black community's) rela-tionship to white leadership in sports. While many whites and some African Americans still touted sports' role as an escalator to social mobility for "ghetto blacks, many African Americans—athletes and others—began to condemn the sport establishment for blatant exploi-tation and racial discrimination. No longer would a belief in sport as the route to increased status go unchallenged. If whites had renewed their faith in sports' ability to elevate the status of the black commu-nity, they were not joined in this belief by many of those principally involved—black athletes.

Proposition 48 and Other Legislation by the NCAA

For at least the last two decades we've told Black kids who bounce balls, run around tracks and catch touchdown passes that these things are ends unto themselves. We've raped them. We can't afford to do it to another generation. (cited in Edwards, 1984, p. 14)

According to Harry Edwards (1984), the above statement, which was made from the floor of the 1983 NCAA convention floor, was, in part, responsible for the adoption of Proposition 48. This required freshmen collegiate athletes, beginning in 1986, to attain a minimum 700 SAT or 15 ACT score and a 2.0 average in 11 core high school courses to receive an athletic scholarship. The minimum SAT and ACT scores have since been raised. It was evident that the debate over new standards for providing athletic grants-in-aid was directly related to African American athletes' success, or lack of success, in academic programs at colleges and universities.

Edwards has been a leader in castigating colleges for their failure to graduate minority student athletes. Colleges, he has often said, bring black athletes to campus to do one thing: play sport. They are not serious about the academic concerns of black athletes, often providing them with "Mickey Mouse" courses and giving them grades for courses never completed or mastered. So, for him there was irony in the fact that opposition to higher academic standards for student athletes came from black college presidents and civil rights leaders who criticized the NCAA for attempting to limit the participation of black student-athletes by imposing rules based on scores earned by taking racially or culturally biased examinations.

Both sides recognized that sport is unlikely to provide *professional* sport opportunities for most African American student-athletes, but those in opposition to Proposition 48 (and later Proposition 42) often point to the role sport has played in the black community for the student who would otherwise be least-disposed to go to college. Sport, they argue, may provide the means necessary (i.e., a scholarship) for the student-athlete to improve his or her station in life. But this is only possible through educational attainment (i.e., graduation from college). From this view sport facilitates upward mobility.

Others believe the athlete and student roles to be incompatible for most student-athletes in revenue-generating sports (Harris, 1991, 1994). A few experience upward mobility—directly or indirectly—through sport involvement, but for far too many, sport participation results in the abuse of student athletes.

As this essay indicates, perceptions about sport and its role in the black community are ever shifting. At times there has been optimism about its capacity to enhance the status of an entire group of people. At other times it has been cautiously embraced as an escalator to a better life. During the 1960s, sport was interrogated as a path to the American Dream. Today there is a brighter outlook than during the sixties among those who believe sport can provide opportunities for advancement outside of the sport world. (The phrase often used now is "don't let sport use you, use it.")

While the role of sport in the black community appears to be unclear, the media seem to be less cloudy about their view of race and sport. They bombard us with endless articles and vignettes about how black athletes had little going for them—they would come from broken or father-absent homes in dreadful neighborhoods where residents succumbed to dashed hopes—until they found, or were found by, sport. This is typically followed by the athlete's "admission" that if it had not been for sport, he (and sometimes she) would be out on the street or working a menial job. (Mississippi State University basketball player Dante Jones and the Seattle Supersonic's Ervin Johnson are but two of the many players who were reportedly rescued from low-paying, unfulfilling jobs by basketball.) And, in the end, the athlete, showing a bit of humility, informs the audience that they, too, can be lifted out of undesirable circumstances, if they would work hard at sport. The sports media would have us hold on to the belief that sport is *the* way to a better life. Many are not at ease with this assessment of sport in the black community.

Notes

1. Direct mobility refers to one's attainment of a player position, while indirect mobility refers, typically, to educational attainment or occupational sponsorship resulting from sport participation.
2. In 1888, George "Little Chocolate" Dixon became the first African American champion in any sport; he was bantamweight and featherweight champion. Joe Walcott followed in 1901 as welterweight champion. Joe Gans won the lightweight bile in 1902 (Rust, 1985).
3. Johnson had a penchant for dating and marrying white women and for being indiscreet about his affairs. Washington and many whites abhorred this and Johnson's ostentatious public manner.

References

Angelou, Maya. 1970. *I Know Why the Caged Bird Sings.* New York: Random House.

Blalock Jr., Hubert M. 1962. "Occupational Discrimination: Some Theoretical Propositions." *Social Problems* 9:240–247.

Coakley, Jay J. 1994. *Sport in Society: Issues and Controversies.* 5th ed. St. Louis: Mosby.

Curry, Timothy J. and Robert Jiobu. 1984. *Sports: A Social Perspective.* Englewood Cliffs, NJ: Prentice-Hall.

Edwards, Harry. 1973. "Black Athletes: 20th Century Gladiators for White America." *Psychology Today* 7:43 52.

————. 1979. "Sport within the Veil: The Triumphs, Tragedies and Challenges of Afro-American Involvement." *Annals of the American Academy of Political and Social Science* 445:116–127.

————. 1984. "The Collegiate Athletic Arms Race: Origins and Implications of the 'Rule 48' Controversy." *Journal of Sport and Social Issues* 8:4–22.

Eitzen, D. Stanley and George H. Sage. 1993. *Sociology of North American Sport.* 6th ed. Madison, WI: Brown & Benchmark Publishers.

Gilmore, Al-Tony. 1973. "Jack Johnson and White Women: The National Impact." *Journal of Negro History* (Jan.):18–38.

————. 1975. *Bad Nigger!: The National Impact of Jack Johnson.* Port Washington, NY: Kennikat Press.

Harris, Othello. 1991."Athletics and Academics: Contrary or Complementary Activities?" Pp. 58–73 in *Sport, Racism and Ethnicity*, edited by Grant Jarvie. London: Falmer Press.

————. 1994. "Balancing Athletics and Academics: Some Reflections from African American Male Student-Athletes." Paper presented at the annual Association of Black Psychologists Meetings (August, Toronto).

————. (in press). "African Americans in Sport From Shadow to Summit." In *Sport and International Politics in the 20th Century*, edited by Jim Riordan. E & FN Spon (Chapman and Hall).

Leonard II, Gilbert M. 1997. *A Sociological Perspective of Sport.* 6th ed. Boston: Allyn and Bacon.

Levine, Peter. 1989. *American Sport: A Documentary History.* Englewood Cliffs, NJ: Prentice Hall.

London, Jack. 1992. "Tommy Burns versus Jack Johnson." Pp. 142–150 in *Jack London*, edited by James Bankes. Dubuque, IA: Wm C. Brown Publishers.

Olsen, J. 1968. "The Black Athlete: A Shameful Story. The Cruel Deception, Part I." *Sports Illustrated* 29(1) (1 July): 15–17.

Roberts, Randy. 1983. *Papa Jack: Jack Johnson and the Era of White Hopes.* New York: Free Press.

Rust Jr., Art and Edna Rust. 1985. *Art Rust's Illustrated History of the Black Athlete.* Garden City, NJ: Doubleday.

Sammona, Jeremy. 1988. *Beyond the Ring: The Role of Boxing in American Society.* Urbana, IL: University of Illinois Press.

2

Cool Pose: Black Masculinity and Sports

Richard Majors

Sport, as a social institution, emerged in the nineteenth and twentieth centuries in response to a shifting constellation of class and gender dynamics. Not only did sport make a crucial contribution to the ideological naturalization of men's superiority over women, popular belief held that working-class men and men of color could not possibly compete successfully with "gentlemen." Thus, as a homosocial environment within which white upper- and middle-class males sharpened their competitive skills, sport became an important institution in which the superiority of hegemonic masculinity was supported and reproduced, while women and other (subordinated) men were marginalized (Cornell, 1987).

Interestingly, since World War II—and especially in the last 15 years—athletic roles within major organized sports in the United States have come to be dominated by black men. The dynamics of this historic shift—and the extent to which the contemporary dominance of certain sports by black males is more a sign of continued racism than a sign of progress—have been examined elsewhere (H. Edwards, 1973, 1984; Tygiel, 1983). The goal of this chapter is to illustrate how contemporary black males often utilize sports as one means of masculine self-expression within an otherwise limited structure of opportunity. After a brief discussion of contemporary black men and masculinity, this chapter will show how what the author calls "cool pose" (i.e., a set of expressive lifestyle behaviors) is often developed and used by black men as a response to the limits that institutionalized racism places on their other opportunities for self-expression. This chapter will argue that sport has become a major institutional context for the expression of cool pose, and that although self-expression through athletics does offer a small number of black males an escape from the limits imposed by poverty and racism, for the majority, sport is a form of self-expression that ultimately can lock them into their low-status positions in society.

Black Men and Masculinity

Despite the recent proliferation of men's studies programs and the resultant publications based on this growing academic interest in masculinity (Brod, 1987; Kimmel, 1987), research on how ethnicity, race, and socioeconomic status affect the development of masculinity remains limited. In particular, black males are either rendered invisible or are viewed as helpless victims of a racist system. With a few exceptions (e.g., Cazenave, 1984; Franklin, 1984; Majors, 1986, 1987), there has been a noteworthy dearth of literature on black men's actual responses (i.e., survival strategies, coping mechanisms, and forms of resistance) to a limited structure of opportunity. The problems facing black males today are so serious, and their consequences so grave, it is tempting to view these men primarily as victims. In fact, Stewart and Scott (1978) have argued that there is a contemporary "institutional decimation of black males," which these authors describe as the "coordinated operation of various institutions in American society which systematically remove black males from the civilian population" (p. 85). Indeed, recent research has shown that young black males are experiencing unprecedented setbacks in their struggles for economic and educational equality in the United States, a nation that holds equal opportunity as one of its founding principles (Gibbs, 1988; Larson, 1988). Black men are among the predominant victims of an entire range of socioeconomic, health, and stress-related problems.

These problems include, but are not limited to, higher rates of heart disease, hyper-tension, infant mortality, mental disorders, psychiatric hospitalization, homicide, unemployment, suspension from school, imprisonment, and morbidity and low life expectancy (Bulhan, 1985; Cordes, 1985; Gite, 1985; Heckler, 1985).

Black males have responded in various ways to this constricted structure of opportunity. What is of interest here is how black males' relationships to dominant definitions of masculinity have figured into their responses to institutionalized racism. Many black males have accepted the definitions, standards, and norms of dominant social definitions of masculinity (being the breadwinner, having strength, and dominating women). However, American society has prevented black males from achieving many aspects of this masculinity by restricting their access to education, jobs, and institutional power. In other words, the dominant goals of hegemonic masculinity have been sold to black males, but access to the legitimate means to achieve those goals has been largely denied black males (Staples, 1982). As a consequence of these conditions, many black males have become *men manqué*; because of the many frustrations resulting from a lack of opportunities in society, many black males have become obsessed with proving manliness to themselves and to others. Lacking legitimate institutional means, black males will often go to great lengths to prove their manhood in interpersonal spheres of life (e.g., fighting, the emotional and physical domination of women, and involvement in risk-taking activities; Majors, 1986; Staples, 1982).

Cool Pose as an Expression of Black Masculinity

Institutional racism and a constricted structure of opportunity do not cause all black males to exhibit antisocial behaviors, nor do these problems succeed in erasing black men's expressions of creativity. In fact, black men often cope with their frustration, embitterment, alienation, and social impotence by channeling their creative energies into the construction of unique, expressive, and conspicuous styles of demeanor, speech, gesture, clothing, hairstyle, walk, stance, and handshake. For the black male, these expressive behaviors, which are a particular manifestation of what the author has elsewhere described as cool pose (Majors, 1986, 1987), offset an externally imposed invisibility, and provide a means to show the dominant culture (and the black male's peers) that the black male is strong and proud and can survive, regardless of what may have been done to harm or limit him. In other words, the expressive lifestyle is a "survival strategy that makes oneself interesting and attractive to others...through [the process of] making oneself an interesting object, through the cultivation of an aura...that elicits rewarding responses from others" (Rainwater, 1966, p. 214).

Although black people have been forced into conciliatory and often demeaning positions in American culture, there is nothing conciliatory about the expressive lifestyle. It is adaptation rather than submission. In that sense, then, cool pose is an attempt to carve out an alternative path to achieve the goals of dominant masculinity. Due to structural limitations, a black man may be impotent in the intellectual, political, and corporate world, but he can nevertheless display a potent personal style from the pulpit, in entertainment, and in athletic competition, with a verve that borders on the spectacular. Through the virtuosity of performance, he tips the socially imbalanced scales in his favor and sends the subliminal message: "See me, touch me, hear me, but, white man, you can't copy me!" The expressive lifestyle invigorates the demeaning life of black men in white America. It is a dynamic vitality that transforms the mundane into the sublime and makes the routine spectacular.

Black Male Expression and Sport

Sport has become one of the major stages upon which black males express their creativity. For example, in football, Butch Johnson and Billy "Whiteshoes" Johnson were two well-known athletes who exhibited expressive lifestyle behaviors on the playing field. Both men were known for their fancy dances and "spikes" in the end zone after a touchdown. To further accentuate themselves (i.e., to be "cool"), these athletes wore wristbands and hung towels from their pants. In basketball, Julius "Dr. J" Erving, Darryl Dawkins, Michael Jordan, and other black players have been known for their expressiveness as well as their considerable skills. Erving may best symbolize the emergence of this expressive style among black basketball players. On the court, Erving was known for his very creative, graceful, and agile performance. His style of play was exemplified by his famous "ceiling-climbing, high-flying, gravity-defying" dunks, for which he would often start his take-off at the foul line.

Cool pose in sport can sometimes be interpreted as cultural resistance to racism. The fists-raised demonstration on the victory stand in the 1968 Olympics was not the only characteristic of Tommie Smith's and John Carlos's protests against racism in the United States—these athletes also ran while wearing black socks and sunglasses. Similarly, Muhammad Ali's expressive style—his boasting, his poetry, his dancing, his ritualistic "hair combing" while holding a mirror after his bouts—can be interpreted not simply as personal vanity but as one athlete's defiant expression of resistance to a society that uses black males as its warriors—both as pugilists in the ring and as soldiers in Vietnam. Because black (and Hispanic) men showed up disproportionately as drafted combat soldiers, and then as casualties in Vietnam (Staples, 1982), it is not surprising that many U.S. blacks identified with the style and substance of Ali's performances. Meanwhile, many whites in the media, the government, and the public were profoundly threatened by it.

Expressive behaviors are not, of course, restricted merely to professional athletes. College, high school, and playground athletes also mimic, develop, and use expressive styles. As Wolf (1972) has noted of young black males,

> The school yard is the only place they can feel true pride in what they do, where they can move free of inhibitions, and where they can, by being spectacular, rise for the moment against the drabness and anonymity of their lives.... When you jump in the air, fake a shot, all without coming back down, you have proven your worth in incontestable fashion...thus, when a player develops extraordinary "school yard" moves...[they] become his measure as a man." (p. 170)

Black males' appropriation of sports as an arena of self-expression is an example of human agency operating within structural constraints. Faced with a lack of resources, facilities, services, goods, information, and jobs, black males who live in poor black communities have taken a previously white-dominated activity and constructed it as an arena in which they find accessible recreation, entertainment, stimulation, and opportunities for self-expression and creativity. Sports play an important and—in some limited ways—a positive role in many black males' lives. However, as we shall see, there is a downside to the relationship between black males and sports.

Black Males and Organized Sports

The sports establishment does not operate as an apolitical, asocial enterprise, but as part of the larger society. As such, sports are not an alternative to "real life," but a reflection of the racist economic and social system that supports them (W. Morgan, 1983). This reflection is often distorted in such a way that, for the individual, sport often appears to be one of the few arenas that provides true equal opportunity. This distortion of reality draws young black males into athletic careers in disproportionately high numbers, and this distortion ultimately guarantees that the vast majority of black males will find sports to be a professional dead end (H. Edwards, 1984).

Despite its apparent equality and integration, sport remains an extension of the dominant racist economic system, which serves to exploit those who are already professional or college athletes and to mislead those who are merely aspiring athletes. In fact, even the apparent integration at the player level is misleading (H. Edwards, 1982; Yetman & Eitzen, 1972). As evidenced by recent statements made by prominent white men in professional sports concerning how blacks supposedly "lack the necessities" to be field managers, racism lives on within organized sports. Indeed, black managers, coaches, and front-office personnel are exceedingly rare, with most sports organizations owned, operated, and managed exclusively by whites. Furthermore, there is racial segregation in sport by playing position (Curtis & Loy, 1978; Eitzen & Tessendorf, 1978), as any devotee of football is especially aware after the media attention Doug Williams received for being the first black quarterback to start in the Superbowl. Black males also find themselves represented in disproportionately high numbers as athletes in sports to which they have had access, such as basketball, football, baseball, boxing, and track. Meanwhile, blacks are underrepresented in sports to which they have not had access, such as golf, auto racing, swimming, hockey, and soccer. As H. Edwards (1984) writes,

> Patterns of black opportunities in American sport are consistent with those in society at large, and for the same reason—deeply rooted traditions of racial discrimination. I contend that racial discrimination in both sport and society is responsible for the disproportionately high presence of extremely talented black athletes in certain sports on the one hand and the utter exclusion of blacks from most American sport and from decision-making and authority positions in virtually all sports on the other. (p. 9)

Despite the large number of black males who participate in sports, less than 6% of all the athletic scholarships given in the United States go to blacks. Just as damaging is the fact that an estimated 25 to 35% of high school black athletes do not even qualify for scholarships because of academic deficiencies. Of those black athletes who ultimately do receive athletic scholarships, as many as 65 to 75% may not ever graduate from college (H. Edwards, 1984; Spivey & Jones, 1975; Talbert, 1976). Among the approximately 25 to 35% of the black athletes who do graduate from college, about 75% of them graduate with either physical education degrees or with degrees in majors that are especially created for athletes. As one might suspect, such "jock degrees" are often not acceptable in the job market, given the growing emphasis on the need for math, science, engineering, and computer training in today's high-tech market. In the final analysis, because such a small percentage of these college athletes will be drafted by a pro team, and those who actually play will find that the average professional career is short, many once-aspiring black athletes will find themselves back out on the streets with academic degrees that may not help them survive—much less succeed—in the "real world."

Summary and Conclusion

It has been argued here that cool pose (expressive lifestyle behaviors) as expressed by black males in sports may be interpreted as a means of countering social oppression and racism and of expressing creativity. Moreover, the demonstration of cool pose in sports enables black males to accentuate or display themselves (i.e., "Here I am, world; watch me, see me, hear me, I'm alive"), obtain gratification, release pent-up aggression, gain prestige and recognition, exercise power and control, and express pride, dignity, and respect for themselves and for their race. However, the emphasis on athletics and on cool pose among black males is often self-defeating, because it comes at the expense of educational advancement and other intellectually oriented activities that are integral aspects of the dominant forms of masculine power and success today.

Furthermore, although cool pose is an example of creative agency in response to one form of social domination (institutionalized racism), cool pose also illustrates the limits of an agency that adopts another form of social domination (hegemonic masculinity) as its vehicle. Because hegemonic masculinity is ultimately about men's domination of women (and some men's domination of other men), black men's adoption of cool pose as a response to institutionalized racism is often self-defeating. This response ultimately does not put black males in positions to live and work in more egalitarian ways with women, nor does it directly challenge male hierarchies. Cool pose demonstrates black males' potential to transcend oppressive conditions to express themselves as men. In rejecting the false promise of patriarchal privilege, black males might move from individual transcendence to social transformation. A critical examination of black males' relationship to ports is an important requisite of this movement.

References

Brod, H. (1987). (Ed.) *The Making of Masculinities: The New Men's Studies.* Winchester, MA: Allen and Unwin.

Bulhan, H. (1985). "Black Americans and Psychopathology: An Overview of Research and Therapy." *Psychotherapy*, 22, 370–378.

Cazenave, N. (1984). "Race, Socioeconomic Status, and Age: The Social Context of American Masculinity." *Sex Roles,* 11, 639–657.

Connell, R. W. (1987). *Gender and Power: Society, The Person and Sexual Politics.* Stanford, CA: Stanford University Press.

Cordes, C. (1985, January). "Black Males at Risk in America." *APA Monitor*, 9/10, 27–28.

Curtis, J., and Loy, J. (1978). "Positional Segregation in Professional Baseball: Replications, Trend Data, and Critical Observation." *International Review of Sport Sociology*, 4(13), 5–21.

Edwards, H. (1973). *The Sociology of Sport*. Homewood, IL: Dorsey Press.

———. (1982). "Race in Contemporary American Sports." *National Forum*, 62, 19–22.

———. (1984). "The Collegiate Athletic Arms Race: Origins and Implications of the 'Rule 48' Controversy." *Journal of Sport and Social Issues*, 8, 4–22.

Eitzen, S., and Tessendorf, I. (1978). "Racial Segregation by Position in Sports." *Review of Sport and Society*, 3, 109–128.

Franklin, C.W. (1984). *The Changing Definition of Masculinity*. New York: Plenum.

Gibbs, J. (1988). "Young Black Males in America: Endangered, Embittered, and Embattled." In J.T. Gibbs (Ed.) *Young, Black, and Male in America: An Endangered Species*. (pp. 1–36). Dover, MA: Auburn House.

Gite, L. (1985, November). "Black Men and Stress." *Essence*. Pp. 25–26, 130.

Heckler, M. (1985). *Report of the Secretary's Task Force on Black and Minority Health*. Bethesda, MD: U.S. Department of Health and Human Services.

Kimmel, G. (1987). "Men's Responses to Feminism at the Turn of the Century." *Gender and Society*, 1(3), 261–283.

Larson, T. (1988). "Employment and Unemployment of Young Black Males." In J. Gibbs (Ed.) *Young, Black, and Male in America: An Endangered Species* (pp. 97–128). Dover, MA: Auburn House.

Majors, R. (1986). "Cool Pose: The Proud Signature of Black Survival." *Changing Men: Issues in Gender, Sex and Politics*, 17, 5–6.

———. (1987). *Cool Pose: A New Approach Toward a Systematic Understanding and Study of Black Male Behavior*. Doctoral Dissertation, University of Illinois, Urbana.

Morgan, W. (1983). "Towards a Critical Theory of Sport." *Journal of Sport and Social Issues*, 7 (Winter/Spring), 24–34.

Rainwater, L. (1966). "The Crucible of Identity: The Lower Class Negro Family." *Daedalus*, 95, 172–216.

Spivey, D., and Jones, T. (1975) "Intercollegiate Athletic Servitude: A Case Study of the Black Illini Student-Athlete." *Social Science Quarterly*, 55, 937–947.

Staples, R. (1982). "Black Masculinity." San Francisco: Black Scholar Press.

Stewart, J., and Scott, J. (1978). "The Institutional Decimation of Black American Males." *Western Journal of Black Studies*, 8, 82–93.

Talbert, T. (1976). "The Black Athlete in the Southwest Conference: A Study of Institutionalized Racism." Doctoral Dissertation, Baylor University, Waco, Texas.

Tygiel, J. (1983). *Baseball's Great Experiment: Jackie Robinson and His Legacy*. New York: Oxford University Press.

Wolf, D. (1972). *Foul: The Connie Hawkins Story*. New York: Warner Books.

Yetman, N., and Eitzen, S. (1972). "Black Americans in Sport: Unequal Opportunity for Equal Ability." *Civil Rights Digest*, 5, 20–34.

3

Betting Against the Odds:
An Overview of Black Sports Participation

Gary A. Sailes

American college and professional sports have gained enormous popularity since the "Sports Golden Age" of the 1920s. As American technology advanced, so did American sport. Its popularity led to its commercialization. Huge stadia were built, athletes were able to command enormous salaries; media interest and coverage increased which led to the emergence of sports heroes. Leagues developed and flourished, All-star games and All-star athletes were born, the collegiate All-American was established, and March Madness became synonymous with college basketball. The Super Bowl, arguably, has the largest television market of any televised event, sport or non-sport. Virtually every American is influenced by sport in some way. American sport is a $300 billion industry with unprecedented interest from fans and active participants in a global market.

American sport was a "whites only" institution until 1947 when Jackie Robinson broke the color barrier in Major League Baseball. Since that historic event, African American athletes have come to the forefront of American sport, particularly in the popular sports, football, basketball, and baseball, at both the collegiate and professional levels. Currently, African American athletes account for 80%, 60%, and 25% of the athletes in professional football, basketball, and baseball, respectively. In college sports, African American athletes account for 67% and 44% of the athletes playing NCAA Division I level basketball and football, respectively (Coakley, 1998). African Americans account for only 12% of the population in the United States, yet they enjoy a distinct over-representation in college and professional sports.

Additionally, African American athletes have a distinctive style of play that separates them from their white counterparts. For example, basketball was forever changed in its configuration when African American males began to dominate that sport. The "whites only" style of play was slowed down and consisted mostly of team play and outside shooting. Individual skills were sacrificed to complement team-oriented play. However, African American athletes played a more athletic and aggressive game which included artistic moves to the basket, slam dunking, improvisational dribbling and passing skills, and aggressive rebounding (Sailes, 1996a; George, 1992).

African American athletes have dominated nearly all the sprint and middle distance events in amateur and professional track and field competition and the heavyweight division in professional boxing. What accounts for the over-representation of African American athletes in college and professional sports? Are there specific social and cultural variables that impact on and shape the sports participation patterns of African American males? Does American sport actually provide the salient opportunities for African American athletes that the media portray? It is the intent of this chapter to examine the different social institutions and inherent variables that impact and shape the sport participation patterns of African American males. It is this distinct pattern of social events that serve as the foundation for the socialization of the African American athlete.

Sociocultural Variables

The cultural and social variables which impact upon, shape the lives of, and establish the values of African American males are complex. Much of African American culture is rooted in its historical and contemporary reaction to white racism and discrimination. Discriminatory institutional barriers are perceived by African American males to be in place at almost every segment of the American opportunity network. Consequently, many African American males feel they are left with few visible opportunities. Consequently, they are forced to look outside the mainstream of American society for opportunities to success (Oliver, 1994).

For many African American males, sports appear to be one of the few allowable and available opportunities for success in a perceived racist and oppressive society (Sailes, 1984; Edwards, 1973). It is felt this accounts for the enormous over-representation of African American males in professional basketball, football, and baseball and in major college football and basketball today. Their resistance to racism and persistence to achieve success in the sports arena has not only exemplified itself in their over-representation, but also in the changes which occurred in American sport as a result of that participation. Many contemporary African American athletes serve as role models, further perpetuating the migration of African American male youth into sport (Sailes, 1984). Lapchick (1982) claims that the black family is seven times more likely than a white family to push a male child into sports. These and other forces impact on the black family and channel black males into sport.

Poverty

The economic and social conditions of the lower class shape their socialization, making it distinct from other economic and social groups. Interpretations of social conditions, cultural values, and educational achievement among the poor are distinct when compared to individuals from higher socioeconomic groups (Oliver, 1994; Hacker, 1993; Wilson, 1980). There are approximately thirty-four million African Americans in the United States today. Approximately one-third live at or below the poverty level (Hacker, 1993; Wilson, 1986).

Members of the lower or working class are more likely to view sport as an avenue for social and economic mobility (Oliver, 1980). Currently, almost two-thirds of African Americans playing NCAA Division I-A football or Division I basketball come from impoverished backgrounds (Sailes, 1987). Perceptions that few opportunities exist through traditional channels contribute to the perception that sports offers the only viable opportunity to achieve success in American society (Sailes, 1987; Rehberg & Cohen, 1975; Edwards, 1973). With many African-American scholarship athletes emanating from lower socioeconomic backgrounds, it is plausible that the social variables that define their cultural values and belief system serve as the foundation for their actions and participation patterns in the sports setting (Coakley, 1998; Leonard, 1998; Sailes, 1984; Edwards, 1973).

Class is a variable which impacts specifically on the sport socialization and value development of African-American males (Sailes, 1984). That distinct socialization is the catalyst which defines their educational and athletic dilemma. Sailes (1993a) noted that African American athletes tended to use the educational setting to achieve sports stardom when in fact they should have used sports to achieve an education. Sailes (1996b) also noted that many athletes attend college with no intention of graduating. In fact, they use college sports to get their shot at professional sports. This is blatant exploitation and a waste of scholarship dollars from an educational perspective. From a business perspective, the athletic department is getting its money's worth. Most NCAA Division I athletic departments make millions off the talent of their student athletes.

Education

Social class also impacts on the quality of education one receives and the development of educational values, which significantly impacts on educational achievement. Crouse and Thrusheim (1988) found that economically disadvantaged African Americans were educationally disenfranchised as a result of their economic status. They disclosed that for every increase in family income of $18,000, SAT scores increased by 200 points. Moreover, it was determined that the longer a family remained impoverished, the greater the likelihood that lower SAT scores, lower grade point averages, lower high school graduation percentages, and unlikely college matriculation would prevail.

The devaluation of education among the impoverished class further contributed to lower educational attainment (Hacker, 1993). It is feared among educators that contemporary African American youth devalue education. Moreover, many African American male youth associate educational achievement with trying to be white (Fleming, 1984). This concept created understandable paradoxes for African Americans intent on maintaining their racial identity and achieving educational success. Many youth drop out or become underachievers in high school in order to achieve acceptance among their peers.

By contrast, sports can contribute to educational development among high school student athletes (Harris, 1993; Sabo, 1988). Athletes tend to perform at higher levels in the classroom and beyond than their nonathletic counterparts (Coakley, 1998; Leonard, 1998). In addition, many high school athletes believe that participation in high school athletics could possibly deliver educational, social, and life-skill benefits and opportunities that would facilitate the transition to purposeful productivity and full-employment later on (Harris, 1993; Oliver, 1980). Moreover, high school athletes had higher aspirations to attend college than their nonathletic counterparts and parents took greater interest in their children's socialization when they were involved in high school sports (McElroy, 1981). Finally, in a report commissioned by the Women's Sports Foundation, it was found that high school sports provided greater opportunities, higher aspirations, developed a stronger sense of self worth, and provided an overall positive experience for its participants compared to nonparticipants (Sabo, 1988).

Others claim the desire to play professional sports is positive because it requires participation in the college sports system which exposes the student athlete to a higher level of education (McElroy, 1981). However, too many student athletes abandon the opportunity to get an education or earn a college degree. They exploit the college system to gain their shot at playing professional sports often leaving college one or two years early and never returning to complete the degree.

The educational agenda of the NCAA is clear: "Hit the books or play somewhere else." The NCAA eligibility requirements for incoming college freshmen to compete in college sports have risen since NCAA Proposition 48 was mandated in 1986. Today, NCAA Proposition 16 mandates that a high school senior must have a cumulative grade point average of 2.5 balanced with an SAT score of 700 or an ACT score of 17 to be eligible. The sliding scale also grants eligibility to a student with a cumulative grade point average of 2.0 and SAT score of 900 or ACT score of 21.

An article in *USA Today* disclosed very disturbing news (Wieberg, 1995). The college graduation rates among African American student athletes were declining. The graduation rate for African American males playing Division I-A football fell from 44% to 42%. For NCAA Division I basketball, the graduation rate slipped from 46% to 42%. Overall, the graduation rate for African American student athletes fell from 43% to 42% (Wieberg, 1995). Moreover, the percentage of college scholarships awarded to African American student athletes has declined every year since 1986 (Wieberg, 1995). Currently, 23.2% of college scholarships are awarded to African American student athletes in comparison to 27.1% in 1986. Additionally, African American representation in Division I basketball declined from 61% in 1986 to 59.5% today. A dramatic decrease in representation also occurred in women's basketball. The number of African American women has declined from 36.9% to less than 31%. Overall, the ratio of whites to blacks on athletic scholarship fell from 2.5 to 1 in 1986 to 3 to 1 today (Wieberg, 1995). These figures possibly suggest a trend that illustrates the decreasing participation of African American athletes at the NCAA Division I level of competition. It could also be an indication that African American high school athletes are not taking the educational mandates of NCAA initial eligibility seriously.

Educational Stereotypes

Educational stereotypes prevail within the sports environment, particularly in the educational setting. Some white faculty and students had low expectations about the achievement of African American students. Low self-concept, low faculty expectancy, and social alienation contributed to low academic achievement among African American students attending predominantly white colleges and universities (Fleming, 1984).

In a related study, college student athletes perceived low academic expectations among faculty regarding student athletes attending NCAA Division I institutions (Sailes, 1993a). Furthermore, these athletes felt their courses were very difficult and that they were underprepared to attend college, felt alienated from the campus environment, were not confident about maintaining eligibility, and felt student attitudes about their academic competence were negative. It was concluded that the combination of low self-concept, low faculty expectation and alienation from the social environment contributed to lower academic achievement, especially among African American athletes. Some athletes do little more academically than what is required to remain eligible to keep their athletic scholarship (Sailes, 1993a). Most NCAA Division I football and basketball players identify more as athletes than as students because the athletic expectancy of coaches is greater than the academic expectancy of their instructors. Only 5% of student athletes participating in a national survey indicated their head coaches encouraged them to do more academically than what was required to maintain their eligibility (Sailes, 1993a). Moreover, student athletes felt the athletic department was more interested in maintaining their eligibility than encouraging them to pursue a purposeful education. Although the NCAA recommends the balancing of athletics and academics, it appears that most athletic departments practice "lip service" regarding the ideals of academic achievement.

Consequently, the singular focus of sports participation to obtain professional sports status overshadows, in some cases, the desire for academic achievement and leads to poor academic achievement and lower graduation rates. Some student athletes blame obsessive coaches and the business mentality of college athletic departments for the lack of academic achievement among college student athletes (Sailes, 1993a).

Professional Sports

According to the NCAA, there are approximately one million high school football players and 500,000 high school basketball players in the United States (Schoemann, 1995). About 150 athletes make it to the National Football League (NFL) and approximately 50 will sign a contract with an National Basketball Association (NBA) team annually! The odds of a high school football player making it to the NFL are about 6,000 to 1. The odds of a high school player making it to the NBA are approximately 10,000 to 1 (Schoemann, 1995).

In a national study of NCAA Division I football and basketball players, Sailes (1994) found that approximately 52% of African American student athletes felt they would play professional sports. Moreover, of those college student athletes, over 95% elected to attend their respective schools to improve their chances of making it to the NFL or NBA. What was more revealing was the fact that African Americans felt more strongly about their chances of signing a professional sports contract than their white counterparts. It appears that African American males are more likely to hit the courts than the books while in college.

The mass media play a significant role in the sport socialization of African American youth (Coakley, 1998; Sailes, 1984). They facilitate the shaping and development of social values and reinforce the norms of American culture (Leonard, 1998). American radio, television, and print media often sensationalize the achievements of elite athletes, most notably in their coverage of NCAA basketball and football, the NFL, the NBA, and Major League Baseball. The so-called "glamorous" personal lives, enormous salaries, and often incredible accomplishments of professional athletes are romanticized to the point of fantasy (Coakley, 1998). It is very likely that some professional athletes have more name recognition among African American youth than our country's economic, political, educational, and business leaders combined.

Professional athletes are more likely to serve as role models for American male youth than other adults (Johnson, 1991). For example, Michael Jordan, NBA superstar and future NBA legend, will be remembered for decades as the greatest athlete to play the game of basketball. His name and reputation as a professional basketball player as well as his contributions to the sport of basketball are recognized globally. The income of the NBA has more than doubled to over three billion dollars annually in the last decade through the careful marketing of its superstars like Jordan, Shaquille O'Neal, and retired Laker Magic Johnson.

The aggrandizement of professional athletes and the sensationalization of professional sports in the United States appear to have a narcotic effect on American youth, luring them into unrealistic expectations about their chances of signing a professional sports contract (Coakley, 1998; Leonard, 1998; Sailes, 1984). Consequently, the chances of a college athlete signing a professional sports contract is less than 1% while the average career of the professional athlete is less than four years (Coakley, 1998). By the time professional athletes reach the end of their sports careers, most other individuals will be starting their professional careers (Leonard, 1998). Moreover, more than 80% of African American professional athletes are financially bankrupt within five years after their retirement (Lide, 1984). With no education or marketable skills, those former athletes struggle to make a living to support themselves and their families.

African American males are more likely to have black professional athletes as role models than their white counterparts. Sailes (1987, 1984) and Edwards (1973) argued that holding professional athletes as role models contributed, in part, to the disproportionate over-representation of African American athletes in the three major professional sports, (football, basketball, and baseball) and their lack of representation in the individual sports (tennis, swimming, gymnastics, and golf). The constant barrage of successful African-American professional athletes fuel the hopes of African American male youth to play professional sports. Consequently, African American males rely on sports for fame and fortune at higher percentages than their white counterparts. This trend is most likely a response to the perception that institutional barriers limit employment opportunities among African American males in other segments of American society (Harris, 1993; Sailes 1987, 1984; Edwards, 1973).

Racial stereotyping in professional sports has had a dramatic impact on the participation of African American athletes. For example, although the participation numbers of African American athletes in professional basketball, football, and baseball are 80%, 65%, and 25% respectively, that representation drops dramatically when one views the positions occupied by African Americans as managers, coaches, and front office personnel. Currently, the NBA, the NFL and Major League Baseball employ 14%, 7%, and 2% African American coaches respectively. The numbers in front office positions are similarly low.

The leadership positions in front office management and on field coaching are not the only places where racial stereotyping occurs. Positional segregation, or stacking, also occurs in professional sports. The racist belief that African Americans are not natural leaders and are better at the reactive speed positions in the periphery of play appears evident when one peruses the stacking literature. African American athletes play the outfield positions in major league baseball, away from the central leadership positions that initiate play like pitcher or catcher. The first line of defense, the infield, also seem replete of African American athletes. In professional football, African American athletes dominate the peripheral positions as running back, wide receiver, defensive backs, and corner backs. These positions are identified as the speed/reactive positions. The leadership positions which initiate the play, center and quarterback, are virtually all white. It is concluded that these positions are reserved for whites who are more intelligent. This factor highlights the disenfranchisement of African American players in their contribution to the development of professional sports as athletes, but are unlikely players in managing and coaching in professional sports (Coakley, 1998; Leonard, 1998).

The concern over the dominance of the African American athlete on the playing field has opened doors to interesting discussions. In the late 1980s when Al Campanis and Jimmy "The Greek" Snyder made their remarks regarding African American athletes on national television, interest in the success of African American athletes has grown. While some researchers have shied away from commentary on the so-called physical superiority of the African American athlete, others have stepped up to the plate and made unqualified and socially repugnant and politically incorrect remarks. Campanis felt that "blacks did not have the necessities to become baseball managers." Snyder asserted "that blacks are better athletes because they have been bred that way. Big black male slaves were mated with big black female slaves to produce a physically superior offspring to work in the fields. This created powerful legs which gave blacks an athletic advantage." Canadian biomechanist Giddeon Ariel asserted, "The black athlete should be proud of his physical prowess because God was on his side" (NBC, 1990). It is interesting to note that these whites were willing to acknowledge black physical superiority, but were not willing to acknowledge intellectual prowess or a tough work ethic. The white status quo places a higher importance on intelligence and work ethic, two traits not bestowed on the African American athlete.

Black Male Machismo

The participation of African American men in American sport has changed the way the game is played. It does not take an expert to see that African Americans play sports different than their white counterparts. Nowhere is this fact more evident than in the sport of basketball.

Historically, basketball was always a city game. Jews dominated the sport in the early 1900s. When African Americans moved into America's inner cities, they took up the game as well. By the time sport became permanently integrated in the 1950s, the configuration of the game changed also (NBC, 1990). While the early images of the game reveal a slowed down version of contemporary basketball, outside shooting was the skill most valued. Today's black gladiators play the game above the rim. Play is characterized by quick artistic moves, aggressive play, slam dunks, and flamboyant passes (George, 1992). Julius "Dr. J" Erving asserted, "Style counts in basketball to the black player. The ultimate play in basketball is when the an artistic move is finished with a powerful move" (NBC, 1990). In other words, an artistic move to get free concluding with a slam dunk is the goal of every African American player.

Basketball is the perfect venue for the African American athlete to release all the frustrations associated with having to live and play in a racially hostile environment. Here, he is able to showcase his talent, be dominant, macho, and get paid a huge salary. In this arena, self-expression, within the team context, is rewarded. The basketball arena is a venue where he can release his anger and his rage to the point of physical exhaustion if need be. This is his boardroom. Here, he is in control.

Conclusions

The social forces which influence the sport socialization of African American youth are varied and complex. The mass media have a great impact in shaping the values and sports aspirations of American youth (Coakley, 1998; Leonard, 1998; Sailes, 1984). It fills the minds of American kids with the notion that professional sports is attainable. The percentages of African American athletes playing professional baseball, basketball, and football are an over-representation of the percentage of African Americans in society. Currently, approximately 80% of the NBA, 60% of the NFL, and 25% of Major League Baseball are African American. However, only 12% of Americans are African American (Coakley, 1997).

These statistics appear to convey the notion that African American opportunity exists in professional sport. However, the converse is true. Too many African American males are buying into the dream and are betting against the odds. They are foregoing the opportunity to earn a college degree to "go pro!" There are far too many casualties who bet against the odds and lose. Consequently, not having educational skills to fall back on makes the situation worse.

Devaluating education is self-destructive behavior. Using higher education to get an opportunity to sign a professional sports contract is not only risky but also exploits the school's economic resources. The scholarships that are awarded to athletes leaving early, who never get drafted, and/or who never graduate would be better utilized by deserving student athletes with serious intentions of acquiring an education and earning a college degree. It is unfortunate and unfair that athletic scholarships are wasted on individuals with no intent of ever graduating.

African American athletes are the gladiators that fill the economic coffers of athletic departments around the country. Schools are making billions of dollars on the athletic talents of these athletes and are exploiting them by not requiring them to attend class, get an education, and earn the degree. A law should mandate that the professional leagues could not draft a player out of college until they earn a degree.

The NCAA and its member institutions should initiate certification mandates, which are established, in part, by graduation rates, and evaluate the member schools on a continuing basis. Coaches must be held accountable for the graduation of their student athletes with sanctions leveled against them or their programs for failure to graduate their student athletes. We should support the higher academic standards mandated and the academic progress rule recently passed by the NCAA which requires all student athletes on scholarship to maintain progress towards a degree and a minimum grade point average.

The recommendations of the Knight Commission, which called for fewer contests during the season, shorter practices, mandatory study tables, the elimination of jock dormitories, tighter restrictions on recruitment, and higher academic eligibility requirements, are reasonable considerations. Agents who require their professional athletes to repay their athletic scholarships to their schools are to be commended.

Athletes should be counseled outside the athletic department and required to major in more than eligibility. Student athletes should be advised of the potential economic consequences that arise from ignoring the educational opportunities that exist at the schools they attend.

The NCAA and its member institutions should remember the mission of the university: to educate its students. Rules should be enforced which guarantee the rights of each student athlete to pursue an education and earn a college degree. If athletes choose not to attend class, let them flunk. It would be the greatest lesson they could learn about life. It is essential that African American student athletes understand that sports is nothing more than a short-lived game and that an education will last a lifetime.

References

Coakley, J. (1998). *Sport In Society: Issues and Controversies*. St. Louis: Mosby Publishers.

Crouse, J. & Thrusheim, D. (1988). *The Case Against the SAT*. Chicago: University of Chicago Press.

Edwards, H. (1973). *Sociology of Sport*. Homewood, Ill.: Dorsey Press:

Fleming, Jacqueline. (1984). *Blacks In College*. San Francisco: Jossey-Bass.

George, Nelson. (1992). *Elevating the Game: Black Men and Basketball*. New York: HarperCollins.

Hacker, Andrew. (1993). *Two Nations: Black and White, Separate, Hostile, Unequal*. New York: Scribners Press.

Harris, L. (1993). *The 1993 Lou Harris Study on High School Athletics*. : Boston: Northeastern University Center for the Study of Sport in Society, November 8.

Johnson, W. (1991). "A Matter of Black and White: A Sports Illustrated Survey of Professional Athletes Revealed Some of the Deep Divisions between the Races." *Sports Illustrated*, August 5th, 44–48.

Lapchick, R. (1982). "The Black Athlete in Contemporary American Sport." Paper presented at the annual meeting of the North American Society for the Sociology of Sport, Boston, November.

Leonard, W. (1998). *A Sociological Perspective of Sport*. New York: Macmillan Publishers.

Lide, W. (1984). "Post Athletic Careers of Professional Football and Basketball Players." Paper presented at the annual meeting of the North American Society for the Sociology of Sport, Las Vegas, November.

McElroy, M. (1981). A Comparison of Sport and Nonsport Occupational Aspirations Among Disadvantaged Youth. *Journal of Sport Psychology*, 3(1), 58–68.

Nabil, P. (1980). The Present-Day Afro-American Major-League Baseball Player and Socioeconomic Mobility in American Society. *Review of Sport and Leisure*, 5(2), 49–68.

NBC. (1990). *The Black Athlete: Fact or Fiction*. Special documentary film.

Oliver, M. (1980). "Race, Class, and the Family's Orientation to Mobility through Sport." *Sociological Symposium*, 2, 62–85.

Oliver, W. (1994). *The Violent Social World of Black Men*. Lexington Books: New York.

Rehberg, R., & Cohen, M. (1975). "Athletes and Scholars: An Analysis of the Compositional Characteristics and Images of These Two Youth Cultures and Categories." *International Review of Sport Sociology*, 10, 91–106.

Sabo, D. (1988). *Report on Minority Sports Participation*. Women's Sports Foundation: New York.

Sailes, G. (1996a). "An Examination of Basketball Performance Among African American Males." *Journal of African American Men*, 1(4), 37–46.

———. (1996b). "A Comparison of Professional Sports Career Aspirations Among College Athletes." *Academic Athletic Journal*, 11(2), 20–28

———. (1994). "The Case Against NCAA Proposition 48." In *The American Black Male: His Status and His Future*, edited by R. Majors & J. Gordon. Chicago: Nelson-Hall, 95–104.

———. (1993a). "An Investigation of Academic Accountablity Among College Student Athletes." *Academic Athletic Journal*, Spring, 27–39.

———. (1993b). "An Investigation of Campus Stereotypes: The Myth of Black Athletic Superiority & the Dumb Jock Stereotype." *Sociology of Sport Journal*, 10, 88–97.

———. (1987). "A Socio-Economic Explanation of Black Sports Participation Patterns." *Western Journal of Black Studies*, 11, 164–167.

———. (1986). "The Exploitation of the Black Athlete: Some Alternative Solutions." *The Journal of Negro Education*, 55(4), 439–442.

———. (1984). "Sport Socialization Comparisons Among Black and White Adult Male Athletes and Non-Athletes." Doctoral dissertation, University of Minnesota.

Schafer, W., & Armer, M. (1971). "On Scholarship and Interscholastic Athletics." In *Sport: Readings From A Sociological Perspective*, edited by E. Dunning. Toronto: University of Toronto Press, 198–229.

Schoemann, Christopher. (1995). "1995–96 NCAA Guide for the College-Bound Student-Athlete. Overland Park, Kans.: The National Collegiate Athletic Association.

Wieberg, Steve. (1995). ""Prop 48 Study Raises Questions of Racial Equity." *USA Today*, July 6.

Wilson, W. J. (1980). *The Declining Significance of Race*. Chicago: University of Chicago Press.

II

The Image of the
African American Athlete

4

The Dominant Images of
Black Men in America:
The Representation of O.J. Simpson

Billy Hawkins

In America, black heterosexual masculinity has been strategically defined and black men have conveniently had their identities pre-arranged for them. The current definition and identities have produced images that are consistently reproduced in various forms of electronic and print media. They are based upon certain historical roles of the sambo and the brute nigger that were ascribed to black men to maintain the social order during the ante-bellum and post-ante-bellum periods. This safeguarding of the public order is continued today in the representation of black men in the mass media: creating in roles that provide convenient identification upon visual contact.

According to Gray (1995):

> Black heterosexual masculinity is figured in the popular imagination as the basis of masculine hero worship in the case of rappers; as naturalized and commodified bodies in the case of athletes; as symbols of menace and threat in the case of black gang members; and as noble warriors in the case of Afrocentric nationalists and Fruit of Islam. While these varied images travel across different fields of electronic representation and social discourse, it is nevertheless the same black body—super-star athlete, indignant rapper, "menacing" gang member, ad pitch-man, appropriate middle class professional, movie star—onto which competing and conflicting claims about (and for) black masculinity are waged. (p. 402)

The competing claims are working to maintain control and profit from the black male body by reproducing historical roles that have worked to keep black men in their place—confined to certain roles that support racial ideologies.

Unlike the claims some researchers (Lester & Smith, 1990) have made in suggesting that the stereotypical portrayal of blacks in newspaper and magazines have been replaced with a more fair and objective representation, there exist a reproduction of stereotypical images. What currently exists is a mysterious re-creation of the sambo and brute nigger roles where comparable images (e.g., the ad pitch-man, menacing gang member, super-athlete, etc.) are developed which provides the mass media with a format for representing black men. This format seems to portray black men most conspicuously in the roles of super-athletes, super-entertainers, and super-criminals. The term "super" is included because of supposed superior genetic predisposition, that is, black men are innately or naturally athletic, rhythmic, humorous, and violent. Two of the historical roles that have been transformed into the current dominant images are the sambo (coon) and the brutal black buck. In an attempt to address the problem of unfair representation in the mass media, this paper will look at how these images originated and how the mass media, specifically the print media, continue to reproduce them through their photo-representations of black men.

Because we live in a society where visual images are paramount (Berger, 1985) and where the mass media is a powerful medium for perceiving reality, as well as perpetuating ideological hegemony (Hall, 1981), we must be cognizant of the ways these forces continue to reproduce images that work to oppress and manage black people. Various studies have considered the reproduction of the ideological images of blacks (Colle, 1968; Hall, 1993), the mass media's perpetuation of racism (Entman, 1990; Jhally and Lewis, 1992; Hartmann and Husband, 1974), the representation of blacks in film (Bourne, 1991; Miller, 1996 and Querrero, 1995), and the disparity in coverage of blacks in different mass media forms (Sentman, 1983; Stempel, 1971; Lester and Smith 1990; Lambert, 1965). This current study will concern itself with showing how news magazines have used various photographic images, which are subtly aligned with historical roles and images, to stereotypically describe, socially control, and exploit black men.

Though subtle and sometimes ambiguous, photographic images play a major role in the maintenance of ideologies that work to socially control various populations in our society. According to Duncan (1990):

> Photographs are so much a part of our daily lives that we rarely think about how they influence us and what that influence is. Yet photographs, like other mass

media images, are politically motivated. Photography is a signifying system that works to legitimate interests of hegemonic groups. (p. 22)

Some researchers have addressed how the electronic and print media reproduces racism (van Dijk, 1991; Entman, 1990), and how the text is framed to influence people's understanding about social reality (Entman, 1993; Iyengar, 1991). However, photographic images present a message, and they can be positioned to influence the way people perceive reality. In other words, as Duncan (1990) states, "they serve to shape consensus, that is, consent to a social arrangement" (p. 22).

Documentaries, like *Ethnic Notions,* and various historical studies (Bogle, 1989) have demonstrated how the mass media have continually adhered to the images of black men as sambos, coons, and brute niggers in their representation of black men. The dominant representation of black men in the mass media today appears to be rooted in the images of sambo and brute nigger. The photo-representation (darkened mug-shot) of O. J. Simpson in *Time* and *Newsweek* is an example of how the print media portray black men negatively regardless of innocence. This paper intends to illustrate how the representation of black men shifts on a continuum between the sambo and brute nigger image based on the needs of the system of white supremacy.

The Sambo (Coon) Image

Before the sambo became a specific identity, it represented a concept that originated during the colonial period in the seventeenth century (Boskin, 1988). Boskin states that "the sambo was conceived on the European continent, particularly, in England, and drew its first life with the initial contact with West Africans during the slave period" (p. 32). According to Pieterse (1992), "The name sambo is derived from a Hispanic-American term meaning half-caste" (p. 153). Characteristics of the sambo image include the following: childish, contented slave, dependency, high-spirited (rhythmically speaking) but lazy, and a natural entertainer (Boskin, 1988; Pieterse, 1992; Elkins, 1959; Leab, 1975). Other terms that referred to the sambo were: uncle (as in Uncle Remus), Boy, Rastus, Coon, Jim Crow, Tambo and Pompey (Boskin, 1988; Pieterse, 1992).

The creation and maintenance of this image was very important to the institution of slavery (Elkins, 1959), and, according to Pieterse (1992), "Sambo was an antidote to Denmark Vesey and Nat Turner." Because there existed a climate among slave-holders that rendered them dreadfully fearful of a slave rebellion, the sambo image was needed and became very popular as a tool to control slave revolts.

Another reason for the popularity and necessity of this image was because it made slavery and segregation seem appropriate for blacks. Since the sambo was a contented slave, happy to serve his/her master, and a helpless child in need of a parent-figure, slavery was seen by plantation owners, anti-abolitionists, and segregationists as beneficial to the slave (Elkins, 1959; Pieterse, 1992; Boskin, 1988). Therefore, according to Boskin (1988), those individuals that were pro-slavery and segregationist encouraged the sambo image because "it was a device through which both slavery and segregation would be made the more palatable" (p. 258).

Since its early beginnings, the sambo image has evolved over time to be incorporated in the following ways: into popular songs such as "Old Black Joe," or "Uncle Ned"; in various advertisements such as "Uncle Ben's Rice," "Uncle Remus Syrup," or the Cream of Wheat man on Nabisco products; and in various minstrels and movies such as "Jim Crow," Zip Coon, "Wooing and Wedding of a Coon," and "Rastus in Zululand" (Boskin, 1988; Leab, 1975; Bogle, 1989; Pieterse, 1992).

Finally, the sambo image, unfortunately, is continually being manifested in the roles played by many black comedians, athletes, actors, and by blacks in advertisements. Many of the black athletes the media gives attention to are those that exhibit buffoon-like behavior (e.g., Dennis Rodman) or those that have been domesticated and have transcended color (e.g., Michael Jordan, Grant Hill, etc.). There are those black comedians and actors that have bought into this image and only seek to profit from it (i.e., the exploited is exploiting his/her exploitation), but their are others who are trying to overthrow or redefine this image from what Boskin (1988) classifies as its "presumed inherent form of humor: the possessor of the uninhibited laugh, the initiator of natural comedy, and the recipient of derogatory jokes" (p. 259).

The Brute Nigger (Savage) Image

The brute nigger image (more specifically termed "savage") also emerged on the European continent as a description for Africans. According to Jordan (1968), "The condition of savagery—the failure to be civilized—set Negroes apart from Englishmen in an ill-defined but crucial fashion" (p. 24). Jordan also suggests that, "They [Europeans] knew perfectly well that Negroes were men, yet they frequently described the Africans as 'brutish', 'bestial' or 'beastly'" (1968, p. 28).

The American terminology for the savage was the brute nigger (Pieterse, 1992). According to Pieterse (1992):

> In the United States, between roughly 1800 and 1950, key images of Black men were the brute nigger, sambo, and uncle.... The brute nigger is the Black male stereotyped as beast, who is "tamed" by means of lynching (emasculation), either physically or symbolically, and transformed into Sambo. (p. 228)

Therefore, this image justified the use of lynching to keep black men in their place—subservient and powerless.

D. W. Griffith's 1915 movie *Birth of a Nation* was one of this country's most notorious films that portrayed black men as savages as well as "sexual violators and political ravagers" (Boskin, 1988, p. 258). Boskin suggests that (1988):

> With respect to the savage, it was held that the Black man was endowed with violent and sexual impulses. It was argued, buttressed with quasi-scholarly data from mid-nineteenth to the later decades of the twentieth century, that dark-skinned people were stunted in their intellectual capacities. This myth gave rise to specific cultural traits ascribed to Black men: to their supposed natural rhythm, their proneness to rioting and fighting. (p. 258)

This image draws more upon the physicality of black men than the sambo image. Both images promote the biological inferiority of blacks (Boskin, 1988), however; the savage has superior physical abilities yet they are untamed and uncivilized, whereas the sambo was a domesticated savage. The brute nigger image supports the ideology that blacks are natural athletes because they have superior physical abilities. This image also supports the notion that blacks are natural criminals because of assumptions that blacks are primates or beast-like in behavior and uncivilized, thus prone to committing violent acts, especially sexual violaters of white women. The Willie Horton image used in 1988 by Vice President Bush was effective in reinforcing the attitudes associated with the brute nigger image.

Therefore, the representation of black men as super-criminals and super-athletes stem from the historical role black men fulfilled as brute niggers or savages. What is hopefully illustrated in this brief overview is the development of these images and some of the ways they have been manifested in the media representations of black men.

Theoretical Considerations and Methodology

These current representations are at work in the United States in what can be called a white supremacist's continuum of images for black men. On one end of this continuum exist the images of sambo and on the other end the brute nigger image. This continuum illustrates how various forms of the media have represented and continue to misrepresent black men. This continuum also demonstrates how the representations of black men can shift depending upon the need of the system of white supremacy. These representations in the mass media range from demonized images to domesticated images. Therefore, similar to the move from the slavery image of sambo to the post-slavery image of brute nigger, the image that works to keep black men in their respective places will be the image used by this system of white supremacy through the media's representation of black men. The use of this continuum will be placed within a cultural studies analysis. According to Turner (1990), "Cultural Studies analyses of media generally emphasize the construction of consensus, the reproduction of the status quo, the irresistibility of dominant meanings" (p. 95).

Are these images being reproduced today? How are these images being re-created in today's photo-representation of black men? To answer these questions, this study will analyze visual data by using an interpretative analysis to examine the cover-page photo-representation of black men from two major U.S. news magazines—*Time* and *Newsweek*. This analysis is a qualitative approach to illustrate how the photo-representations of black men continue to support white culture's continuum of images for black men.

FIGURE 1
U.S. White Supremacist's Continuum of Images for Black Men

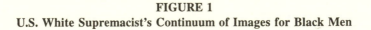

Sambo (Coon) Image:
Domesticated savage, subservient knows his/her place, happy and contented slave, natural entertainers childish.

Brute Nigger (Savage) Image:
Demonized, untamed, bestial, superior physical abilities, highly sexed and violent primates.

The cover pages were chosen because these are the first pages (and sometimes the only page) many subscribers as well as nonsubscribers see. At a news and magazine stand, it is the cover pages that often capture the attention of individuals, and encourage them to buy or not to buy. The cover pages of *Time* and *Newsweek* were chosen because they ranked fourth and seventh, respectively, among the 25 largest magazines in the United States (*Advertising Age*, 1995). This ranking was based on revenues and circulation.

Photo-representations of black men were viewed from 2,656 issues (1,328 of each magazine). The analysis initially placed each photo-representation of black men into one of the following categories: black athletes, black criminals, black entertainers, black suspects or in criminal positions (rioting, handcuffed, etc.,), black political or religious leaders, and black businessmen. The latter two categories recorded the positive photo-representation of black men in these magazines. The black politician and religious leader groups were combined because those individuals represented as religious leaders (e.g., Jesse Jackson or Louis Farrakhan) also fit the description of politician, whether by choice or demand. This seems to be a pattern which dates back to slavery when most of the literate slaves were ministers, and throughout the struggle for equality in America, the leaders (both male and female) of this struggle often emerged from the black church.

The interpretations of these photo-representations of black men were then placed into categories based on their similar characteristics with the sambo image or the brute nigger image. This interpretive analysis is not suggesting that all readers/viewers of these photos will interpret them the same way: this is one of the limitations with an interpretive methodology. According to Duncan (1990): "The reader brings his/her personal set of experiences, history, and social and cultural contexts to the text, and all of these influences shape the reader's interpretation of the text" (p. 27). In a similar fashion, each viewer of these cover page photos will have various interpretations based upon their social and cultural contexts, their experiences and histories. With this analysis, this study attempts to illustrate the connection between historical images and current representation of black men.

Results

Of the 2,656 total issues of both *Time* and *Newsweek*, Black men were represented on only 98 of the cover pages (3.7%); *Time* magazine had 46 (3.5%) photo-representations of black men and *Newsweek* had 52 (4%) photo-representations of black men. The breakdown of these photo-representations are illustrated in Table 1.

TABLE 1
Total and Percentages of Photo-representation of Black Men
in *Time* and *Newsweek*

	Time	Newsweek
Black Athletes	15 (32%)	11 (21%)
Black Criminals	1 (2%)	1 (2%)
Black Entertainers	7 (15%)	11 (21%)
Black Political/ Religious Leaders	10 (22%)	9 (17%)
Black Suspects or Black Men in Criminal Positions	10 (22%)	16 (31%)
Black Businessmen	3 (7%)	4 (8%)

In comparison to other categories, both magazines had a high percentage of photo-representation in the category of black politicians and religious leaders. However, these cover page photo-representations of black men as politician and religious leaders often accompanied derogatory headings. For example, one of the magazines had a photo-representation of Andrew Young with the heading, "The Outspoken Andrew Young." Two other issues had Vernon Jordan on the cover with the heading, "Whatever Happened to Black America," and a cover page photo of Idi Amin with the heading, "The Wild Man of Africa." Finally, there was an issue with a photo-representation of Minister Louis Farrakhan with the heading, "Minister of Rage."

These numbers are somewhat deceiving because if we were to examine the numbers exclusively it becomes evident that black male representation exists, though sparingly. However, this representation is framed in a way that continues to support dominant ideologies. In the above examples, Andrew Young is framed as a loud mouth, Vernon Jordan as a hopeless politician working for a hopeless cause (black America), Idi Amin is framed as a savage or an uncivilized black man with political power, and Minister Farrakhan as another angry black man. It is often taken for granted that when marginalized groups have sought equal representation, they assumed that representation would be fair. This is a prime example of where having sufficient representation is not enough because it can often be derogatory, just as degrading as having no representation, or it can work to maintain the social order. Increased representation of black men and other marginalized groups should not rest upon mere numbers but a thoroughly accurate representation that does not support stereotypical images.

If we were to examine the categories of black athletes, black entertainers, black criminals, and black suspects, the percentages are high— 71% of the cover pages for *Time* magazine and 75% for *Newsweek* magazine. This reflects an average of 74% of cover-page photos representing black men as athletes, entertainers, criminals, or suspects, and only 26% of the photo-representations of black men as politicians, religious leaders, and businessmen.

To look at the categories in terms of the historical images they represent, we would see a perpetuation of these negative images that work to control a social group. As mentioned earlier, the sambo is characterized as a happy, contented slave, a jester-like being that entertains his master in some outlandish fashion. The characteristics of the brute nigger are that he is physically strong, bestial, with violent behavior. Therefore, the sambo is represented in the black male entertainer and to some degree the black male athlete (especially professional sport athletes that exhibit buffoon-like behavior to excite the crowd, or those that have supposedly transcended color), while the brute nigger is represented in the black male criminal, the black male suspect, and the black male athlete.

It is very unusual to have these images available in one individual and accessible to the media for easy display. Historically, Jack Johnson was portrayed in the media as a super-athlete, super-criminal, and super-entertainer. As a super-athlete, Jack Johnson reigned as heavyweight champion from 1908 to 1915 (Ashe, 1988). As a super-entertainer, he performed vaudeville acts in Europe after he had won the heavyweight championship (Ashe, 1988). Johnson gave the media the opportunity to display him as a super-criminal when in 1912 he was "formally indicted by a grand jury for violating the Mann Act" (Ashe, 1988, p. 39). Within this indictment, Ashe list several counts brought against Johnson: "three counts of prostitution; two counts of debauchery; three counts of unlawful sexual intercourse; two counts of crimes against nature; and one count of inducement to prostitution" (1988, p. 39).

Another individual that gave the media opportunity to perpetuate these images was Jim Brown. In a similar fashion, Jim Brown represented the super-athlete (professional football with the Cleveland Browns), super-criminal (fights, alleged rapes, and abusing a white girlfriend), and super-entertainer in various movies: "The Dirty Dozen," "Rio Conchos," and "Three the Hard Way" (Brown, 1989).

Currently, the reproduction of these three images is represented in O. J. Simpson. Simpson's athletic prowess started at an early age when sport was the main avenue to keep young black kids out of trouble and possibly afford them an opportunity for social mobility. O. J. Simpson, through time, talent, and effort focused on football, took this avenue that led to 11 years in the NFL. Simpson, like Jim Brown, left a successful football career in professional football and stepped into Hollywood.

His Hollywood experiences presented him with some fortunate experiences, such as appearing in the television miniseries *Roots*, and some unfortunate opportunities of reproducing the sambo image; the reproduction of this image was evident in the series *The Naked Gun*, where Simpson played a buffoon-like cop or what Noverr (1995) considers "a bumbling policeman" (p. 311). His acting opportunities also included supporting roles in several television specials, comedy series, and films made specifically for television (Noverr, 1995). Simpson also became a commentator for NBC and ABC Sports. He also had the opportunity to be a spokesman for Hertz Rent-a-Car and a pitchman in several commercials for Hertz (Noverr, 1995).

Simpson's career exemplified that of a super-athlete and a super-entertainer who possessed a very profitable image—one that transcended color. Unfortunately, this lustrous career as an actor, commentator, spokesman, and pitchman came to an abrupt end in 1994. It was during this year that Simpson emerged with the image of super-criminal when on June 27, 1994, both *Newsweek* and *Time* magazines cover-page photos depicted Simpson in a darkened mug shot unshaved and dreary eyed. Perkins (1994) referred to the *Time* photo-representation of O. J. Simpson as a form of "Willie Horton journalism" (p. A15). The losses to the Brown and Goldman families are tragic and unfortunate occurrences, and in no way am I trying to trivialize these fatalities by highlighting this unfair and unethical form of journalism.

Conclusion and Implications

It is not my assertion that these representations of black men in these news magazines are intentional, but rather reflect a social conditioning process that shapes and focuses the lens that produces and reproduces these images. The photo-representation (mugshot) of O. J. Simpson by *Newsweek* and *Time* magazine and the high percentages of photo-representation of black men as suspects, entertainers, and athletes are by no means mistakes but convey a continual working and manifestation of white culture's continuum of images for black men. It is this racist ideological structure that is in place in the United States strategically working to keep black men, specifically, and blacks in general, in stereotypical and disadvantaged positions.

It is difficult to ignore the similar lifestyles of Johnson, Brown, and Simpson as just coincidental. All three were successful athletes, made a transition to being entertainers (Jack Johnson's entertainment career was rather brief), and they all broke the sexual taboo of having affairs with white women or marrying white women. America's most wanted have often been black men that have fit the above descriptions, especially those that have broken the sexual taboo.

Similar to the Willie Horton's media representation, the photo-representation of O. J. Simpson was a great opportunity to perpetuate the idea of what will happen to a black man in America if given enough rope. Since the days of D. W. Griffith's *Birth of a Nation* there still exists a fear that is ingrained within the consciousness of many white Americans produced from the myth of lustful desires that black men have for white women. Two of the reasons this photo-representation was and is so devastating are because it re-affirmed this myth, and it confirmed for many white Americans what they already believed and feared about black men, that is, that black men, no matter how polished they become through the whitening or domestication process of the American system, are still brutes—lustful of and killers of white women.

It is unfortunate that millions of black men, despite their innocence, will always be guilty because they fit the description of being black and male. Fitting the description makes black men accessible for false arrest and convictions. Thus, this description makes it easy for a white woman in North Carolina to kill her two children and blame a black man. Fitting the description makes it horrifyingly simple for a nursing home in Michigan to target and suspend seven blacks with no justifiable reason (other than they were black men) after a 92-year-old women said she was raped. Finally, the dominant images of black men in this country populates our prisons and fuels the public perception that black men and crime are synonymous terms (Smothers, 1990; Kelly, 1996).

The photo-representations of black men by the print media have created images that strongly encourage people of various races and from various countries to be cautious when in or near their presence, and preferably to avoid their presence for fear of a potential threat. As Walton (1989) suggests, "I might meet Bernhard Goetz on the subway; my car might break down in Howard Beach; the armed security guard might mistake me for a burglar in the lobby of my building. And they won't see a mild-mannered English major trying to get home. They will see Willie Horton" (p.77). This explains the power of these negative images, and their ability to justify the mistreatment of black people in general. These photo-representations along with other forms of media representations of black men will also work to maintain a system of white supremacy.

Because of these prescribed images, Simpson and others will always be guilty until proven innocent and even when proven innocent they will always be a lifetime suspect. He is, as the June 27, 1994, *Time* magazine headlines states, "An American Tragedy." A tragedy in the sense of fulfilling the roles many Americans have about the potentialities of black men, and a tragedy where America has failed in keeping its most notorious public enemy (the black male) in his place. He is also a tragedy in the sense that the domestication or "whitening process" of America, which many black men must go through to reach this point of transcending color and profitability has left him torn and hopelessly adrift between two worlds. The white world into which he has assimilated now rejects him and the black world, which he rejected in order to assimilate, he now seeks for consolation.

This representation of black men or "Willie Horton" journalism is also an American tragedy because it contributes to the continual demise of black men and the efforts of all black people. To be limited to the images of athletes, entertainers, and criminals on the social canvas of this country is a grave injustice committed to black men. The lens that framed these images sees black men as little more than high flying athletic mutants, crouch-grabbing rappers and singers, and as menaces to society. This is unfortunate but unless the lens that continually frames black men in negative and stereotypical roles is re-focused to capture a view that is more realistic of our daily experiences and endeavors, America will continue to be deceived and abort its obligation of living up to its potential and motto as being the land of opportunity.

One way of focusing and capturing an accurate representation of black men starts with deconstructing the myth that this is a land of opportunity. A land of opportunity evokes thoughts of equal access and nonbiased or nonprejudicial assumptions. Dominant forms of American media's misrepresentations of black men must move its narrow lens beyond the historical images that worked to maintain a system of slavery and Jim Crow and adopt a wider lens that accepts and respects the positive images of black men. This transition will take place when the black community no longer consents to and reproduces those negative images themselves (a personal and collective emancipation from the ideological hegemony that they have submitted to), and when they no longer support the media industries that continually profit from the misrepresentations of black men. The continual misrepresentations of black men will require a perpetual opposition. Images and a continual means of cultural resistance by black writers, directors, scholars, photographers, producers, and so forth, who are consciously aware and concerned about freedom from ideological oppression.

References

Advertising Age (1995, May 8). "25 Largest Magazines in the US," vol. 66 (19).

Ashe, A. (1988). *A Hard Road to Glory: A History of the African American Athlete 1619–1918, Vol. 1.* New York: Amistad.

Berger, J. (1985). *Ways of Seeing.* London: British Broadcasting Corp. & Penguin Books.

Bogle, D. (1989). *Toms, Coons, Mulattoes, Mammies, and Bucks: An Interpretive History of Blacks in American Films.* New York: Continuum.

Boskin, J. (1988). "Sambo and Other Male Images in Popular Culture." In *Images of Blacks in American Culture: A Reference Guide to Information Sources*, edited by J. C. Smith. New York: Greenwood Press, 257–272.

Bourne, S. C. (1991). "The African American Image in American Cinema." *Black Scholar*, 21 (2), 12–19.

Brown, J. (1989). *Out of Bounds.* New York: Kensington Publishing Corp.

Colle, R. D. (1968). "Negro Image in the Mass Media: A Case Study in Social Change." *Journalism Quarterly*, 45, 55–61.

Duncan, M. C. (1990). "Sports Photographs and Sexual Difference: Images of Women and Men in the 1984 and 1988 Olympic Games." *Sociology of Sport Journal*, 7 (1), 22–43.

Elkins, S. M. (1959). *Slavery: A Problem in American Institutional & Intellectual Life.* Chicago: The University of Chicago Press.

Entman, R. (1990). "Racism and Local TV News." *Critical Studies in Mass Communication*, 7 (4), 332–345.

————. (1993). "Framing: Toward Clarification of a Fractured Paradigm." *Journal of Communication*, 43 (4), 51–58.

Gray, H. (1995). "Black Masculinity and Visual Culture." *Callaloo*, 18 (2), 401–405.

Hall, R. E. (1993). "Clowns, Buffoons, and Gladiators: Media Portrayals of African-American Men." *Journal of Men's Studies*, 1 (3), 239–251.

Hall, S. (1981). "Television as Expression of Ideology." *Communication Research Trends*, 2 (3), 5–6.

Hartmann, P., & Husband, C. (1974). *Racism and the Mass Media*. Totowa, N.J.: Rowman & Littlefield.

Iyengar, S. (1991). *Is Anybody Responsible? How Television Frames Political Issues*. Chicago: University of Chicago Press.

Jhally, S., & Lewis, J. (1992). *Enlightened Racism: The Cosby Show, Audiences, and the Myth of the American Dream*. Boulder, CO: Westview Press.

Jordan, W. D. (1968). *White Over Black: American Attitudes toward the Negro, 1550–1812*. New York: W. W. Norton & Company.

Kelly, M. P. F. (1996, July 2). "Do You See a Kid or a Criminal?" *Christian Science Monitor*, p. 18, col. 1.

Leab, D. J. (1975). *From Sambo to Superspade: The Black Experience in Motion Pictures*. Boston: Houghton Mifflin.

Lester, P., & Smith, R. (1990). "African-American Photo-Coverage in *Life, Newsweek* and *Time*, 1937–1988." *Journalism Quarterly*, 67, 128–136.

Lambert, V. (1965). "Negro Exposure in *Look's* Editorial Content." *Journalism Quarterly*, 42, 657–659.

Miller, C. (1996). "The Representation of the Black Male in Film" (on-line). Available from: http://www.gti.net/cmmiller/blkflm.html.

Noverr, D. A. (1995). "O. J. Simpson: (July 9, 1947–)." In *African-American Sports Greats: A Biographical Dictionary*, edited by D. L. Porter. Westport, CT: Greenwood Press, pp. 309–312.

Perkins, J. (1994, June 29). "Simpson Case Leaves a Trail of Shame." *Atlanta Constitution*, p. A15.

Pieterse, J. N. (1992). *White on Black: Images of Africa and Blacks in Western Popular Culture*. New Haven: Yale University Press.

Querrero, E. (1995). "The Black Man on Our Screens and the Empty Space of Representation." *Callaloo*, 18 (2), 395–400.

Sentman, M. A. (1983). "Black and White: Disparity in Coverage by *Life* Magazine from 1937 to 1972." *Journalism Quarterly*, 60, 501–508.

Smothers, M. L. (1990, May 12). "Black Males are Branded by 'the Stereotype'." *Amsterdam News*, p. 6, col. 1.

Stempel, G. G. (1971). "Visibility of Blacks in News and News-Picture Magazines." *Journalism Quarterly*, 48, 337–339.

Turner, G. (1990). *British Cultural Studies: An Introduction*. Boston: Unwin Hyman.

Walton, A. (1989, August 20). "Willie Horton and Me: Experience of Being a Black Male." *The New York Times Magazine*, 138, 52.

Van Dijk, T. A. (1991). *Racism and the Press*. London: Routledge.

5

Black Sports Images in Transition: The Impact of Tiger's Roar

Christopher P. Uchacz

> *He [Tiger] will transcend the game...and bring to*
> *the world...a humanitarianism...which has never*
> *been known before. The world will be a better*
> *place to live in...by virtue of his existence...and*
> *his presence.... I acknowledge only a small part*
> *in that...in that I know I was personally selected*
> *by God himself...to nurture this young man...and*
> *bring him to the point where he can make his*
> *contribution to humanity.... Tiger will do more*
> *than any other man in history to change*
> *the course of humanity.*
> —Earl Woods (Smith, 1996, p. 31)

There can be no denying that Tiger Woods has become one of the most visible and celebrated athletes of the 1990s. His signing of several lucrative endorsement contracts with the likes of Nike, Titleist, American Express, and Rolex, coupled with the media's extensive fascination with his celebrity status, has established Woods as one of the most intriguing cultural symbols of our time. Tiger has become a prime exemplar of Kellner's (1995) belief that everyday life is mediated by the spectacles of media culture that dramatizes our conflicts, celebrates our values, and projects our deepest hopes and fears. In other words, Tiger's cultural value or celebrity status is connected to ways of making sense of our social world (Marshall, 1997, p. 51), as becomes the case when examining the social construction of race.

The examination of race must be engaged within the contextually specific realms of culture and politics because "they emerge as part of a historically specific relationship of oppression in order to justify the existence of the relationship" (Callinicos, 1993, p. 18). In order to begin to understand Tiger's cultural impact on American society, it will become necessary to ground this analysis within the historical context of the present or 1990s America. Doing so will provide an objective examination of the political, economic, social, and cultural components of this specific conjunctional moment in time while beginning to "unpack" the racial politics of the 1990s or Clinton's America. Tiger's ability to represent the current status of racial identification within the political climate of Clinton's America is integral to this project; a project which must draw upon "the past in a nostalgic sense in order to provide 'us' with a sense of who 'we' are as individuals and members of [American] society" (Nauright, 1996, p. 227). In other words, this chapter will re-present the discourse connected to the historical context of the 1980s or Reagan's America in order to disclose the identity politics of race as they have been re-articulated in the 1990s, a time of rapid social, political, and economic transformation.

In order to deconstruct the racial politics, as they have been and are currently being constructed in the 1990s or Clinton's America, it is essential to provide a contextual analysis through the examination of the existing racial codes that define the representation of Tiger's multi-racial body. More specifically, Tiger's multi-racial body will be interrogated in order to articulate how it has been taken up and mobilized in order to challenge or perpetuate the current categorization of race in the United States. In order to do so, this chapter will address issues which will examine how race has come to be understood and subsequently categorized in 1990s America; how Tiger's multi-racial body challenges or perpetuates the current status of racial categorization; and how media representations of Tiger articulate a deliberate racial discourse in the United States.

Further, it can be argued that Tiger's multi-racial body has become representative of a more racially diverse and tolerant generation of young Americans who, according to Clinton, are destined to lead the United States into the twenty-first century. However, before trying to "unpack" the racial politics of Clinton's America, it will be necessary to provide an overview of the current racial climate of the 1990s as it has been, and is being constructed. This is important as it will be within this context that a preliminary "reading" of Tiger's multi-racial body, and how its presence challenges or perpetuates the current process of racial categorization in the United States, will be provided.

Clinton's America: The Re-Articulation of Race in the 1990s

"How 'we' have come to remember the past will become integral to how 'we' come to make sense of our experiences in the present" (Nauright, 1996, p. 227). Kathleen Stewart (1988) agrees as she maintains that the past "creates a frame of meaning, a means of dramatizing aspects of an increasingly fluid and unnamed social life" (p. 227). It is here that it will become critical to begin to unpack the historical antecedents that have, to date, influenced Americans and their subsequent understanding of race in the 1990s. Drawing on the racial politics of the 1980s, will provide a "reference point" in order to begin to develop a preliminary understanding of race in the 1990s. However, it is important to keep in mind that while it is wrong to suggest that no progress has been made in race relations in the United States since the Civil Rights Movement of the 1960s, it is equally wrong to assume that all is well.

Former President Ronald Reagan and his government believed in and promoted the idea, amongst other ideas (i.e., the New Christian Right, the family, and "new" [read old] traditional American values), that racism and the need for affirmative action were things of the past. Yet, in the politically conscious times of the 1990s we are often afraid to confront the obvious, that this type of racist ideology is alive and well in America. As a direct result, a part of how we have come to understand race in the 1990s has been directly influenced by the racial politics and practices of the 1980s, or Reagan's attempt at the re-construction of a more "traditional" or "white" America.

During the 1980s, it was both Reagan's and the New Right's particular brand of racialized politics which were responsible for the exhibition of "emotional hostility towards blacks, was resistive to the political demands of blacks, and argued that racial discrimination no longer impeded achievement in urban America, as it had in the past" (Reeves & Campbell, 1994, p. 91). It was during this particular political/historical moment of the 1980s that racism was no longer thought of as a problem, yet, the divide between "white" America and "black" America was continuing to grow larger.

Nauright (1996) sheds some light on both Reagan's and the New Right's motivations as he claims that "in times of social, cultural, and political shifts, people frequently draw on elements of their past cultural identity in order to cope with various societal changes" (p. 228). One could argue that this is what occurred throughout the Reagan government and the New Right during the 1980s, a time when the minority (read black) body was portrayed as the irrevocable root of all evil in American society. Urban America was portrayed as the weak American link that had the potential to drag an entire nation into social or cultural bankruptcy.

It was this re-construction of the "deviant" or "diseased" black body that Reagan attributed to the downfall of the American family and to the moral fiber of an entire nation. As a means of marginalizing this corrupted segment of American society, Reagan and the New Right were quick to re-instill notions of the traditional or nuclear family, a lifestyle which, they feared, was becoming a thing of the past. This further exemplifies Nauright's (1996) belief that "dominant power group(s) can legitimate their position by promoting a sense of cultural security through cultural practices common to many members of society" (p. 228). Traditional family structures exemplified by the "Cleavers," the "Cunninghams," and the "Huxtables" were often referred to as presenting a nostalgic sense of security and the feeling everything was all right in American society.

In the same manner that Levi-Strauss (1966) argued that modern societies think of the world in binary opposites, Americans seemingly conceive of race as it is encompassed within a "white" versus "black" binary; a binary re-created by the Reagan administration and the New Right in the 1980s. It is this particular relationship that is often used as a means of differentiation between social, cultural, economic, racial, and class boundaries. As a result, this "black" vs. "white" dyad has come to saturate American common sense with notions of "white" privilege and power in contrast to the dehumanization of the pathologized "black" body as "Other."

According to Giroux (1994), "whiteness" has come to "represent itself as a universal marker for being civilized and in doing so, posits the 'Other' within the language of pathology, fear, madness, and degeneration" (p. 75). For this reason, distinctions between "them" (read black) and "us" (read white) are enforced through the popular representation of the savage, bestial, and uncivilized "black" American, in difference to its restrained, cerebral, and civilized "white" American nemesis. The representation of "blacks" as "Other" establishes the belief that African Americans, in some way, "do not demand the equal respect that is increasingly acknowledged as the right of [all] human beings" (Callinicos, 1993, p. 28).

Both Denzin (1991) and Giroux (1994) refer to the racial politics of Reagan's backlash, or the politics of the New Right, as a "new cultural racism." This is a racism that acknowledged people of color (read black) as being significantly more likely to commit violent criminal acts than members of the white majority (Dumm, 1993). More often than not, these sorts of violent criminal acts were located in the urban segment of America and very rarely in the safer segment or "white" suburbs. As a result, mass-mediated discourses signified African American culture as being inherently deviant, unproductive, irresponsible, uncivilized, promiscuous, all in contrast to the hegemonic white norm (Andrews, 1996).

It was also during the 1980s that crime/violence became re-racialized and located within the various urban centers of America. "Racially coded violence and greed, embodied in the figure of the African-American gang member, is the apparent and decisive factor in the decimation of the inner city" (Cole, 1996, p. 368). This led directly to the subsequent delinquency and criminalization of African-American males who lived in urban America. Although this "reading" of delinquency was not created during the Reagan era, it was re-articulated as an insidious counter discourse to the institution of the "family" where the suburban, nuclear, and white family was portrayed as the "All-American" ideal.

It was this type of reading of "black" youth which developed a commonsense understanding of the inherent delinquency which, more than ever before, had come to plague "blackness" as a racial marker continuing on into the 1990s. The media was integral in the perpetuation of this particular representation of "black" urban youth, and, as a result, Denzin (1996) asserts that the "majority of Americans [come to] know and understand the American racial order through media representations of the Black, ethnic other" (p. 319). In other words, the media's portrayal of the pathology of delinquency has been articulated through the body of the young, "black," poor urban youth of America.

For example, the Fox Network show "Cops" reveals to us how popular culture still perpetuates the representation of the criminalized "black" body. The show repeatedly presents, to the American public, clips of responsible police officers upholding their duty to rid the streets of deviant and primarily African American drug dealers, gang members, thieves, or vagrants. In addition, the police officers on the show are deliberate in voicing their disdain for the increase in domestic disputes which are on the rise in American society. "Cops" successfully articulates to its viewers that the primary instigators of domestic violence are "blacks," displaying them as the destroyers of the moral fabric of contemporary America.

Still in the 1990s, the pathologized "black" body maintains a central position in the racial climate of Clinton's America. This re-creation of a "cultural racism," as re-constructed during the Reagan administration of the 1980s, is still alive and well as is evidenced by the media's representation of the deviant "black" body. In support of this theory, Denzin (1996) maintains that "race in America today is largely a matter of advertising, commercials, and the media" (p. 319). One only need examine professional sports and how the media often represents "black" athletes as the pathologized "Other" as found in society in general.

There is a stereotypical media representation of the pathologically violent and criminal "black" body which is evident in the world of sport as articulated in society. According to Andrews (1996), "the contemporary constructions of the pathologically criminal and naturally sporting black body are founded upon a common assumption of the innate physicality of the black body" (p.135). The inherent "physical" nature becomes dangerous as it perpetuates a commonsense notion that "blacks" are physically aggressive, destructive, and violent, all characteristics of the criminalized "black" American male. This particular articulation cannot exist without having a significant effect on the representation of race in American society. Denzin (1996) supports this thought arguing that "the most significant feature of the contemporary American racial order is the one given in the professional sporting arena" (p. 319), more specifically in the National Basketball Association (NBA).

NBA officials have successfully sold a league that is 80% "black" to a predominantly white audience (Taylor, 1997b). In doing so, the NBA has embraced a specific culture that originated in inner-city or urban America. This culture has a certain "street" credibility which influences the manner in which race is currently articulated within American society. As a result, the NBA has never been completely separated from "its popular, racially charged connotation as an aberrant domain" (Andrews, 1996, p. 144). The NBA, in part, reinforces notions of an "inherently" deviant lifestyle, a lifestyle the media tells us is articulated through the pathologized black body found in America. Andrews (1996) uses the NBA as a:

> euphemism for an American nation, the racial paranoia and insecurity pervading popular discourse depicted by the unruly and disrespective behavior of young African-American males as being threatening to the stability of the NBA as the

criminal irresponsibility of the young urban African-American male was to the American society as a whole. (p. 150)

A good example of this is the very recent altercation between Latrell Sprewell, a player for the NBA's Golden State Warriors, and his coach, P. J. Carlesimo. Sprewell was witnessed to have assaulted and threatened to kill Carlesimo during a December 1, 1997, practice (Taylor, 1997a). There can be no denying that Sprewell committed one of the most outrageous acts on the court or the field of play that threatened American professional sports, and its representation of the "black" athlete. At the same time, his [Sprewell's] actions confirmed the "bad boy" image of the NBA and has further perpetuated the media's representation of the pathologized black body. As a result, the NBA has again been "targeted by the reactionary popular media as yet another site for representing African-American males as signifiers of danger and social depravity" (Andrews, 1996, p. 150).

However, in 1990s America the focus of race is no longer simply a focus on "blackness." Giroux (1997) argues that "whiteness" has also become an increasingly visible symbol of racial identity in America. It has become hard to disagree with Giroux (1997) that perhaps "whiteness" is becoming a racial marker for 1990s America, much in the same manner as "blackness" has, but for different reasons and through different mechanisms.

"Whiteness" as a category of racial identity was appropriated by diverse conservative and right-wing groups, as well as critical scholars, as a broader articulation of race and difference (Giroux, 1997). The discourse of "whiteness" signifies the resentment and confusion of many whites who ultimately feel victimized by the racial politics of the 1990s. This resentment or "victimization" exists on the premise that there has been an increase in the incidence of "unqualified" minorities benefiting (i.e., achieving gainful employment) from affirmative action policies at the expense of qualified, hard-working whites. It is this type of "white" resentment that argues that there has been a reversal in the current social order where "white" males are now the minority and the once previous minorities are benefiting in their place.

This discourse expresses the idea that "white" males have, ironically, become the marginalized and oppressed figures in the contemporary social formation of the United States. As a result, the 1990s have "spawned" the bitter "white" male who has become "part of a broader resistance to multi-cultural democracy and diverse racial culture" (Giroux, 1997, p. 287). In the next section, this analysis will draw upon this particular conjunctional moment in order to develop an understanding of how Tiger's multi-racial body challenges or perpetuates current notions of the pathologized "black" body. Further, through Oprah Winfrey, it will attempt to articulate how she attempts to provide a counter-discourse to racism in the United States.

Tiger Woods: A Cultural Symbol for Oprah's America?

Shortly after his stunning victory at the 1997 Masters Championship, Tiger made his first appearance on "The Oprah Winfrey Show," which aired on July 29, 1997. Several times throughout the hour-long interview, Oprah referred to Tiger as "America's Son." It was here that the importance of Tiger's multi-racial body becomes clear as does Oprah's own political agenda. As Oprah's interview of Tiger progressed, it became increasingly obvious that she was making direct reference to his multi-racial identity while acknowledging that this particular representation had the potential to become a social marker for a more racially diverse United States.

Through her talk show, Oprah has successfully established a forum where she has created a very "down to earth" or "at home," atmosphere which has become a sort of media haven for celebrities of Tiger's status. Oprah has been described as a comforting, nonthreatening bridge between black and white cultures, which has effectively minimized or depoliticized her race, presenting her as an exemplar of American success (Peck, 1994). Her project, at least with Tiger Woods and other "black" cultural icons, is clear and deliberate—she is trying to deconstruct the notion of "race" that Americans have come to understand and perpetuate. This conscious interaction with Tiger becomes Oprah's attempt to "de-racialize" Tiger's identity in order to construct a "race-free" America.

One of the first questions Oprah asks Tiger during the initial segment of the show was "what do you call yourself?" (Winfrey, 1997). Tiger's reply was quick, "growing up, I came up with this name...Cablinasian." This was a category that Tiger created as a young child in order to celebrate his multi-racial identity. It was a play on the combination of his *Ca*ucasian, *bl*ack or African-American, Native American *In*dian, and *Asian* ancestry. It is this racial combination that, as will be further argued, has become "uncategorizable" by American standards of racial categorization.

Further, Oprah announces to both studio and television audiences that "Tiger is exactly what our world needs right now" (Winfrey, 1997). She fails to expound on her frame of reference for this comment; however, it becomes logical to assume that she is again making reference to Tiger's potential to elicit social change, a change that will mark a new level of racial tolerance as Americans move into the twenty-first century. In addition, Tiger's multi-racial or "Cablinasian" identity becomes representative of his "real" threat to the categorization of race in contemporary American culture.

Here we can see Tiger's potential for becoming (or perhaps he has already become) a "human vehicle" for cultural change where others, like Oprah Winfrey, are establishing sites of social awareness meant to lead to social reform or change in the American consciousness. There can be no denying that Tiger Woods has become a legitimate cultural symbol of 1990s America as Stuart Hall (1981) explains that "the meaning of the cultural symbol is given in part by the social field into which it is incorporated, the practices with which it articulates and is made to resonate" (p. 235). As a primary result of the racial politics of the 1980s, contemporary 1990s American culture has effectively "naturalized" the categorization of race as it exists within a "white" versus "black" dualism.

It is this seemingly simplistic conception of race that the representation of Tiger's multi-racial body challenges. For example, upon winning the Masters Championship, the media was quick to hail Tiger as the first "black" man to win the most coveted of golf's major tournaments. However, this particular representation of Tiger's "blackness" is instantly problematic as it systematically denies his Caucasian, Native American Indian, and Asian ancestries. It becomes important here to ask who the representation of Tiger as a "black" man benefits and why? This issue will be explored at greater depth in the next section.

At this point it is necessary to clarify or make the distinction that the scope of this chapter is not trying to define Tiger's "race," but rather has set out to examine what Tiger's multi-racial body signifies within contemporary American society. American culture has become steeped in a history marred by racism and segregation as is evidenced in the current racial politics of Clinton's America—a conjunctional moment that, Oprah Winfrey would argue, Tiger has the potential to disrupt.

Immanuel Wallerstein (1991) reminds us that race is often perceived as a genetic category which has a distinct, visible physical form. As a result, Americans categorize people into certain racial groups based on the color of a person's skin. This becomes problematic for a couple of reasons. First, we must be aware that there are many underlying issues that are often not visible on the surface of what we see or are studying, as is the case with Tiger Woods. Although he may look "black," we know that his multi-racial or "uncategorizable," body has become the object of study that represents something other than itself. Further, the categorization of race, by American standards, incorporates a set of restrictive labels that dictate different social, cultural, political, and economic restraints, as is often mediated through the minority body.

For example, the federal government recently rejected the addition of a "multi-racial" category to be used in its federal programs. Individuals who wish to report their multi-racial identity will be asked to check each of the categories that apply. This year's American test Census provides only five categories of race: American Indian/Alaska Native, Asian, Black or African-American, native Hawaiian, or White (Schmid, 1997). What has happened to the "Hispanic" category? Why have the categories changed? The point here is not to enter into a debate concerning the legitimacy of "categorization," but to acknowledge that Tiger's multi-racial identity challenges this complex issue.

The next section of this chapter will re-address and further draw upon Oprah's political agenda, to de-racialize America. It will attempt to link Oprah's agenda to that of Nike as a means of exhibiting a socially responsible/caring image. In addition, it will also provide an alternative reading of Tiger's multi-racial body as it is appropriated by Nike.

"I am Tiger Woods":
A Brief Textual Analysis of a Nike Ad Campaign

Since turning professional and signing a lucrative endorsement contract with Nike, Tiger Woods has been featured in several highly innovative and controversial ad campaigns, in both television and print. Among these campaigns is a series of ads that focus specifically on youth and their presence within the golf community. Although the game of golf is steeped in several racist and exclusionary practices, these Nike ads seem to be breaking new ground by acknowledging and promoting youth and their desire to claim a space of their own within the institution of golf. A critical "reading" of a particular Nike ad will address Nike's attempts to "hail" American youth, while at the same time attempting to position Tiger's multi-racial body as a representation of America's potential to move towards a more racially tolerant society.

Here the focus will be on a recent ad campaign launched by Nike featuring Tiger Woods and his apparent fascination with the youth of America. This ad will be referred to as the "I am Tiger Woods" campaign featured in both television commercials and print advertisements. Again, Nike has successfully marketed a star athlete, Tiger Woods, in order to promote the global "swoosh," Nike's logo, which has come to stand for such things as "cutting edge," "style," "image," "attitude," "commitment," "responsibility," "loyalty," and, most importantly, "Nike."

Although the game of golf is grounded in racist and other exclusionary practices (i.e., practices centered around gender and generational issues), the "I am Tiger Woods" campaign seems to be Nike's attempt to break new ground by acknowledging and promoting a racially diverse group of young children and their desire to "be like Tiger."

The "I am Tiger Woods" print campaign provides the consumer with a collage of images of a racially diverse group of young boys and girls as they negotiate their way around an unknown golf course. All of the images in this collage have been super-imposed on top of a large black and white close-up of Tiger's face. His face is expressionless and he is seemingly looking out of the ad, directly into the consumer's eyes. Tiger's demeanor in the ad is both pensive and non-threatening. In fact, Tiger's presence seems to articulate to the consumer that he is somehow watching over the children, and thus so is Nike and its global swoosh.

One of the most striking images from this ad presents four young boys, their backs to the consumer, walking up an unknown fairway towards an extremely bright skyline. The image is in black and white which further accentuates the brightness of the sky. The fact that they are walking on an "unknown" fairway becomes important as it signifies that this place could be on any golf course in the United States. The image of these young boys walking from "anywhere" to a bright light can be interpreted as a walk into a pastoral future, a path that will lead to better times that await them in the twenty-first century. The accompanying phrase "I am Tiger Woods" becomes important as it is Tiger's multi-racial identity that is being appropriated by the young boys in order to ask America to "come walk with us" into a brighter, more racially tolerant future or "Nike Nation." Although this last image is highly seductive, it fails to address the urban spaces of America; spaces which have come to be defined by a not so new "cultural racism." However, there is another image presented within this same Nike ad campaign which depicts three young boys who are black and Hispanic looking, walking from one city street corner to another. Each of the three boys has a set of golf clubs strapped across his shoulders.

It becomes clear that this particular image is Nike's attempt to "hail" urban youth, an attempt to give these kids a chance to remove themselves from a racialized and segregated space, enabling them to integrate into new, previously inaccessible spaces, and Tiger alludes that this can happen through golf. Perhaps in this case, the boys walking across the street signifies a crossing of a boundary that has traditionally separated them from the other portions of America. Tiger's multiracial identity articulates to urban youth that there is hope; a hope to overcome a 1990s version of "cultural racism" that still divides America. It is clear, that Nike, through Tiger's multi-racial identity, is attempting to seduce American youth into "buying" into Nike's social awareness and subsequent desire for social change.

Oprah's quote, "Tiger is exactly what our world needs right now," becomes important here. As has been depicted here, Tiger is being positioned in American culture as a multi-racial exemplar or role model in order to lecture America about racial tolerance in the United States. His own racial tolerance was recently displayed in the media following comments made by Fuzzy Zoeller at the Master's. Zoeller's reference to Tiger as a "boy" coupled with his comments about "fried chicken" and "collard greens or whatever the hell they eat" ("Woods Accepts Zoeller's Apology," 1997) created quite a commotion within the media. We can learn from Tiger's handling of the incident. Rather than striking back at Zoeller, through the media, in a resentful manner, Tiger was more restrained and tolerant as a means of overcoming what I might call Zoeller's "white resentment." Through Tiger's handling of this incident, Americans, especially American youth, can witness racial tolerance at work.

Conclusion

It is clear that Tiger's multi-racial body can be articulated in many different ways. Oprah Winfrey would likely argue that Tiger's multiracial body is quickly becoming a signifier that suggests that America may be moving towards a more racially tolerant future, a future where, quite possibly, race won't matter, a time when we will be able to forget about racial intolerance. President Clinton argues that we must focus on the youth of America, to teach them about racial tolerance, as well as the racial intolerance that has been instrumental in the development of "cultural racism" and "white resentment" as defining parameters of race in America. If Tiger continues to handle himself in a responsible and "tolerant" manner, young children will be tempted to model their behavior after his. They will learn to engage in a critical pedagogy of self-formation that allows them to cross racial lines in order to begin to forge multi-racial coalitions based on critical engagement with 'Others'" (Giroux, 1997, p. 299).

In addition, Nike has created a forum where the new American racial order has been imagined, created, presented, and played out (Denzin, 1996). It is clear that through its representation of Tiger Woods, Nike is attempting to create a socially responsible image by re-framing the ongoing debate about racism in the United States. Nike has tapped what Susan Willis (1991) refers to as (Tiger's) "new ethnicity" where individuals have the ability/power to represent all races and are held up as ideals where their use indicates an attempt to erase the political significance of race. Tiger's Cablinasian identity makes him a "real" floating racial signifier in contrast to Andrews' (1996) articulation of Michael Jordan, an African American, as a "floating racial signifier."

Tiger's multi-racial body, combined with the media's representation of his "blackness" has become a nemesis to what Andrews (1996) refers to as the "stereotypical representations of deviant, promiscuous, and irresponsible black males that punctuated the ubiquitous populist racist discourse" (p. 138). Tiger's mediated "blackness" creates an ideal that provides a reprieve from the pathologized "black" body. Tiger's body is a body that is not "too" black or pathologically flawed by American standards.

Tiger's multi-racial identity can be used as an example of a change in the racial discourse of American society. Tiger represents an "uncategorizable" body which has the ability/power to transcend the current racial codes which dictate categorization while challenging stereotypical notions of race (read "blackness") in order to depoliticize race as Americans have come to understand it.

References

Andrews, D. L. (1996). "The Fact(s) of Michael Jordan's Blackness: Excavating a Floating Racial Signifier." *Sociology of Sport Journal*, 13(2), 125–158.

Callinicos, A. (1993). *Race and Class*. London: Bookmarks.

Cole, C. L. (1996). "American Jordan: P.L.A.Y., Consensus, and Punishment." *Sociology of Sport Journal*, 13(4), 366–397.

Denzin, N.K. (1991). *Images of Postmodern Society: Social Theory and Contemporary Cinema*. London: Sage.

————. (1996). "More Rare Air: Michael Jordan on Michael Jordan." *Sociology of Sport Journal*, 13(4), 319–324.

Dumm, T. L. (1993). "The New Enclosures: Racism in the Normalized Community." In *Reading Rodney King: Reading Urban Uprising*, edited by R. Gooding-Williams. New York: Routledge, 178–195.

Giroux, H. (1994). *Disturbing Pleasures: Learning Popular Culture*. New York: Routledge.

————. (1997). "Rewriting the Discourse of Racial Identity: Towards a Pedagogy and Politics of Whiteness." *Harvard Educational Review*, 67(2), 285–320.

Hall, S. (1981). "Notes on deconstructing 'the popular.'" In *People's History and Socialist Theory*, edited by R. Samuel. London: Routledge & Keegan Paul, 227–240.

Kellner, D. (1995). *Media Culture*. London and New York: Routledge.

Levi-Strauss, C. (1966). *The Savage Mind*. London: Weidenfeld & Nicolson.

Marshall, P.D. (1997). *Celebrity and Power*. Minneapolis: University of Minnesota Press.

Nauright, J. (1996). "Sustaining Masculine Hegemony: Rugby and the Nostalgia of Masculinity." In *Making Men: Rugby and Masculine Identity*, edited by J. Nauright and T. Chandler. London: Frank Cass, 227–244.

Peck, J. (1994). "Talk About Racism: Framing a Popular Discourse of Race on Oprah Winfrey." *Cultural Critique*, Spring, 89–126.

Reeves, J. L., and Campbell, R. (1994). *Cracked Coverage: Television News, the Anti-Cocaine Crusade, and the Reagan Legacy*. Durham and London: Duke University Press.

Schmid, R. E. (1997, November 2). "Government Rejects Multi-racial Category for Federal Programs," http://www.foxnews.com/sunday/index.htm

Smith, G. (1996, December, 23). "The Chosen One." *Sports Illustrated*, 28–52.

Stewart, K. (1988). "Nostalgia—A Polemic." *Cultural Anthropology*, 3(3), 227.

Taylor, P. (1997a, December 15). "Center of the Storm." *Sports Illustrated*, 60–67.

————. (1997b, December 15). "The Race Card." *Sports Illustrated*, 70–71.

Wallerstein, I. (1991). "The Construction of Peoplehood: Racism, Nationalism, Ethnicity." In *Race, Nation, Class*, edited by E. Balibar and I. Wallerstein. New York: Verso, 71–85.

Willis, S. (1991). *A Primer for Daily Life*. London: Routledge.

Winfrey, O. (1997, July 29). "The Oprah Winfrey Show" (television program). Chicago: Harpo Productions.

"Woods Accepts Zoeller's Apology, Ends Racial-Comment Controversy." (1997, May 3). *Golfweek*, 39.

6

Race Logic and "Being Like Mike": Representations of Athletes in Advertising, 1985–1994

Mikaela Dufur

Scholarly works, novels, news broadcasts, and movies all suggest that black Americans still struggle for recognition and equality in the 1990s. A black child in the public schools today is less likely to attend college, make a reasonable salary, reside in decent housing and live a long, healthy life than are her or his white schoolmates (Hochschild, 1995). Blacks are underrepresented in the professions, government and big business, while they are over-represented in manual labor (Tomaskovic-Devey, 1994). One arena in which blacks seem to have made significant progress, however, is sport. Since Jackie Robinson broke baseball's color barrier in 1947, black athletes participation in many major professional and Olympic sports has increased sharply. For example, although blacks make up only 12 percent of the population of the United States today, they make up 80 percent of the players in the National Basketball Association (Lapchick, 1996).

As black athletes' participation in sport grows, opportunities for blacks to partake of the huge amounts of money pouring into sport increase, too. Sport is big business, and one of the areas that is growing most rapidly is corporate sponsorship and endorsement opportunities. Companies brawl over who gets to put names on a new arena or this week's stop of the professional beach volleyball tour. Even more lucrative for individual athletes are the product endorsements. Between the years of 1983 and 1987, endorsement monies for athletes multiplied fourfold to more than 500 million dollars annually (Finch, 1987). Led by Michael Jordan, black athletes receive a substantial chunk of these endorsement dollars.

But do these greater athletic and endorsement opportunities for blacks translate into a better way of life for black athletes or black America in general? Are black athletes portrayed differently from their white counterparts in these expensive advertisements? Black athletes today still experience racial discrimination, and one type of this discrimination comes in the form of advertising themes and images. In this paper, I examine whether black athletes are portrayed in the marketing media as succeeding only because of innate abilities or unusual strength and speed, rather than because of the qualities of intelligence or hard work that are so valued in the broader business world. I use content analysis of 210 advertisements featuring well-known athletes to investigate whether black athletes are more likely to be portrayed as succeeding because of innate physical abilities, while white athletes are more often portrayed as succeeding because of hard work, intelligence or leadership qualities. Further, I examine whether black athletes are more likely to be portrayed as angry, violent, or hypersexual.

Theory

An examination of this issue requires an understanding of black participation in sport and in advertising today. Research outlined below shows that black athletes are still the victims of discrimination within their own sports, while other studies demonstrate that black models in general, even those outside of sport, are portrayed in stereotypical manners in advertising.

Some sporting executives claim that black athletes experience significant upward mobility because of their participation in athletics. While it is true that athletes today often make a good deal of money, it is not true that their prestige or occupational level increases along with their salaries. More blacks are entering these professional sports than in previous years, but there is evidence that entrance for blacks into high-level leadership positions is still largely blocked. Yetman and Berghorn (1988) found that in 1985, only 8.4 percent of Division I men's college basketball teams were coached by blacks, while more than 50 percent of the athletes on these teams were black. Blacks coached only 3 percent of women's Division I college basketball teams, while 25 percent of players on these teams were black. Coakley (1994) notes that minority applicants fill few management positions in high school, college, and professional football, including administrative or front office positions, a finding echoed by Lapchick (1996) for professional football and baseball. Because of the large number of black participants in sport, we might expect more blacks to fill these positions.

In addition, it is true that many more blacks play professional and collegiate sports today than did 25 years ago; however, studies show that discriminatory practices that existed then continue today. Loy and Elvogue's classic study (1970) showed that black baseball players were likely to be placed in peripheral positions, or positions that were thought to require fewer cognitive or leadership skills than did central positions. White players, on the other hand, dominated central positions. This practice of assigning based on race logic and stereotypes, known as stacking, explains much of the difference in sport positions by race.

Over the ensuing years, researchers showed that stacking persists in many sports. Yetman and Berghorn (1988, 1993) demonstrated that while black athletes had made inroads into central positions in collegiate basketball, this progress was due mostly to the huge increases in the number of black athletes participating and was not proportional to the numbers of new athletes entering the sport. Stacking still exists in women's collegiate volleyball (Eitzen and Furst, 1989), professional baseball (Smith and Self, 1989; Lavoie and Leonard, 1994), and professional (Schneider and Eitzen, 1986; Kooistra, Mahoney, and Bridges, 1993) and collegiate (Jones et al., 1987; Lewis, 1995) football. These studies suggest that while many black athletes have achieved notoriety and success in the white-dominated forum of sport, racial stereotypes of minorities' supposed lack of leadership and intellectual qualities still flourish.

Just as in sport, black models, endorsers and executives have had to struggle to attain status in the advertising world. Advertisements are influential in shaping the popular culture of all American communities, including the black community. As black athletes have supposedly made strides toward equality, black models in advertising have supposedly made breakthroughs in print and broadcast marketing. Pollay (1992) notes that black models appeared in cigarette advertising four times more often in 1965 than they did in 1955. Some black models also moved from portraying rigidly stereotyped roles in commercials, such as domestic servants, to more professional or family-oriented roles (Culley and Bennett, 1976).

None of these scholars, however, claim that these changes mean that black models have reached an era of full equality and participation. Culley and Bennett (1976), for example, found that fewer than 7% of ads in popular magazines included blacks. Humphrey and Schuman (1984) found an improved situation, but still describe under-representation. They further noted that ads often show white authority figures helping black models and portray few close friendships between black models. Although these studies seem somewhat dated, current evidence supporting them underscores the pervasive influence of these racial stereotypes; Sharpe and Curry (1996), examining a large sample of magazines, find that blacks (both models and feature subjects) are still more likely to be portrayed as athletes or entertainers than are white models.

In addition, black models or athletes in advertising are at least as likely, if not more so, to go through the process of licking (Williamson, 1978; Ewen, 1982). Licking refers to manipulating images into forms that tap viewers' preconceived notions, allowing the viewers to place the image into their social world and move instantaneously to further interpretation. Because of the limited number of images an advertisement can use, licking images into stereotypes is a quick way to allow consumers to move beyond the primary image of the ad to the important information—the product that is being sold. Eurocentric race logic provides a number of prevalent stereotypes of African Americans that can be readily used in advertising, including black man as comic, violent, savage or primitive and hypersexual (Jackson, 1994).

In addition, even the positive roles that black models are filling now are sometimes designed to suggest harmful choices. Some black scholars such as George (1992) and Leviatin (1993) suggest that ads extolling the virtues of black athletes are encouraging black youths to make poor choices about education and to pursue sports careers based on unrealistic expectations. Further, portrayals of blacks as successful athletes only may mask existing inequalities, both within sport and in more general society (McKay, 1995). Sieter notes that black children in television advertising are often relegated to the realms of hip-hop music and sports:

> Black children appear in nearly all the advertising for infant sports shoes, thus emphasizing their presumed "inborn" athletic ability. A television commercial for Apple Jacks uses a rap soundtrack and a basketball game to envision the "teamwork" of whites and blacks playing together. One of the black boys makes the final slam dunk of the cereal box in the end: the only starring role repeatedly offered to black boys...achievement in sports and in music are obviously a proud and valuable aspect of black culture. But in advertising they are distorted because they appear not as aspects of culture but as innate, natural talents. (1995, p. 104)

Despite this evidence that black endorsers might be "licked" into negative, stereotypical images, witty and stylish ads starring a few major black athletes espouse the idea that product endorsements are new opportunities for black athletes to enjoy economic mobility and to present positive images to society. However, it is rarely the athlete who is controlling his or her image; instead, advertisers who have great stake in "licking" images into a few stock symbols in order to sell products are creating and controlling the images athletes present in advertisements. Because of this reliance on easily recognizable stereotypes in advertising, I hypothesize that endorsements containing well-known athletes will draw on ingrained sports stereotypes and will present black athletes as succeeding because of physical attributes (such as size, strength or speed) while more often presenting white athletes as succeeding because of character or intellectual traits (such as intelligence, work ethic, acquired skill or leadership abilities). Further, I hypothesize that the racial stereotypes imposed on athletic endorsers will also be drawn from the broader culture and that black athletes will be more likely to be portrayed as angry, violent or highly sexualized than will be white athletes. In order to test these propositions, I examine advertisements from *Sports Illustrated.*

Sample and Methods

I draw all advertisements in this study from *Sports Illustrated,* a mass circulation magazine published by Time-Warner Communications. The magazine has the fifth highest circulation in the United States, making it an excellent forum for study. The magazine has a readership primarily of young males (ages 15–35) and has a slightly over-represented group of black readers (20 percent) (Simmons Market Research Bureau, 1992).

In order to test the above hypotheses, I examined issues of *Sports Illustrated* from four different periods throughout the year: February, April, June, and November. I selected these periods because they covered the largest portions of each of the major sports seasons to which *Sports Illustrated* devotes the most space—college and professional football, college and professional basketball, and professional baseball. In addition, other sports that receive substantial coverage, such as auto racing, golf and the so-called "Olympic sports" were also covered during these periods. A sample of issues published during these months was drawn from the ten-year period from 1985 to 1994. I used the 1985 date because it is the year in which Nike began a concerted—and expensive—effort to flood the athletic shoe market with Michael Jordan's image (Stauth, 1993). The Jordan campaign is often cited as the advertising coup that convinced Madison Avenue that black athletes could sell to both black and white America. If this is the case, ads after 1985 should include increasing numbers of black athletes.

I coded advertisements containing black athletes for stereotypical images. The athlete's gender, ethnicity and sport were recorded, as were the product the athlete was endorsing and the company selling the endorsed product. I coded athletes in ads into categories based on given or implied reasons for or chances of success: athlete is successful because of: (1) innate physical traits, such as (a) strength, (b) speed, or (c) body composition; or (2) acquired or intellectual traits, such as (d) intelligence, (e) work ethic, (f) leadership ability, or (g) skill. Although the main cues used to determine these stereotypes were in written ad copy, I also coded visual cues such as clothing, exposure of or focus on specific body parts, and positioning of the athlete in practicing or learning situations. I also noted whether the athlete was portrayed in a violent, angry, or sexualized manner, based on visual cues such as facial expression, clothing or costuming inappropriate to the sport, body position, body dissection, explicit textual messages, or actions of others portrayed in the ad. Such cues might include partial nudity for athletes who usually compete fully clothed, facial expressions that suggest screaming or growling, or text that implies threat or aggression. I coded several categories for facial expression, including smiling/laughing, speaking, shouting, angry, serious and sad/crying, and for body position, including standing/face toward camera, standing/face away from camera, sitting/face toward camera, and posed directly across from camera, posed below camera and posed above camera. I recorded textual messages and actions of others in the ad on the coding sheet for later analysis. Specific examples of these portrayals are provided below in the analysis of ads.

I further coded ads for whether the athlete was posed or shown in an action photo, whether the ad was in color or black and white, the size of the ad, use of special effects or unusual angles and the presence of other people in the ad. Text in the ads was coded for use of the athlete's name (including whether only first or last name was used), explicit description of the product or the athlete, presence of qualifiers for the athlete (e.g., "world champion" or "100–RBI man"), and superimposition of text on the athlete. With a few exceptions, such as color photography vs. black and white, these categories are not mutually exclusive.

I coded only ads containing well-known, recognizable athletes; I counted ads containing no athletes for purposes of obtaining percentages, but these were not coded for the above items. Because arguments concerning the impact of advertising images revolve around exposure to those images (Culley and Bennett, 1976), repeated ads, both including and not including athletes, were counted each time they appeared in *Sports Illustrated to* capture repeated exposure.

Although lack of resources prevented the use of more than one coder for this project, this work may be used as a starting point for the analysis of athletes' images in advertising. While use of a single coder cannot approach the breadth of reactions to a particular text that more extensive sociological or marketing research may, as Duncan (1990) notes in her analysis of photographs accompanying articles in *Sports Illustrated,* the kind of content analysis presented here may be used as a means of centering and sensitizing future research.[1]

Results

A total of 5,120 advertisements appeared in the sampled issues; 210 (or 4.1 percent) of these contained well-known athletes. Eight of these ads contained athletes of Hispanic, Asian, or other/unknown origin; because this small number made comparisons questionable, I excluded them from this analysis. The April and June issues have on average the higher number of ads, while the February and November issues tend to have fewer ads. Although black athletes appear in nearly 40 percent of the ads containing well-known athletes, the majority (62 percent) of those ads appear after 1988. This pattern does not coincide with the topical content of the magazine as a whole; black athletes, while underrepresented in photographs and feature articles (Lumpkin and Williams, 1991), appear more often than do black endorsers. For example, the May 11, 1987, issue contains a long feature article on the Lakers' Michael Cooper and a commentary by Reggie Jackson on racism in sports. There are, however, no ads in this issue that picture black models or athletes. During the summer in which this issue was published (May 4 through August 25), there are no blacks in the ads. In addition, almost all athletes featured in the ads (210 out of 218, or 96.3 percent) are male. Again, considering their small number, I excluded ads containing female athletes from the sample in the interest of simplicity in comparison. This left a sample of 210 ads containing well-known athletes as endorsers.[2]

In some cases, the differences between the representation of black and white athletic endorsers are small (Table 1). Both groups are about as likely to be photographed in color or to be posed for the photograph. Only three more black athletes than white athletes were enhanced by special effects or special angles (although the difference in percentages, affected by the total number of ads, is slightly greater—23 percent as compared to 15 percent).

A further breakdown of the ads is telling. Surprisingly, white athletes were more likely than were black athletes (by a margin of 67 percent to 41 percent) to have accompanying qualifiers describing why they should be respected spokespersons. Fifty-seven percent of the black athletes in the advertisements were portrayed as succeeding because of physical abilities such as strength, speed or size, while only 4 percent of their white counterparts were portrayed as succeeding primarily because of such attributes. Conversely, 47 percent of the white athletes were portrayed as succeeding because of character- or intellect-based traits such as intelligence, leadership, acquired skills or work ethic. Only 20 percent of the black athletes enjoyed similar representation. Thirty-six percent of the black athletes were portrayed as violent or angry, while only 4 percent of white athletes were so portrayed. Similarly, 28 percent of black athletes were rendered in a hypersexual image, but only 4 percent of white athletes received the same treatment. Twenty-five percent of black athletes had text superimposed over their images, as compared to 13 percent of white athletes, and 52 percent of black athletes shared their ad with other people (who were more often than not unknown models), while only 25 percent of white athletes shared the stage. Perhaps most disturbing, all 16 advertisements in which body dissection occurred employed black athletes as endorsers.

Although these numbers are helpful in understanding the general trends in advertising, the most powerful testimony of the stereotypical and damaging images used to sell products—and black athletes' bodies—comes from the ads themselves. Soloflex's Ken Norton, Sr., ad in the June 3, 1985, issue is an example of the use of the hypersexual black man stereotype. Norton is pictured naked from the waist up and in tight spandex shorts from the waist down, with no boxing paraphernalia in sight. A white hand with long, painted fingernails—presumably a woman's hand—reaches into the frame to caress Norton. These images play directly into traditional stereotypes of black men's bodies and supposed sexual prowess. The small-print text seems to belie the image presented, as it focuses on the work required to unlock the body's potential; in this way the ad is

TABLE 1

Percentages of Advertisements Featuring Black Athletes, Ads Featuring White Athletes, and All Ads Featuring Athletes That Contain Stereotypical Portrayals and Layout Characteristics Ads Featuring All Ads

Characteristic	Black Athletes ($N = 91$)	Ads Featuring White Athletes (N - 119)	Featuring Athletes ($N = 210$)
Hypothesized Stereotype Portrayals			
Qualifiers	41	67	56
Physical Means of Success	57	4	27
Character or Intellectual Means of Success	20	47	35
Violent/Angry	36	4	18
Sexualized	28	4	12
Body Dissection	75	80	78
Ad Layout Characteristics			
Posed	15	28	22
Action	80	83	82
Color	20	17	18
Black and White	23	15	19
Special Angle or Effects	18	0	8
Superimposed Text	25	13	18
Others Present in Ad	52	25	37

unlike others focusing on black athletes' physical prowess. But the overriding message of the ad, presented in its bold-type headline, is linked to its presentations of Norton's body—"a hard man is good to find."

Although Jim Palmer and Bart Connor, both white, do appear in Jockey underwear ads in which they wear only briefs, these two athletes represented all five of the ads in which white athletes were portrayed in a sexualized manner (an example of the Connor ad appears in the June 9, 1986, issue). In addition, test in the Jockey ads suggested that the athletes are discussing their own sexuality, a sharp contrast with the Norton ad, which is purely voyeuristic. Finally, the Jockey ads include pictures of the white athletes participating in their respective sports; the Soloflex ad and others of its ilk generally do not include such links to the athletes' on-field accomplishments.

Another prevalent stereotype in these ads is black athlete as biologically gifted, and, by "logical" extension, therefore succeeding because of physical rather than mental attributes. Beginning in 1988, black athletes suddenly appear in as many as 40 percent of the ads in *Sports Illustrated*. Because of this sudden proliferation, both Madison Avenue and society struggled to create a new identity for the black athlete and a new way to categorize the images being presented. Fueled by comments such as Jimmy "The Greek" Snyder's assertions that the breeding of slaves for strength and power in the 1800s caused superior athleticism in blacks today (Davis, 1987), advertisers appear to have associated black athletes' success with innate ability and strength. The Nike Bo Jackson ad in the April 17, 1989, issue is a good example of this trend. This black and white ad focuses on Jackson's largely nude body, drawing attention to Jackson's physical attributes. The props include football shoulder pads and a baseball bat, emphasizing the fact that Jackson plays two sports, an indicator of unusual ability. The text also refers to Jackson's sports as "hobbies," or playthings that do not require much effort. The ad implies that Jackson does not have to work hard to succeed; he simply takes advantage of his natural gifts.

A Pepsi ad using budding star Shaquille O'Neal in the February 14, 1994, issue demonstrates that advertisers continue to draw upon these stereotypes to sell products. The ad focuses entirely on O'Neal's size and strength, picturing him as larger than surrounding buildings and as effortlessly lifting a large vending machine under one arm. Not only does the ad again highlight a black athlete's strength and size, inborn qualities, but it does not even make the pretense of including text to soften the stereotype. The ad also places O'Neal in an asphalt jungle covered with graffiti, bringing to mind the image of black man as criminal as the basketball player makes off with a machine full of soda.

A November 15, 1994, Nike ad using Reggie White as endorser is a classic example of body dissection and resulting objectification. White's face is never seen in the ad; instead, an extreme close-up of White's arm and torso, photographed in black and white and covered with copious amounts of sweat, takes up an entire full-page ad. The text of the ad is superimposed on White's biceps, and focuses on what White is "doing" with those muscles. Such dissection de-emphasizes White's humanity and recasts his body as a tool to be used for winning.

By contrast, few white athletes appear in ads that emphasize their physique or the things their bodies can do, despite the fact that they also create their success through physical means. Instead, 47 percent of white athletes are represented as succeeding because of intellect, leadership, or work ethic. The Champion clothing ad showing the Chicago Bears' Tom Waddle in the November 23, 1992, issue emphasizes this kind of portrayal. Waddle is shown in practice gear, sweaty and dirty, as though he has just finished a demanding workout. His hands are taped and bandaged. The text of the ad demonstrates Waddle's work ethic, even to the point of downplaying his physical abilities: "Other players are more physically blessed than I am. But if I have an advantage over them, it's that I don't mind taking the hits. And if getting hit is a God-given talent, I guess I have it." The text plays into implicit race logic by suggesting that while a white player may not have an inherent physical advantage, he can make up for this perceived deficit through his greater willingness to work and sacrifice for the team. Based on the sample examined here, it is difficult to imagine a lesser-known black athlete who is not as "physically blessed" as other athletes being used in an endorsement.

Finally, more than a third of the ads containing black athletes portray those athletes as angry or violent. The Scottie Pippen AT&T ad in the April 27, 1992, issue underscores the use of this stereotype. This ad portrays Pippen dunking and shows him with his mouth open, screaming, in an angry snarl. Such ads draw from and promote the stereotype that black men are beyond social control or even dangerous. White athletes, on the other hand, were rarely portrayed in such a manner. When they do appear angry, as in the Diet Pepsi Chris Nilan ad in the February 15, 1990, issue, the cues are almost always in the text. Nilan stares directly into the camera, mouth closed in a tight line, dressed in black leather and with his skates flung over one shoulder. There is no indication of verbalization of anger, as is the case for the screaming Pippen; instead, Nilan's "anger," as described in the text, is meant to signal intensity. The qualifier placed just under Nilan's picture, which announces he has amassed "2,447 career penalty minutes," is meant to express the anger and violence present in the athlete. The text on the facing page announces, "If you're gonna mess with Chris' favorite soft drink, you better do it right." Unlike the Pippen ad, this ad explicitly outlines the intention of violence, perhaps because no stereotype of white man as violent exists to make the athlete easy to lick into a quickly classifiable image.

Discussion

Madison Avenue's use of ingrained racial stereotypes to sell products has a negative effect on the black athlete and the black community in general. Several noted black scholars such as George (1992) and Leviatin (1993) assert that shoe companies' aggressive marketing of black athletes to black youths has led these youths to disdain more conventional forms of success in their pursuit for athletic glory.

These assertions are supported by studies (Kassarjian, 1973; Meyer, Donohue, and Henke, 1978) showing that blacks interpret marketing models as role models. Black children often view black models as more athletic than other models (Meyer et al., 1978), and this effect is exacerbated when the majority of blacks in advertisements are athletes. In a more recent study, Wilson and Sparks interviewed black and nonblack youths concerning television commercials starring professional athletes and found that some of the black youths used the athletes "as a reference point, defining a style that further influenced their masculinity" (1996, p. 415). Lee and Browne (1995) find a similar pattern, with only peers outstripping advertisements as influences. If the reference points available to black youths as role models are not only typically portrayed as athletes and entertainers (Sharpe and Curry, 1996), but as succeeding because of natural athletic prowess rather than intellect and hard work, what message does this send black youths about how America views them? Does this kind of message suggest to black youths that the surest way to success is through athletic ability, which—according to these ads—is supposedly innate in blacks? Coakley (1994) notes that black youths are more likely to perceive sport as a means of mobility. than are white youths, despite the long odds against having a career in professional sports; additional research like that done by Wilson and Sparks (1996) may reveal whether the stereotypes employed in these advertisements help to perpetuate these non-productive goals.

What do these repeated racial stereotypes mean to other groups? Does the continued use of stereotypes such as black man as anti-intellectual, violent or hypersexual reify their use in general society? Whittier (1991) shows that both white and black viewers quickly recognize and accept stereotyped portrayals in advertising and suggests that this repeated exposure to stereotypes acts as a confirmation to the viewer of the veracity of the viewer's assumptions about race and ethnicity. In their study of youths who viewed athletic apparel commercials, Wilson and Sparks (1996) found that non-black youths did not identify with the celebrity athletes to the same extent as did their black contemporaries. These youths did believe, however, that the styles displayed in the commercials influenced black youths. While use of these stereotypes may not be as influential to other youths' self-image and goals as they are to black youths, they are damaging if they create a false impression of genetic cultural differences. These assumptions about differences between black and white athletes continue to manifest themselves in the form of stacking, salary differences and limited opportunities for minorities to coach or manage teams.

The question of whether sport can—or should—move away from commodification is beyond the scope of this brief paper, but sport and advertising executives, as well as the athletes themselves, should be aware of the potency and possible consequences of the stereotypes they employ to sell shoes and sports drinks. Future studies along the lines of Wilson and Sparks' (1996) should delve into the influence repeated exposure to these stereotypes in a sport setting has on consumers, both black and white. Additional work should examine ways to control for the athlete's sport and relative skill; for example, it is possible that white athletes may be more likely to be presented with qualifiers because advertising opportunities are open to relatively less-skilled or less-known white athletes, while black athletes must be of stratospheric fame and skill even to merit an ad. The number of white athletes in ads may be greater because white athletes are more likely to be found in a diverse number of sports, and therefore spread some of the exposure. In addition, these studies would do well to explore the characteristics of the audiences these ads hope to attract. Are white athletes more or less likely than black athletes to advertise expensive products such as cars or cruises? Does perceived class of both athlete and audience influence who is being used to endorse products? Finally, a specific examination of the interaction between gender and race would be intriguing. As further studies show the existence of racial differences in advertising images and the power both advertising and sport have to shape popular opinion, it is hoped that advertisers and athletes alike will take the responsibility of presenting positive images of athletes of all races.

Notes

An earlier version of this paper was presented at the 1996 meeting of the North Central Sociological Association in Cincinnati, OH. Direct correspondence to the author, Department of Sociology, The Ohio State University, Columbus, OH 43210 or dufur.2@ocu.edu. I thank Special Issue Editor Tim Curry, an anonymous *Sociological Focus* reviewer, Patricia Drentea, Shelley Lucas, Jim Ainsworth-Darnell, Mel Adelman, Eileen O'Brien, Gladys Farmer, and the OSU Sociology Research Laboratory.

1. A separate coder evaluated 50 of the advertisements, 25 of which the author had coded as showing the characteristics above and 25 from a "control group" that did not include the characteristics listed above. The independent coder is of a different sex, racial background, and regional background than is the author. In addition, the independent coder is older than the author and has fewer years of formal education. Interrater reliability for this small subsample ranged from 1.0 for items like athlete's sex and race to .88 for athlete is portrayed as hypersexual or is portrayed in a sexual manner. The independent coder was slightly less likely than the author to identify athletes as being portrayed in an overtly sexual manner, but was slightly more likely to identify athletes as being portrayed as angry. The second coder did not find any athletes in the "control sample" whom he felt had been excluded; he did not recognize two of the athletes included.

2. Two of the female athletes in ads were Asian, while two were Hispanic; two were black and two were white.

References

Coakley, Jay J. (1994). *Sport in Society: Issues and Controversies*. Chicago: Mosby.

Culley, James D., and Bennett, Rex. (1976). "Selling Women, Selling Blacks." *Journal of Communication*, 26(4): 160–174.

Davis, Laurel R. (1987). "The Articulation of Difference: White Preoccupation with the Question of Racially Linked Genetic Differences among Athletes." *Sociology of Sport Journal*, 7: 179–187.

Duncan, Margaret Carlisle. (1990). "Sports Photographs and Sexual Difference: Images of Women and Men in the 1984 and 1988 Olympic Games." *Sociology of Sport Journal,* 7(1): 22–43.

Eitzen, D. Stanley, and Furst, David. (1989). "Racial Bias in Women's Collegiate Volleyball." *Journal of Sport and Social Issues*, 13(1): 46–51.

Ewen, Stuart. (1982). *Channels of Desire: Mass Images and the Changing of the American Consciousness*. New York: McGraw-Hill.

Finch, Peter. (1987). "Nothing Sells Like Sports." *Business Week*, August 31: 48–54.

George, Nelson. (1992). *Elevating the Game*. New York: Harper and Collins.

Hochschild, Jennifer L. (1995). *Facing Up to the American Dream: Race, Class, and the Soul of America*. Princeton, NJ: Princeton University Press.

Humphrey, Ronald, and Schuman, Howard. (1984). "The Portrayal of Blacks in Magazine Advertisements." *Public Opinion Quarterly*, 48(3): 551–563.

Jackson, Peter. 1994. "Black Male: Advertising and the Cultural Politics of Masculinity." *Gender, Place, and Culture*, 1(1): 49–59.

Jones, Gregg A., Leonard II, Wilbert Marcellus, Schmitt, Raymond L., Smith, D. Randall, and Tolone, William H. (1987). "Racial Discrimination in College Football." *Social Science Quarterly*, 68(1): 70–83.

Kassarjian, Harold H. (1973). "Blacks as Communicators and Interpreters of Mass Communication." *Journalism Quarterly*, 50 (2): 285–292.

Kooistra, Peter J., Mahoney, J. S., and Bridges, Leisha. (1993). "The Unequal Opportunity for Equal Ability Hypothesia: Racism in the National Football League." *Sociology of Sport Journal*, 10: 341–349.

Lapchick, Richard E. (1996). *1996 Racial Report Card*. Boston: Northeastern University Center for the Study of Sport in Society.

Lavoie, Marc, and Leonard II, Wilbert M. (1994). "In Search of An Alternative Hypothesis of Stacking in Baseball: The Uncertainty Hypothesis." *Sociology of Sport Journal*, 11(2): 140–154.

Lee, E. Bun, and Browne, Louis A. (1995). "Effects of Television Advertising on African-American Teenagers." *Journal of Black Studies*, 25(5): 523–536.

Leviatin, David. (1993). "The Evolution and Commodification of Black Basketball Style." *Radical History Review*, 55: 154–164.

Lewis Jr., Richard. (1995). "Racial Position Segregation: A Case Study of Southwest Conference Football, 1978 and 1989." *Journal of Black Studies* 25(4): 431–446.

Loy, John W., and Elvogue, Joseph F. (1970). "Racial Segregation in American Sport." *Sociology Quarterly*, 26: 1125.

Lumpkin, Angela, and Williams, Linda D. (1991). "An Analysis of *Sports Illustrated* Feature Articles." *Sociology of Sport Journal* 8(1): 16–32.

McKay, Jim. (1996). "'Just Do It!' Corporate Sports Slogans and the Political Economy of 'Enlightened Racism.'" *Discourse*, 16(2): 191–201.

Meyer, Timothy P., Donahue, Thomas, and Henke, Lucy L. (1978). "How Black Children See TV Commercials." *Journal of Advertising Research* 18(5): 51–58.

Pollay, Richard W. (1992). "Separate but Not Equal: Racial Segmentation in Cigarette Advertising." *Journal of Advertising*, 21(1): 45–57.

Schneider, John, and Eitzen, D. Stanley. (1986). "Racial Segregation by Professional Football Positions, 1960–1985." *Sociology and Social Research*, 70(4): 259–262.

Seiter, Ellen. (1995). "Different Children, Different Dreams: Racial Representation in Advertising." In *Gender, Race and Class in Media,* edited by Gail Dines and Jean M. Humez, pp. 99–108. Thousand Oaks, CA: Sage Publications.

Sharpe, Cicely, and Curry, Timothy Jon. (1996). "Black Americana in Popular Magazines: The Effects of Audience Characteristics and the Persistence of Stereotypes." *Sociological Focus*, 29(4): 305–318.

Simmons Market Research Bureau. (1991–1992). "Total Audiences." *Study of Media and Markets*, M-1: 1–30.

Smith, Earl, and Seff, Monica A. (1989). "Race, Position Segregation and Salary Equity in Professional Baseball." *Journal of Sport and Social Issues*, 13: 92–110.

Stauth, Cameron. (1993). *The Golden Boys*. New York: Pocket Publishers.

Tomaskovic-Devey, Donald. (1994). *Gender and Racial Inequality at Work: The Sources and Consequences of Job Segregation*. Ithaca, NY: ILR Press.

Whittier, T. (1991). "Viewers' Reactions to Racial Cues in Advertising." *Journal of Advertising Research*, 3(6): 37–46.

Williamson, Diane. (1978). *Decoding Advertisements*. New York: Marion Boyara.

Wilson, Brian, and Sparks, Robert. (1996). "'It's Gotta Be the Shoes': Youth, Race and Sneaker Commercials." *Sociology of Sport Journal*, 13(4): 398–427.

Yetman, Norman R., and Berghorn, F. J. (1993). "Racial Participation and Integration in Intercollegiate Basketball: A Longitudinal Perspective." *Sociology of Sport Journal*, 10: 310–331.

Yetman, Norman R., Berghorn, F. J., and Hanna, William E. (1988). "Racial Participation and Integration in Men's and Women's Intercollegiate Basketball: Continuity and Change, 1958–1985." *Sociology of Sport Journal*, 5: 107–124.

III

Athletic Performance:
A Question of Black is Best

7

Race and Athletic Performance: A Physiological Review

David W. Hunter

That African American athletes, particularly males, dominate or are far over-represented numerically in certain sporting events—or conversely, that European Americans are under-represented in some events—is obvious to even the casual observer. Track and field, football, baseball, basketball, and boxing—sports which tend to be characterized by high-intensity anaerobic component—have a disproportionately high number of African American participants who are outstanding achievers.

According to Census Bureau data, individuals classified as African Americans comprise 12.1% of the population of the United States. Based upon statistics from the Center for Study of Sport in Society (Coakley, 1994), 68% of the players in the National Football League, and more than 75% the players in the National Basketball Association are African American. The percentages of African Americans who are "starters" is even higher. Major league baseball's rosters are 16% African American. In National Collegiate Athletic Association Division I-A, 40% of the football players and 60% of the basketball players are African American (Coakley, 1994). During the Los Angeles Summer Olympic games, African Americans won 40 of the 49 American medals in track and field, and 10 of the 11 American medals in boxing (Hoobing, 1984). These athletic successes are even more interesting when they are juxtaposed against the list of organized and professional events in which African Americans have made little or negligible contributions: rowing, cycling, skiing, skating, hockey, swimming, tennis, golf, fencing, and gymnastics.

There are several prominent schools of thought for the explanation of this successful participation in some events but not in others. Included among these are biological, genetic, sociological, and psychological explanations, as well as combinations of these. The assertions that African and African American athletes have some type of biological advantage over other groups has been well chronicled for many years. Jimmy (the Greek) Snyder, said:

> The Black is a better athlete to begin with, because he's been bred to be that way. Because of his high thighs that go up into his back. And they can jump higher and run faster because of their big thighs.... The Black is the better athlete and he practices to be the better athlete and he's bred to be the better athlete because this goes all the way to the Civil War, when, during the slave trading, the owner, the slave owner, would breed his big Black woman so that he would have a big Black kid. (Shapiro, 1988)

Al Campanis suggested that African Americans had less buoyancy and thus were not suited for swimming (Campanis, 1987). And more recently Roger Bannister, who in 1954 became the first person to break the four-minute mile barrier, asserted that black African and African American sprinters have "certain natural advantages" over white rivals. However, Bannister, a retired physician, gave no evidence to support his position (Associated Press, 1995). It is interesting that all of these assertions have been made based upon casual and empirical observations, not on scientifically based evidence or solid reproducible data.

Sociologists have offered several theories focused on environmental factors, which influence sports participation of African Americans. Edwards (1973) contends that American society is stratified on the basis of skin color, and one's access to power, prestige, and money are greatly impacted by race. African Americans have been and continue to be channeled toward socially acceptable occupations such as sport and entertainment. Edwards further suggests that African Americans seek occupations that are known to be obtainable by them:

> Black society, as does the dominant White society, teaches its members to strive for that which is defined as the most desirable among potentially achievable goals.... the talents of Afro-American males are disproportionately concentrated toward achievement in this one area. In high prestige, occupational positions outside the sports realm, Black role models are an insignificant few.... Thus, given the competition among athletic organizations for top-flight athletes, it is expected that a high proportion of the extremely gifted Black individuals would be in sports. Whites, on the other hand, because they have visible alternative role models and greater potential access to alternative high-prestige positions, distribute their talents over a broader range of endeavors. Thus,

the concentration of highly gifted Whites in sports is proportionately less than the number of Blacks. (Edwards, 1973)

Phillips (1976) suggests that African Americans have excelled in sports activities for which the best facilities, coaching, and competition are available in schools. For sports in which African Americans are rare, the best facilities, coaching, and competition are found in private clubs. This creates an illusion of African American superiority because African Americans excel in the most visible sports (basketball, football, baseball). Coakley (1994) further notes that African Americans in the United States have excelled in sports requiring little expensive equipment and formal training. For example, basketballs are relatively inexpensive and a large number of participants can play a game with one ball.

Similar analogies have been made for baseball and football. Carlston (1983) offers an environmental explanation for racial differences in basketball, noting "the oft-observed racial differences in sports performance are not really racial at all but rather, reflect the differing environments in which White and Black players generally develop their skills" (Carlston, 1983). The hypothesis furthers that the inner-city basketball courts where a high percentage of African American males frequent, are generally crowded with players competing for valuable playing time on limited facilities. By contrast, the noncity player may spend many hours practicing alone in his driveway, shooting time after time without any need to protect the basketball during shots or manipulative movements while dribbling. The contention is that the different learning conditions in African American and Caucasian communities may lead to different performances, styles, and priorities.

Harrison (1995) has postulated that cultural experiences, environment, stereotypes, efficacy, expectations of others, as well as self-expectations, create a self-schemata on participation and physical activity choices. African Americans tend to be influenced by role models in their immediate environment. Additionally, African Americans are noticeably attracted to activities in which other African Americans participate in large numbers. Applying the theory that if African American youth are repeatedly exposed to certain movement patterns and activity, these movements become part of the self-schema, Harrison develops a logical model suggesting that activity choices are rooted in the way people view themselves in relation to others, their culture, experiences, priorities, and perceived choices available to them. As African American males have become increasingly successful in a few highly visible sports, young African Americans focus their attentions on developing their skills in the same sports.

Coakley notes, "This has not only contributed to the high proportion of Blacks in certain sports, but it also accounts for the tendency among many young Black males to put all their motivational 'eggs' into just a few sport 'baskets'" (Coakley, 1994).

If one group excels over another at an endeavor that requires physical ability for superior performance, it makes sense to examine the possibility that the superior group possesses some physical attributes and advantages that cause the superiority. If one is to make such assertions, objective, scientifically based, reproducible data are needed to support them. Therefore the study of racially based physiological comparisons of study invites knowledge, while lack of investigation leads to observations and speculations that serve to perpetuate folklore. The purpose of this article is to review the body of anthropometric and physiological literature regarding race and athletic performance. This review is specifically limited to comparisons of black Africans and African Americans to Caucasians and European Americans with regard to race.

Race and Human Genetic Variation

One of the major potential confounding factors when studying differences between groups is to define the groups. The very concept and definition of race is disputed in many quarters. Some authors believe the concept of race is useful in generalizing and communicating about genetically different groups of humankind, while others view it as invalid, transient, and undefinable. To accept the notion of race in a definable way for the purpose of scientific research, the definition should include, and be rooted in, contemporary human genetics and evolutionary population biology. The term *race* would suggest a biologically distinct group that has a relatively large percentage of its genes in common. The profound difficulty of such a purely scientific approach is that cultural factors are not accounted for. Yet in our modern world the two are inextricably linked. In other words, many groups are distinctive both culturally and biologically. A further confounder in this line of inquiry is that one must try to detect and understand how much of the genetic variation in humans is common to all human beings or specific to a given population or race.

It is important to recognize that Africans and African Americans do not come from some "magical" common gene pool. Historical information suggests that over 98% of the captured Africans for slavery came from a very extensive area of West Africa and West-Central Africa, from Senegal to Angola (Reed, 1969), a distance of more than 3,000 miles. Further, genetic literature is consistent with the fact that there are more differences within any one group as a whole than there are between two different groups. Nei and Roychoudhury (1974) state, "The interracial net codon differences relative to the interracial codon differences was small, indicating that the genic variation between the three races (Caucasoid, Negroid, Mongoloid) is small compared to that within the same race."

Genetic research by Reed (1969) suggests "the American individual to whom the term Negro (Black, African American) is applied is almost always a biracial hybrid. Usually between 2 and 50 percent of his genes are derived from Caucasian ancestors, and these genes were very probably received after 1700." As such, there is virtually no portion of the African American gene pool that does not have some Caucasoid genes. The genetic divergence of the so-called major races is very slight when compared to the amount of variations found among local populations within the same race. In fact differences among populations within the so-called major races account for about 88% of the genetic variation, while differences between the races themselves account for the remaining 12% (Newt, 1991). Bouchard (1988) states, "It is now generally recognized that the majority of genetic variants are shared by all humans and that only about 10% of the genetic variations is specific to populations or races.... In other words, genetic differences between racial groups tend to be small, particularly when one looks beyond skin color and facial characteristics." Thus it is extremely difficult to define the concept of race from a strictly genetic definition. Since individuals are not classified by their strict genetic typology when performing an athletic event (nor anything else for that matter), and since all such classification systems are on a continuum, any such classification is arbitrary. The classification of race in this article is based upon previous researchers' groupings, and as such, the concept of race in this article has been defined as it is defined in a social and biocultural context.

Anthropometry and Morphology

There have been numerous comparisons of height between African Americans and European Americans (Todd, 1928; Metheny, 1939; Herskovitz, Cameron, and Smith, 1931; Davenport and Love, 1921;

Jones, 1941). These studies report remarkably consistent results of no significant differences in overall height between the two races. For example, Davenport and Love (1921) studied World War I soldiers and reported height for African Americans of 171.9 centimeters (cm.) and 172.8 cm. for European Americans. Likewise, Jones (1941) studying Los Angeles school system students, reported that 18-year-old African American males were 174.0 cm. and European American males were 174.2 cm. The 18-year-old African American females averaged 159.3 cm., while the European American females were 161.8 cm.

Proportionality, the relationships of body segments and dimensions, have been compared relative to race. It is now generally accepted that African Americans as a group tend to have proportionally longer limbs, shorter trunks, and narrower pelvic girdles than do Caucasians relative to overall height (Himes, 1979; Ross and Ward, 1984; Malina, 1969; Tanner, 1964; Davenport and Love, 1921; Herskovitz, 1930). There are some fairly consistent African American–Caucasian differences in average body proportions that appear repeatedly in the literature. These comparisons hold only for groups of African Americans and Caucasians, whereas comparisons between individuals are far less predictable. Africans and African Americans generally have smaller sitting heights relative to stature than do Caucasians; that is, African Americans have relatively longer bones. Similarly, arms are usually longer in African Americans than Caucasians, relative to sitting height and total stature. Africans and African Americans tend to have longer distal (tibia) limb segments proportionately to proximal segments (femur) compared to Caucasians (Himes, 1988). An extensive study by Metheney (1939) using 47 direct and derived anthropometric measurements on 51 African American and 51 Caucasian male college students was analyzed. The African American group was found to exceed the Caucasian in weight, arm length, forearm length, hand length, elbow breadth, chest depth and width; while the Caucasian group exceeded the African American in sitting height, total fat, and hip width. The author conservatively draws the conclusions that these findings of bodily proportions might give African Americans a slight kinesiological advantage in certain events.

One of the areas in which a great deal of data have been collected for comparison is morphology. One of the most prominent and useful classification systems of physique is somatotype. The somatotype is a quantitative description of three components of physique—relative fatness, relative leanness, and relative muscularity. De Garay, Levine, and Carter

(1974) studied athletes participating in the 1968 Olympics and reported large and systematic differences in mean somatotypes among groups of different sports, but few differences in mean somatotypes found among racial groups within a sport. Likewise, Tanner (1964) and Carter (1984) reported wide variations in somatotype of elite Olympic athletes, and it appears that the variation does not follow racial classifications closely. Himes (1988) states, "Studies of twin and other familial similarities have shown an appreciable genetic effect on somatotype components. Nevertheless, the total environmental effect on somatotype components approximates the total genetic effect. Thus, simple attribution of racial or group differences in somatotype to genetics alone is probably inappropriate."

Another area of interest is in the comparison of lean body mass, fat, and bone density between racial groups. Harsha, Freichs, and Benson (1978) reported that African American youth are less fat than their Caucasian counterparts aged six to sixteen. Similar results have been reported by Burdeshaw (1968) in college-aged women. In a study using Cuban black and white youths it was concluded that blacks have greater height and weight measurements, but thinner skinfold measurements than their white counterparts (Laska-Mierzejewska, 1970). Cohn et al. (1977) measured body elemental composition by means of measuring total body calcium, phosphorus, sodium, chlorine, and potassium. The results showed both African American men and women to be leaner than their sex-matched Caucasian counterparts. Schutte et al. (1984) formulated the hypothesis that the lean body mass is denser in African Americans than in European Americans, and suggested that separate formulas should be used in converting density to body composition for African American subjects. It is generally accepted that bone density tends to be greater in black African and African American groups relative to whites (Trotter et al., 1960; Himes, 1988), with differences generally 8% to 12% greater in African Americans.

Skeletal Muscle Physiology

Skeletal muscle characteristics were studied and compared between African and Caucasian males by Ama et al. (1986), who took muscle biopsies of the vastus lateralis of 23 black African and 23 Caucasian males to compare fiber type and enzyme activities. Results indicated that Caucasians had a higher percent type I (8%) and lower percent type II a (6.7%) fiber proportions than Africans. No significant differences were observed between the two racial groups in the type II b fiber proportion or in the three fiber areas. Enzymes catalyzing reactions in phosphagenic (creatine kinase) and glycolytic (hexokinase, phosphofructokinase, and lactate dehydrogenase) pathways had significantly higher activities, about 30% to 40% in the black African group than in the Caucasian group. No significant difference was noted in the activities of oxidative enzymes. The authors concluded that there are differences between blacks and Caucasians in muscle fiber types I and II a proportions. However, the authors pointed out that while a difference of this magnitude may indicate that racial differences exist, these differences were only slightly larger than the error of the sampling and measurement, and should be considered with caution. What is significant is that this provided some evidence, relative to anaerobic enzyme activities, to suggest that these black individuals were well endowed to perform in sport events of high intensity and short duration. In spite of this strong theoretical evidence, performance testing from these researchers have not shown differences in anaerobic power between such groups (Ama, Lagasse, Bouchard, and Simoneau, 1990). The African subjects in Ama's (1986) study were of West African heritage. Comparing East African runners with Scandinavian runners, Saltin et al. (1995) reported extremely similar percentages of muscle fiber types (Type I 72.5%, Kenyans, 69.1%, Scandinavians; Type II a 24.5%, Kenyans, 28.2%, Scandinavians; Type II b 1.3%, Kenyans, 2.7%, Scandinavians) between the two groups. However, these data are quite different from that of Ama et al. (1986). This has led some to speculate that there are differences in fiber type percentages in individuals from West Africa or West African heritage versus East Africans and Caucasians (Saltin, 1996). Further investigation with significantly larger samples are needed to verify these assertions.

Motor Performance

Motor skill tests and speed studies are plentiful with respect to racial comparisons in children. Huttinger (1959) reported that African American fourth, fifth, and sixth graders were significantly faster than their European American counterparts in the 35-yard dash. Milne, Seefeldt, and Reuschlein (1976) showed similar results in elementary school-aged children in the 30-yard dash. Differences of statistical significance were observed as early as kindergarten for speed. However, Milne et al. did not show any other significant differences in motor skills with respect to race. Ponthieux and Barker (1965) reported that African American male elementary students were significantly superior in five of seven components of the American Alliance for Health, Physical Education, Recreation, and Dance Youth Fitness Test. African American females were significantly superior to their Caucasian counterparts in four of seven, while the Caucasian females were superior in two. In general the literature suggests that African American children, particularly males, perform better on average in sprinting and jumping tasks (vertical and broad jump) than do Caucasian children (Malina, 1988). There seems to be no consistent trends in agility tasks, primarily shuttle runs, between African American and Caucasian children. The available studies of ball throwing for distance, primarily the softball throw, indicates better performance for African American youth in the majority of studies. Several other tasks including ball-put, sit-ups, pull-ups, parallel bar dips, and balance do not provide consistent trends to suggest performance differences between African American and Caucasian children and youth (Malina, 1988).

Aerobic and Anaerobic Power

There have been a number of published investigations comparing aerobic metabolism between racial groups (Davies, Barnes, Fox, Ola Ojikuta, and Samueloff, 1972; Davies, Mbelwa, Crockford, and Weiner 1973; DiPrampero and Cerretelli, 1969; DiPrampero, Pinera Limas, and Sassi, 1970; Leary and Wyndham, 1965; Robinson, Dill, Harmon, Hall, and Wilson, 1941a; Robinson, Dill, Wilson, and Nelson, 1941b; Wyndham et al., 1966; Wyndham et al., 1963; Wyndham and Heyss, 1969). While a few of these studies have shown a very small difference in absolute maximal oxygen consumption (VO_2 max) between African American and Caucasian subjects, none of them report any statistical differences in VO_2 max when the figures are expressed in milliliters per kilogram of body weight per minute (ml/kg-min^{-1}), or milliliters per kilogram of lean body weight. Robinson, Dill, Harmon et al. (1941) found practically the same VO_2 max in Caucasian and African-American sharecroppers who were living under the same environmental conditions and with similar levels of habitual activity (Caucasian 49.6 +/– 0.52 ml/kg-min^{-1}; African American 49.9 +/– 0.52 ml/kg-min^{-1}).

Wyndham et al. (1963) compared South African Caucasian, Bantu, and nomadic Bushmen, and reported no significant difference in VO_2 max for males in a similar state of physical training. Leary and Wyndham

(1965), using Caucasian and Bantu athletes of international class, found the Caucasian athletes to be taller and heavier than were the Bantu athletes. The mean maximum oxygen intake of these two groups was similar (Caucasian 61.1 ml/kg min^{-1}; Bantu 63.2 ml/ kg min^{-1}). This same study compared "fit young men" for oxygen consumption and again found no statistical differences between the groups (Caucasian 48.3 ml/kg min^{-1}; Bantu 47.7 ml/kg min^{-1}). Davies et al. (1972) studied 47 Caucasian, 72 West Africans of Yoruba heritage, 31 Jewish Kurdish, and 32 Jewish Yeminites of Israel. They reported that when standardized for body mass and composition, the maximal oxygen intake for each paired group was identical. It was concluded:

> If differences between aerobic power output exist between ethnic groups, they must be small and therefore of doubtful biological significance.... they are certainly less than the large intersubject variations which exist between members of the same race.... thus it would seem that provided the groups are comparable there is little evidence to support the existence of racial differences in physical working capacity of man. Further it is our view that such evidence that has been adduced in the past for ethnic differences can be explained in terms of environmental rather than racial factors.

Based upon numerous investigations, it can be safely concluded that interpopulation differences in maximal aerobic power have little to do with ethnic or racial origin of subjects (Boulay et al., 1988).

DiPrampero and Cerretelli (1969) measured both maximal aerobic and anaerobic power in a group of 156 black Africans. Additionally, anthropometric data were collected and all of the results were used for comparison to previously published literature. No significant differences were found between the Africans and previous reports when expressed relative to body weight. The Margaria step test was employed in the assessment of anaerobic power. The results proved to be quite interesting with the control group, Italians from Margaria's study, scoring appreciably higher in maximal anaerobic power than did the Africans whether expressed absolutely or relative to lean body weight. DiPrampero, Pinera Limas, and Sassi (1970) studied maximal aerobic and anaerobic power and body composition of Olympic athletes. They reported no differences based upon race for aerobic or anaerobic power.

More recently Hunter, Bartels, and Lanese (1989) compared various indices of anaerobic power between 136 African American and European American adolescent males. Results indicated no differences in anaerobic power based upon the Wingate anaerobic test (African American 12.65 watts per kilogram +/− 1.24; European American 12.62 watts per kilogram +/– 1.32), Margaria step test (African American 15.90 watts per kilogram +/– 1.79; European American 15.95 watts per kilogram +/– 1.99) or 40-yard dash when subjects are equated for body weight and lean body weight (African American 4.822 seconds; European American 4.935). This investigation did, however, report small but statistically superior performances in the vertical jump by the African American males (African American 0.562 meters +/– 0.080; European American 0.507 meters +/– 0.072). Based upon the power of the tests it was concluded that there was no difference in anaerobic power production between African American and European American males in multiple contraction explosive events.

Ama, Lagasse, Bouchard, and Simoneau (1990) reported similar results and conclusions using isokinetic knee-extension testing, results indicating no significant differences in short- and long-term anaerobic performance of knee extensor muscles between sedentary black African and Caucasian subjects. The authors reported that these observations were consistent with data from a previous study from their laboratory, which showed no significant differences between sedentary black African and Caucasian males in all-out ergocycles tests of short duration.

Nerve Conduction Velocity

It is not uncommon to read in athletic magazines and books, Dintman (1984) for example, that African Americans have faster nerve conduction velocities than do Caucasians. However, this assertion seems to be based upon a single study by Browne (1935). With the specific intent to determine why African American athletes seem to excel over Caucasians in sprinting events, Browne looked at the patellar tendon reflex times of African Americans and Caucasians. The patellar tendon reflex time was chosen because it had previously been shown that fast sprinters possessed short reflex times of this nature. The obtained difference between reflex time for the groups was 0.0087 second (+/– 0.0016) in favor of the African American group. This difference was found to be statistically significant.

While this study was an excellent approach in determining possible neuromuscular differences, which might account for race related characteristics, which could predispose one group to success in certain events more than others, extreme caution must be used in drawing conclusions. This investigation was flawed with respect to selection of subjects. Caucasian subjects were all selected from an institution of higher learning, whereas African American subjects were selected from a "school recreation association," and therefore were already active participants in athletic and recreational events. For this reason, and because these results were obtained over sixty years ago, this study needs to be replicated using equivalent groups and modern technological equipment.

This study is emphasized here because it is still often cited as some type of definitive in the discussion of this topic. Schureman (1934), and Todd, McGraw, and Kuenzel (1925), studied the relationships of nerves and their ability to produce responses and found no significant differences between races.

Williams and Scott (1953) studied motor development in infants, and suggested that motor acceleration is not a racial characteristic. More advanced research by Thies, Billinghurst, and Richardson (1967) looked at motor nerve conduction velocity in healthy young East Africans of both African and Indian descent using a percutaneous technique to stimulate the ulnar nerve and peroneal nerve. Neither sex nor race had any significant effect upon nerve conduction velocity. After comparing their data with previous investigations, the authors concluded that East Africans have motor nerve conduction velocities that are indistinguishable from values of Europeans, Caucasian Americans, or Japanese.

Discussion

There have been numerous reports of scientific comparisons of race and physiology relative to athletic performance. In general, results suggest either no differences or small differences between African American and Caucasian groups. When exploring race and athletic performance from a biological perspective, it is important to keep in mind that if there are physiological differences between racial groups, they must be of sufficient quantity and quality to affect performance. For example, if African American superiority in a sport such as basketball is explainable by some physical advantage possessed by African Americans more than Caucasians, two conditions would have to be obtained. First, researchers would have to discover some physical variable, or more likely combination of variables, that are associated with basketball excellence for all performers, independent of racial background. Second, this variable or combination of variables would have to be associated with race. That is, it will have to be more prevalent among African Americans than Caucasians or vice versa. To date such variables have not been established. While there are many theoretical advantages, particularly from a biomechanical perspective, which could impact performance, these characteristics have not been shown to be reliable predictors of performance. For example, Metheny (1939) suggested that the body proportions of her subjects might give the African Americans a slight kinesiological advantage. Unfortunately, data which have tested such anthropometric factors as criteria for increased performance, independent of race, provide very low correlations of these factors as predictors of performance (Oyster and Wooten, 1971).

Motor skill performances and physiological function are not one and the same. With regard to skill testing it is important to acknowledge that motor skill test performances in activities such as running, jumping, and throwing do not reflect physiological functions or predispositions independent of other factors, such as practice and habituation. Thus any performance is only partly impacted by physiology. For example, that many athletes from Switzerland have been successful in skiing, that many Japanese athletes have been successful in judo, that many male athletes from Bulgaria have been successful in weight lifting, or that many Canadians have been successful in ice hockey does not necessarily reflect that they are more physiologically endowed for these events relative to others. What it does suggest is that they have various requisites, including but not independent of physiology, for successful performance in these events.

Roughly 12% of the United States population is African American, yet several professional and college sporting events are comprised of greater than 50%, 60%, and even 70% African American males. If this African American overrepresentation is to be explained by some physical, physiological, or anthropometric advantage, the advantages would have to appear in African Americans relative to European Americans at extremely high magnitudes. For example, to achieve the 68% representation in the National Football League, would require African Americans to possess a fifteen to one advantage. In professional basketball (77% African American), a 27 to 1 advantage would be required of African Americans over Caucasians for the performance trait to explain the discrepancy (Phillips, 1976).

Studies that have reported quantitative physiological differences between racial groups report relatively small differences between the groups. Possibly the most impressive difference reported is that by Ama et al. (1986) who found 30% to 40% higher anaerobic enzyme activities in African male subjects when compared to their Caucasian counterparts. Yet this 40% difference hardly comes close to the magnitudes needed to significantly impact the disproportionate overrepresentation of Africans and African Americans in highly anaerobic sports. In no single case does the performance difference or mechanical model come remotely close to approaching the requisite powers needed to account for the discrepancies.

If African and African Americans possess some type of biochemical or biomechanical qualities that predispose them to success in events such as basketball, baseball, football, and sprinting, it is quite curious that they do not also dominate other activities as well. Sporting activities such as tennis, volleyball, weight lifting, high jumping, pole vault, and baseball pitching—areas where African Americans are not well represented—have remarkably similar bioenergetics (Fox, Bowers, and Foss, 1993) and movement patterns to the aforementioned. As Malina (1991) suggests, discussion of racial variations in sport performance should be set within both a biological and social context. Performance in sport should thus be viewed neither in an exclusively biological nor in an exclusively social or cultural manner. If we are to understand the factors related to success in sport, a biocultural approach is imperative.

Future research is needed, yet unfortunately many researchers are reluctant to explore this area because of its potentially controversial nature. However, investigation and study lead to knowledge, while lack of investigation leads to observations and speculations that serve to perpetuate folklore. Because a number of the studies cited are relatively old, several of them need to be replicated with modern technologies and approaches. Additionally more females should be included in samples since, if the factors are indeed racial in nature, they should cross gender lines. From a statistical standpoint, much larger samples are needed to make significant conclusions in these studies.

The importance of anatomical and physiological differences has not yet been exhaustively studied, but at the present time the many studies that have been done indicate that physical endowment explanations are not very promising. The available scientifically based physiological data do not seem to support the observed performance differences among racial groups—certainly not to the magnitudes that would be needed to account for the disproportionate representations and successes. It seems more likely that physiological function is only one slice of the pie to explain performance and participation discrepancies. Performance is not achieved through some monolithic characteristic, but rather through a wide variety of biocultural factors.

References

Ama, P. F. M., Simoneau, J. A., Boulay, M. R., Serresse, O. Theriault, and Bouchard, C. (1986). "Skeletal Muscle Characteristics in Sedentary Black and Caucasian Males." *Journal of Applied Physiology,* 61, 1758–61.

Ama, P.F.M., Lagasse, P., Bouchard, C., and Simoneau (1990). "Anaerobic Performances in Black and White Subjects." *Medicine and Science in Sports and Exercise,* 22, 508–11.

Associated Press. (1995, September 14). "Claim: Sprinter's Race a Factor." *Daily Press,* p. B1.

Bouchard, C. (1988). "Genetic Basic of Racial Differences." *Canadian Journal of Sport Sciences,* 13, 104–8.

Boulay, M. R., Ama, P. F. M., and Bouchard, C. (1988). "Racial Variation in Work Capacities and Powers." *Canadian Journal of Sport Sciences,* 13, 127–35.

Browne, R. L. (1935). "A Comparison of the Patellar Tendon Reflex Time of Whites and Negroes." *Research Quarterly,* 11, 121–26.

Burdeshaw, D. (1968). "Acquisition of Elementary Swimming Skills by Negro and White College Women." *Research Quarterly,* 39, 872–79.

Campanis, A. (1987, April 6). *ABC Nightline Interview.* American Broadcasting Company.

Carlston, D. E. (1983). "An Environmental Explanation for Race Differences in Basketball Performance. *Journal of Sport and Social Issues,* 7, 30–51.

Carter, J. E. L. (1984). "Somatotypes of Olympic Athletes." *Medicine Sport Science,* 18, 80–109.

Coakley, J. J. (1994). *Sport in Society: Issues and Controversies.* St. Louis: Mosby.

Cohn, S. H., Abesamis, C, Zanzi, I., Aloia, J., Yasumura, S., and Ellis, J. (1977). "Body Elemental Composition: Comparison between Black and White Adults." *American Journal of Physiology,* 232, E419–E422.

Davenport, C. B., and Love, A. G. (1921). "Army Anthropology." *Medical Department of the United States Army in World War,* 15. Washington: Office of the Surgeon General, Department of the Army.

Davies, C. T. M., Barnes, C., Fox, R., Ola Ojikuta, R., and Samueloff, A. (1972). "Ethnic Differences in Physical Working Capacity." *Journal of Applied Physiology,* 33, 726–32.

Davies, C. T. M., Mbelwa, D., Crockford, G., and Weiner, J. (1973). "Exercise Tolerance and Body Composition of Male and Female Africans Aged 18–30 Years." *Human Biology,* 45, 31–40.

de Garay, A. L., Levine, L., and Carter, J. E. L. (Eds.). (1974). *Genetic and Anthropological Studies of Olympic Athletes.* New York: Academic Press.

Dintman, G. B. (1984). *How to Run Faster.* New York: Leisure Press.

DiPrampero, P. E., and Cerretelli, P. (1969). "Maximal Muscular Power (aerobic and anaerobic) in African natives. *Ergonomics,* 12, 51–59.

DiPrampero, P. E., Pinera Limas, F., and Sassi, G. (1970). "Maximal Muscular Power, Aerobic and Anaerobic, in 116 Athletes Performing in the XIXth Olympic Games in Mexico." *Ergonomics,* 13, 665–74.

Edwards, H. (1973). *Sociology of Sport.* Homewood, IL: Dorsey Press.

Fox, E. L., Bowers, R. W., and Foss, M. L. (1993). *The Physiological Basis for Exercise and Sport* (5th ed.). Madison, WI: Brown and Benchmark.

Harrison, L. (1995). "African Americans: Race as a Self-Schema Affecting Physical Activity Choices." *Quest,* 47, 7–18.

Harsha, D. W., Freichs, R. R., and Benson, G. S. (1978). "Densiometry and Anthropometry of Black and White Children." *Human Biology,* 50, 251–80.

Herskovitz, M. J. (1930). *The Anthropometry of the American Negro.* New York: Columbia University Press.

Herskovitz, M. J., Cameron, V., and Smith, H. (1931). "Physical Form of Mississippi Negroes." *American Journal of Anthropology,* 16, 193–201.

Himes, J. H. (1979). "Secular Change in Body Proportions and Composition. In Roche, A. (Ed.), "Secular Trends in Human Growth, Maturation, and Development." *Monographs of the Society for Research in Child Development: 179,* 28–58.

———. (1988). "Racial Variation in Physique and Body Composition." *Canadian Journal of Sport Sciences,* 13, 117–26.

Hoobing, R. (Ed.). (1984). *The 1984 Olympics: Sarajevo and Los Angeles.* Washington, D.C.: United States Postal Service.

Hunter, D. W., Bartels, R. L., and Lanese, R. R. (1989). "A Comparison of Anaerobic Power between Black and White Males." *Medicine and Science in Sports and Exercise,* 21, S52.

Huttinger, P. W. (1959). "Differences in Speed between American Negro and White Children in Performance of the 35-Yard Dash." *Research Quarterly,* 30, 366–68.

Jones, O. L. (1941). "Race and Stature: A Study of Los Angeles School Children." *Research Quarterly,* 12, 83–97.

Laska-Mierzejewska, T. (1970). "Morphological and Developmental Differences between Negro and White Cuban Youths." *Human Biology,* 42, 581–97.

Leary, W. P., and Wyndham, C. H. (1965). "The Capacity of Maximum Physical Effort of Caucasians and Bantu Athletes of International Class." *South African Medical Journal,* 39, 651–55.

Malina, R. M. (1969). "Growth and Physical Performance of American Negro and White Children." *Clinical Pediatrics,* 8, 476–83.

———. (1988). "Racial/Ethnic Variation in the Motor Development and Performance of American Children." *Canadian Journal of Sport Sciences,* 13, 136–43.

———. (1991, June). "Ethnic Variations in Human Performance." Paper presented at the 38th Annual Meeting of the American College of Sports Medicine, Orlando, FL.

Metheney, E. (1939). "Some Differences in Bodily Proportions between American Negro and White College Students as Related to Athletic Performance." *Research Quarterly,* 10, 41–53.

Milne, C., Seefeldt, V., and Reuschlein, P. (1976). "Relationship between Grade, Sex, Race and Motor Performance." *Research Quarterly,* 47, 726–30.

Nei, M., and Roychoudhury, A. (1974). "Genic Variation within and between the Three Major Races of Man, Caucasoids, Negroids, and Mongoloids." *American Journal of Human Genetics,* 26, 421–43.

Newt, P. (1991, June). "Ethnic Variations in Human Performance." Paper presented at the 38th Annual Meeting of the American College of Sports Medicine, Orlando, FL.

Oyster, N., and Wooten, E. P. (1971). "The Influence of Selected Anthropometric Measurements on the Ability of College Women to Perform the 35-Yard Dash." *Medicine and Science in Sports,* 3, 130–34.

Phillips, J. C. (1976). "Toward an Explanation of Racial Variation in Top-Level Sports Performance." *International Review of Sport Sociology,* 11, 39–53.

Ponthieux, N., and Barker, D. (1965). "Relationship between Race and Physical Fitness." *Research Quarterly,* 36, 468–72.

Reed, T. E. (1969). "Caucasian Genes in American Negroes." *Science,* 165, 762–68.

Robinson, S., Dill, D. B., Harmon, P. M., Hall, F. G., and Wilson, J. W. (1941a). "Adaptations to Exercise of Negro and White Sharecroppers in Comparison with Northern Whites." *Human Biology,* 13, 139–58.

Robinson, S., Dill, D.B., Wilson, J., and Nelson, M. (1941b). "Adaptations of White Men and Negroes to Prolonged Work in Humid Heat." *American Journal of Tropical Medicine,* 21, 261–87.

Ross, W., and Ward, R. (1984). "Proportionality of Olympic Athletes." *Medicine Sport Science,* 18, 110–43.

Saltin, B. (1996). "Exercise and the Environment: Focus on Altitude." *Research Quarterly for Exercise and Sport,* 67, Supplement to No. 3, S1–S10.

Saltin, B, Kim, C., Terrados, N., Larsen, H., Svedenhag, J., and Rolf, C. (1995). "Morphology, Enzyme Activities and Buffer Capacity in Leg Muscles of Kenyan and Scandinavian Runners." *Scandinavian Journal of Medicine and Science in Sports,* 5, 222–30.

Schureman, O. P. (1934). "The Phrenic and Accessory Phrenic Nerves in American Whites and Negroes." *Anatomical Research,* 58, 86.

Schutte, J., Townsend, E., Hugg, J., Shoup, R., Malina, R., and Blomqvist, C. (1984). "Density of Lean Body Mass is Greater in Blacks than in Whites." *Journal of Applied Physiology,* 56, 1647–49.

Shapiro, L. (1988, January 16). "'Jimmy the Greek' says Blacks are Bred for Sports." *The Washington Post,* pp. A1, A10.

Tanner, J. (1964). *Physique of the Olympic Athlete.* London: George Allen and Unwin.

Todd, T. W. (1928). "Entrenched Negro Physical Features." *Human Biology,* 1, 59.

Todd, T. W., McGraw, W. H., and Kuenzel, W. M. (1925). "Measurement of the Brachial and Lumbro-Sacral Plexuses in Man." *American Journal of Physical Anthropology,* 8, 281–91.

Thies, R. E., Billinghurst, J. R., and Richardson, H. D. (1967). "Motor Nerve Conduction Velocities in Healthy Young East Africans." *Journal of Applied Physiology,* 23, 321–23.

Trotter, M., Broman, G. E., and Peterson, R. R. (1960). "Densities of Bones of White and Negro Skeletons." *Journal of Bone and Joint Surgery,* 42-A, 50–58.

Williams, J. R., and Scott, R. B. (1953). "Growth and Development of Negro Infants." *Child Development,* 24, 103–21.

Wyndham, C. H., Strydhom, N. B., Morrison, J. F., Peter, J., Williams, C. G., Bredell, G., and Joffe, A. (1963). "Differences between Ethnic Groups in Physical Working Capacity." *Journal of Applied Physiology,* 18, 361–66.

Wyndham, C. H., Strydhom, N. B., Morrison, J. F., Williams, C. G., Bredell, G. A., and Heyns, A. (1966). "The Capacity for Endurance Effort of Bantu Males of Different Tribes." *South African Journal of Science,* 62, 259–63.

Wyndham, C. H., and Heyss, A. J. (1969). "Determinants of Oxygen Consumption and Maximum Oxygen Intake of Bantu and Caucasian Males." *Internationale Zeitschrift für Angewandte Physiologie,* 27, 51–75.

8

The Athletic Dominance of African Americans—Is There a Genetic Basis?

Vinay Harpalani

Race—the concept of human classification based on physical differences—is probably the most controversial topic in American life. Race affects all aspects of society. The public is enraged and torn apart by allegations of institutional racism, while in academia hotly contested debates center on methods of race categorization and racial differences. One issue that has fascinated both the public and academic world is the debate about African American dominance in athletics. Specifically, the question is: Do people of African descent have a genetic makeup that allows for superior athletic performance? There has been heated controversy over this question, to the point where many scientists are afraid to address it. The specter of racism has clouded modern science for many years, from the craniometic measurements of Morton and Broca in the nineteenth century to the publication of Herrnstein and Murray's *The Bell Curve* (1994). Indeed, science is still misused to justify political agendas, often of a racist nature.

However, this clouded past should not prevent scientists from investigating genetic bases of African athletic dominance. Roger Bannister, the first person to run a four-minute mile, commented correctly that political correctness should not suppress an objective analysis of this issue (*Nature*, 1995, 183). If there is a genetic basis for African dominance, it is best to acknowledge and learn about it. This way, scientific data could replace racial stereotypes in shaping peoples' beliefs about the issue. Scientists should study both biological and socioeconomic factors involved in race differences in athletic performance. These studies would provide valuable insight for many academic fields, including anthropology, sociology, ethnohistory, and genetics. The question of African dominance in athletics touches all of these areas and many others. It lies at the heart of the nature-and-nurture issue in a way that captures the emotions and attention of the entire public.

This article analyzes various studies of race differences in athletic performance, presenting material in a historical context and focusing primarily on the possibility of a genetic basis for these differences— the most controversial issue. However, environmental explanations are also reviewed. African Americans are the main subject of inquiry. First, statistics illustrating the success of African American athletes is presented; subsequently, the article explores various biologically based hypotheses to explain this success. Anthropometric and anatomical data are considered, and the Kane vs. Edwards debate of a quarter of a century ago is evaluated. The article then moves on to investigate ethnohistorical explanations for postulated genetic differences between African and European Americans. These include the ideas of slave selection and slave breeding. Next, the available data on muscle fiber differences and genetic correlates of sports performance are evaluated. The sociological theories of African American sports dominance, which include both psychological and economic factors, are then presented. Throughout the article, the author's analysis is included and future studies are proposed. The conclusion presents general thoughts and cautions for future researchers in this area.

Today, the dominance of African American athletes in many sports is unquestioned; African Americans are over-represented in both professional and amateur athletics. They represent approximately 12% of the United States population; yet they comprise 75% of the athletes in the National Basketball Association, over 50% of professional football players, and close to 25% of professional baseball players. African Americans also represent approximately 60% of college basketball players and 40% of college football players (Sailes, 1991, 480). In addition, African American/Afro-Caribbean athletes have dominated track and field. Athletes of African descent hold world records in the men's and women's 100-meter dash, 200-meter dash, 400-meter dash, long jump, the men's 110-meter hurdles, high jump, and triple jump, and the women's 100-meter hurdles. Moreover, most of these records have been held by various African American/Afro-Caribbean athletes for at least the past forty years, some for twice as long (Ashe, 1993, 542–551). Many of the sports in which African Americans have had the most success require a great deal of speed, agility and, to a slightly lesser degree, strength. The physical and anthropometics studies of this issue have focused on these qualities.

The debate over African American athletic dominance began in the latter half of the nineteenth century, when many African American athletes began to distinguish themselves in organized sports. This was also a time when physical anthropologists across the world were intently studying and comparing bodily features associated with different races. Heavyweight boxing champion Jack Johnson and University of Pennsylvania track star John B. Taylor were among the first prominent African American athletes at the beginning of the twentieth century (Wiggins, 1989, 159–160). The debate intensified in the 1930s when Jesse Owens and other athletes of African descent gained international prominence for their achievements in track and field. Several racist and racially stereotyped theories were formulated to explain their success. Dean Cromwell, the famous University of Southern California and Olympic track coach said of the African American athlete, "...his ability to sprint and jump was a life-and-death matter to him in the jungle. His muscles are pliable, and his easygoing disposition is a valuable aid to the mental and physical relaxation that a runner and jumper must have" (Wiggins, 1989, 161). In a more reasonable assertion, Yale track coach Albert McGall suggested that African American sprinters had an advantage because of a projecting heel bone (calcaneus) more common among them (Wiggins, 1989, 161). However, even this assertion was not supported by evidence.

W. Montague Cobb, a well-known African American physical anthropologist from Howard University, was among the first to investigate the physical differences between races with respect to athletic performance. In 1936, Cobb published a paper analyzing characteristics of successful African American athletes and comparing several physical characteristics for African and European Americans with those of track star Jesse Owens (Cobb, 1936). Cobb studied various attributes of African American athletes who had run the 100-yard dash in 9.6 seconds or less. He found the members of this group contained a variety of physiques, ranging from short to tall, slender to stocky, from well-built to those "who could hardly have served as models for the Greeks" (Cobb, 1936, 6). The group included long- and short-legged runners, who also varied in calf muscle size. The athletes also ranged in style, from fast starters to slow starters and from long striders to short striders. In addition, they varied in temperament, from maintaining calm before an important track meet to becoming extremely nervous before the event (Cobb, 1936, 6–7). Cobb also noted that none of the African American sprinters came from traditionally African American colleges, as would be expected if African Americans were innately superior runners. Those colleges did not have training facilities of the same quality as major universities. This highlighted the importance of training and incentive in athletic success (Cobb, 1936, 7).

Cobb acknowledged several average physical differences between African and European Americans (Cobb, 1936, 52). African Americans have relatively longer limbs and a greater leg-to-thigh length ratio. Cobb stated that the latter could be significant in broad jumping. He also cited a study that the nerve fibers of African Americans were larger in cross section, possibly implying better muscle coordination. In addition, Cobb referred to differences in calf muscle prominence and foot length (Cobb, 1936, 52–53).

Overall, however, Cobb concluded that no racial group had an inherent physical advantage in track and field events (Cobb, 1936, 54). His study indicated that Jesse Owens, the most famous African American track star of the 1930s, did not possess most of the features postulated to give African Americans an advantage in sprinting and jumping. Cobb also presented faults with the calcaneus advantage hypothesis of McGall (Cobb, 1936, 53–55).

Cobb's observation that prominent African American athletes possess a variety of physical characteristics is certainly noteworthy. His statement about training and incentive is also well noted. However, Cobb did not provide quantitative data for most of assertions about African American sprinters. His notions of long and short, slender and stocky, and so on, appear to have been subjective. Cobb only provides quantitative measurements for Jesse Owens, and any study with a sample size of only one is extremely prone to error. Cobb, himself, acknowledges that it would have been more desirable to compare many athletes of all races in his study (Cobb, 1936, 52).

In 1939, Eleanor Metheny, a renowned physical educator form the State University of Iowa, published the next major study of physical and athletic performance differences between races (Metheny, 1939). Metheny conducted anthropometric measurements on 51 African American and 51 European American students at the State University of Iowa, finding many statistically significant differences. She concluded that African Americans surpassed European Americans in the following characteristics relative to body stature: weight, shoulder breadth, chest depth and width, neck and limb girths, and length of arm, forearm, hand, leg, and lower leg. European Americans were higher in sitting height, total fat, and hip width (Metheny, 1939, 50–51).

Metheny went on to postulate athletic consequences of her study (Metheny, 1939, 51–52). She hypothesized that several physical features of African Americans yielded advantages in various sports. Greater body weight due to heavier bones and more musculature, coupled with lower body fat, conferred an advantage in contact sports such as football. Longer forearms and hands were advantageous in throwing and allowed greater momentum in jumping. Longer legs and narrower hips, coupled with greater musculature, gave African-American athletes advantages in running. Metheny also stated that African Americans were disadvantaged in endurance events because of shallow chest and lower breathing capacity. However, Metheny did recognize the wide individual variations within racial groups and noted several relevant elements, including reaction time and psychological elements, not assessed by her study.

The work of British physician James M. Tanner supported Metheny's ideas. Based on anthropometric measurements of 137 athletes at the 1960 Rome Olympics, Tanner also concluded that athletes of African descent have advantages in sprinting and jumping while having disadvantages in endurance events such as the marathon. Renowned anthropologists Carleton Coon and Edward Hunt also supported many of these conclusions (Wiggins, 1989, 166–167). However, Tanner, Coon, and Hunt acknowledged socioeconomic reasons for African dominance in certain sports. Moreover, neither Metheny nor Tanner provided any concrete correlations between racial variation in physical characteristics and athletic performance (Wiggins, 1989, 167).

Many studies have supported the anthropometric measurements of Metheny and Tanner (Jordan, 1969; Malina, 1975; Himes, 1988). In addition, research has indicated that African Americans have faster reaction time than do European Americans on average, although it is unclear whether this effect is inherited or acquired through training (Jordan, 1969, 96). Studies have shown that African Americans dissipate heat more effectively than do European Americans, due to longer limbs and greater quantity of sweat glands (Jordan, 1969, 97). Other research had demonstrated that African American children outperform European American children in sprints, broad and vertical jumps, throwing (Malina, 1988), and other events (Sokolove, 1988, 22). In addition, African Americans appear to exhibit advanced skeletal and motor development in comparison to European Americans (Malina, 1988, 137).

In the January 18, 1971, issue of *Sports Illustrated*, senior editor Martin Kane reviewed the literature on African American dominance of sports in an article entitled, "An Assessment of Black is Best" (Kane, 1971). Although Kane acknowledged that socioeconomic factors were involved, the majority of his article was devoted to average biological differences that may contribute to African American sports dominance. Kane cited the work of Robert Malina, a University of Texas anthropologist. Malina stated that longer limbs, a narrower pelvis, and more slender calves, on average, may confer advantages to African Americans in some athletic events. The African American athlete has a greater power-to-weight ratio than does the European American athlete, regardless of the athlete's size. This would yield an advantage in events such as sprints and jumps (Kane, 1971, 79). Malina's suggestions were similar to those of Eleanor Metheny, cited earlier (Metheny, 1939). Kane also cited the work of Edward Hunt. Hunt claimed that African American athletes have "hyperextensibility" (e.g., double-jointedness) and speculated on the advantages it confers: "The Negro has more tendon and less muscle than the white. The black man's heel doesn't protrude as much and his leg and foot give him tremendous leverage for jumping" (quoted in Kane, 1971, 75). Kane noted other studies similar to those considered previously as evidence of the genetic superiority of African American athletes. One new factor cited was research indicating that African Americans, on average, have larger adrenal glands—an important element in sports performance—although Kane stated that this research was "highly speculative" and far from conclusive (Kane, 1971, 74).

In addition, Kane cited psychological factors for the dominance of African American athletes, including ideas that reflect prejudiced racial stereotypes. The unscientific testimony of Lloyd (Bud) Winters, a former San Jose State University track coach, was the main basis for implication of psychological factors. Winters stated,

> [T]he black athlete, as a rule, can go through his daily motions or his sleep period normally, and when the big moment comes he can react normally. In white athletes the conscious mind often takes over and the tensions mount.... As a class black athletes that have trained with me are far ahead of whites in that one factor—realization under pressure. It's their secret. (quoted in Kane, 1971, 76)

Kane referred to similar testimony by track coach Stan Dowell, who had worked with many Olympic athletes (Kane, 1971, 76).

Finally, Kane referred to historical factors that may have been responsible for the biological advantages of African American athletes. He speculated that Africans may have had a "superior physique" without any breeding or selection. Kane based this speculation on a study that showed Ugandan infants had extremely precocious muscular development compared to European infants (Kane, 1971, 79). Kane also mentions two common hypotheses: slave selection and slave breeding. The slave selection hypothesis was exemplified by the comments of Calvin Hill, an African American professional football player and Yale graduate:

> I have a theory about why so many pro stars are black. I think it boils down to survival of the fittest. Think of what African slaves were forced to endure in this country merely to survive. Well, black athletes are their descendants. They are the offspring of those who are physically and mentally tough enough to survive. (quoted in Kane, 1971, 78–79)

The slave breeding hypothesis, similarly, was embodied in this statement by Lee Evans, an African American Olympic track star: "We were bred for it...on the plantations, a strong black man was mated with a strong black woman. We were simply bred for physical qualities" (quoted in Kane, 1971, 79). Kane did not give any further evidence for the slave breeding, but he did give undocumented suggestive evidence for slave selection. Kane stated that 50% of slaves died approximately five years after their capture, implying that only the strongest survived. Although he noted harsh conditions as the cause of this selection, Kane noted the contrary claim that because of their value, captured slaves were often "better fed than white crewmen, who were considered more expendable" (Kane, 1971, 81). Both the slave selection and slave breeding hypotheses will be discussed later.

Harry Edwards, a sociologist from the University of California at Berkeley, was extremely critical of Kane's article. Edwards classified Kane's evidence for African American athletic superiority into three components: racially linked physical and physiological characteristics, race-related psychological factors, and racially specific historical factors. He attempted to systematically refute each component (Edwards, 1973, 193–200).

In reply to Kane's assertion of race-linked physical and physiological characteristics, Edwards offered several criticisms. First, he claimed that the evidence for physical differences between the races was derived from exceptional African American athletes and not from a random sample of the African American population. Second, Edwards noted that anthropologists have not been successful in deriving criteria to divide humans into discrete "races." Third, he pointed out that because of the many complex factors that determine athletics performance, it is difficult to draw any conclusions about such performance based on observable variables (Edwards, 1973, 193–196).

In response to the notion of race-linked psychological factors, Edwards cited studies indicating that African American athletes are significantly more agitated and concerned than are European American athletes (Edwards, 1973, 196). Edwards's refutation of Kane's third factor, racially specific historical occurrences, consisted of three parts. First, Edwards contended that genetic selection of slaves would have acted upon both physical and mental characteristics. Second, he contended that due to racial interbreeding, modern African Americans are not "pure" descendants of African slaves but rather have a combined African and European constitution. Third, Edwards once again noted that many factors besides physical ability are required for successful athletic performance (Edwards, 1973, 197–198).

Many of Edwards's criticisms were valid. Particularly commendable was his reproach of the race-linked psychological factors, which were based on the racial stereotypes of two track coaches rather than any scientific data. However, Edwards's criticisms did not negate the possibility that genetic determinants may account partially for the dominance of African American athletes. His assertion that there are no biological criteria to separate races into discrete units, while constituting a valid point, is not a refutation of Kane's work. Races can be redefined as social categories based on combined biological and ethnohistorical classification. This classification is somewhat arbitrary, but nonetheless useful. In fact, forensic anthropologists are quite proficient in identifying races in this sense (Sauer, 1992).

Edwards's contention that modern African Americans are not "pure" descendants of African slaves is another valid point that does not refute Kane's work. It is true that present-day African Americans have a combined African and European descent. However, due to racist policy, most people who had any degree of African descent were classified as African American. Perhaps "slave descent" would be a more accurate term to use in the context of this article, since Kane's argument referred to slavery as the possible historical cause of African American athletic dominance. Most people with any degree of slave descent were classified as African Americans, even when they were also of European descent. The slave descent, according to Kane's argument, would confer some amount of physical advantage; this would be true regardless of any other accompanying descent. Perhaps an extension of this argument would affirm that the greater the degree of slave descent, the greater the physical advantage; however, this has yet to be studied.

But what about the validity of Kane's argument? Is there any evidence for the slave selection and slave breeding hypotheses? The slave selection hypothesis will be considered first. This hypothesis has not been studied directly with regard to athletic performance. However, it has been proposed to explain the predominance of hypertension in African Americans (Wilson and Grim 1991). African Americans have higher average blood pressures than do indigenous West Africans. Wilson and Grim propose that major causes of death of slaves during importation were salt-depletive diseases, including diarrhea and fevers. They suggest that slaves with enhanced ability to conserve salt may have had a survival advantage under these conditions, and that this may be partially responsible for the high incidence of hypertension among African Americans. It is interesting to note that some scientists had suspected hypertension to be correlated with a greater proportion of fast-twitch muscle fibers, which will be discussed later. However, this has not been demonstrated to date. The main point of relevance here is Wilson and Grim's statement:

> The published historical evidence on the transatlantic slave trade and New World slavery (from the 16th century to the 19th century) reveals that conditions existed for "natural selection," and therefore, genetic changes were virtually inevitable in the slave populations. (Wilson and Grim, 1991, 1–122)

This suggests that slave selection did take place; it does not, however, correlate it with any specific genetic changes that would yield an athletic advantage to those of slave descent. It is also important to note that Wilson and Grim's work is controversial; other sources claim it is completely invalid (see Curtin, 1992). Indeed, environmental factors, not the least of which is racism, certainly play a major role in the increased incidence of hypertension among African Americans.

The slave breeding hypothesis has been discussed more extensively, particularly with regard to African American athletic superiority. On January 15, 1988, Jimmy "the Greek" Snyder, a famous commentator, remarked in an interview that the success of African American athletes originated with selective breeding by slave owners, mirroring the comments by Lee Evans cited earlier (White, 1988). These remarks led to Snyder's firing and sparked a nationwide debate. Some, such as history professor James Horton, claimed that slave breeding was a rare practice (Rowe, 1988, 33). Others, such as anthropologist Michael Blakey, said that slave breeding was common but was not a sophisticated endeavor. Blakey stated, "That kind of breeding couldn't possibly lead to any difference in athletic ability" (quoted in Rowe, 1988, 33). On the other hand, Alvin Poussaint, a black psychiatrist at Harvard Medical School, and others mentioned earlier, had maintained that slave breeding was one of the causes of African American athletic dominance (*Time*, 59). Who was correct?

Gerald S. Norde wrote an entire doctoral dissertation on slave breeding (Norde, 1985). Norde considered the work of major scholars who had written about slave breeding. He divided scholarly views of slave breeding into three categories: 1) slave breeding by plantation owners did not occur; 2) slave breeding by plantation owners occurred occasionally; and 3) slave breeding by plantation owners was a common practice (Norde, 1985, 1). Norde concluded that the third view was correct; slave breeding was a common practice (Norde, 1985, 171). Moreover, the major motive behind slave breeding was profit. Norde noted advertisements for the sale of thousands of female slaves on a daily basis. Many of these advertisements stated that the female slaves were "'good' or 'fine' for breeding" (quoted in Norde, 1985, 172). For example, the following is an excerpt of an advertisement in the *Charleston Mercury*: "She is very prolific in her generating qualities and affords a rare opportunity for any person who wishes to raise a family of strong and healthy servants" (quoted in Rowe, 1988, 33). These kinds of advertisements provide some evidence for selectivity in slave breeding—selectivity for desirable physical qualities. One can speculate that, even without conscious breeding, this kind of selectivity could have conferred genetic advantages for present-day African American athletes. This is mere speculation, and the advantages in any case may not be that great.

However, even slight genetic advantages for African American athletes could translate into significant overrepresentation in certain sports. To give a hypothetical example, assume there is an index to measure a given athletic ability, for instance speed. Perhaps this index would consist merely of several timed 100-meter runs, controlling for environmental influences. For arguments' sake, we will assume that African Americans have a slight advantage in speed, due to genetic factors. A multifactorial trait like speed or any athletic endeavor would probably be normally distributed. The slight advantage may cause a small shift in the African American normal curve, such that the top 0.1% of individuals on the speed index (i.e., the fastest 0.1% of the population) would consist almost exclusively of African Americans (see Figure 1). These would be the world-class sprinters, and this would explain why most of them are African American. This hypothetical example could apply to any highly competitive sport, as only athletes at the very top of the distribution could compete at the world-class level. Thus, even a slight genetic advantage conferred by slave breeding could have contributed significantly to the great proportion of world-class African American athletes. Perhaps most, if not all, world-class athletes are at the very top of this ability distribution, with differential performance determined by motivation, training, and so on. This explanation implies that the athletic dominance of African Americans (as a group) is caused by genetic factors, while the success of individual African American athletes is determined by motivation, training, and other environmental factors.

However, currently there is not sufficient evidence to validate this hypothesis. The hypothetical shift in the normal distribution could also be caused entirely by environmental factors. Therefore, the role of slave breeding in African American sports success is still equivocal.

Kane (1971) also mentioned that Africans may have had an athletic advantage even without selective breeding (79). This will be discussed after relevant fast-twitch muscle data is considered.

Due to new studies and controversial remarks by Jimmy "the Greek" Snyder, among others, the debate over African American athletic dominance resurfaced in the late 1980s. The new studies took the question of biological basis to the next level. Previous studies had focused on anthropometric and gross anatomical measurements. The impetus for these studies was one of the dominant theories in sports sciences at the time. This theory contended that the proportion of slow-twitch and fast-twitch muscle fibers, rather than body physique, was the main factor in determining speed and jumping ability (Sokolove, 1988, 30). Slow-twitch (type I, oxidative) muscle fibers contract slowly and are necessary for endurance events (e.g., long-distance running). Fast-twitch (type IIa and IIb, oxidative and glycolytic respectively) muscle fibers contract much faster and are necessary for events requiring sudden bursts of energy (e.g., sprinting and jumping).

Two studies in the 1980s focused on comparing muscle fiber types between athletes of African and European descent. Physician Drew Gaffney and exercise physiologist and Olympic gold medalist Peter

Snell conducted one study at the University of Texas Southwestern Medical Center. This study included 50 subjects, one-half African American and one-half European American, who were biopsied to determine the proportions of fast- and slow-twitch fibers in their muscles. Ten of the subjects were sprinters from local universities. The results did not indicate a significant difference between African Americans and European Americans, or between sprinters and nonsprinters. These results were surprising, but may have been attributable to small sample size (Sokolove, 1988, 35–36).

The other study, by Ama et al. (1986), yielded different results. This study consisted of 46 male subjects, 23 European Canadians and 23 Africans from Cameroon, Senegal, Zaire, Ivory Coast, and Burundi. All subjects were matched for age, weight, height, and body mass index. They were also determined by questionnaire to be involved only in sedentary activities at the time of the study. Muscle biopsies were taken from the vastus lateralis of the subjects and assayed fiber type proportion, fiber type areas, and various metabolic enzyme activities. The results indicated that the Africans were significantly higher in fast-twitch muscle fiber proportion and area (for both type IIa and IIb). Africans also had significantly higher activity levels for glycolytic enzymes hexokinase, phosphofructokinase, lactate dehydrogenase and for the phosphagenic enzyme creatine kinase. European Canadians had a significantly higher proportion and area of slow-twitch muscle fibers. No significant difference was observed for oxidative (Krebs cycle) enzymes. These results supported the notion that athletes of African descent are, on average, better equipped for sprinting and jumping events. Because the subjects were controlled for many extraneous physical characteristics and environmental effects, the conclusion was that differences were probably due to genetic factors (Ama et al., 1986). Previous studies had demonstrated that sprinters typically have higher proportions of fast-twitch fibers and higher muscle glycolytic enzyme activities (Costill et al., 1976). However, Ama et al. (1986) did caution that their results, although statistically significant, were only slightly beyond the standard margin of technical error for such assays.

Does the data of Ama et al. support Kane's earlier contention that Africans may have superior athletic abilities even without breeding? This question cannot be answered without further investigation. Another issue that should be addressed is the success of Africans in long-distance running. Kenyan athletes, when allowed to compete, have generally dominated middle- and long-distance running events in the

Olympics since the late 1960s (Moore, 1990). Indeed, great long-distance runners have come from countries in all parts of Africa, from Ethiopia to South Africa to Morocco. Moore (1990) partially attributed the roots of some Kenyan success to evolutionary forces: "Down through the generations...the raiding life killed off slow runners and made fathers of the swift.... Always the culture exalted endurance" (Moore, 1990, 78). The phenomenon of African success in long-distance running, along with the evolutionary explanation given as its basis, appears to contradict the previously noted fast-twitch muscle findings. Perhaps there is an encompassing explanation for both occurrences, such as differential selection, but this has yet to be found.

The fast-twitch muscle theory was the centerpiece of a 1989 NBC special hosted by Tom Brokaw entitled: "The Black Athlete: Fact or Fiction" (Sailes, 1991, 481). This special caused another nationwide controversy. Many observers criticized the lack of consideration for environmental bases of African American sports dominance (Moore, 1989; Sailes, 1991). While these criticisms may have been valid, many of the critics seemed to dogmatically hold the view that genetic factors could not be involved in the success of African American athletes. The fast-twitch muscle theory must be investigated further before any conclusions can be made.

Another round of studies have gone to the next level, focusing directly on the genetic basis of sports performance. According to Malina (1986), many motor characteristics show moderate heritability. Bouchard (1986) concluded that genetic factors have an important impact on aerobic power and capacity. Lortie et al. (1986) found that muscle fiber distribution and area are more affected by environmental than genetic factors. A later study by Simoneau and Bouchard (1995), however, found that the variance of measured muscle fiber proportion of European Americans is 40% attributable to environmental factors and 45% to genetic factors, with the remainder of variance due to measurement error. Bouchard (1988, 107) noted that two types of genetic effects can influence sports performance: effects that determine innate ability and effects that determine sensitivity to training. Bouchard (1988, 107) also noted that sports performance is a complex phenotype with numerous genetic influences. At this point, these influences cannot be correlated with any racial genetic differences, which themselves are quite ambiguous to whatever extent they exist.

Although this article has focused on biological explanations, environmental factors are significant and noteworthy. Many sociological theories of African American sports dominance have been proposed. In 1943, clinical psychiatrist Laynard Holloman implicated psychological factors in the supremacy of African American boxers. Holloman's theory, according to Wiggins (1989, 163), involved hatred of European Americans by African Americans:

> [H]atred and desire for revenge against whites was one reason for the supremacy of black athletes in certain American sports. Black fighters dominated boxing, for instance, because it was an ideal way for them to express their hatred for the white man through getting revenge.

Holloman also speculated that compensation for feelings of inferiority was another motivating factor in African American athletic excellence (Wiggins, 1989, 163).

Alvin Poussaint claimed that athletic success was a means for African Americans to express masculinity and power (Wiggins, 1989, 172). Because they were stripped of social power, African American males turned toward displays of physical power. This manifested itself in athletic success (Poussaint, 1972, 115).

Poussaint, (1972, 116) also noted that prominent African American athletes served as role models for African American youth. Jay Coakley suggested that because many of these role models participated in a limited number of sports (e.g., basketball, football, boxing, and track), African Americans have been channeled into those sports (Wiggins, 1989, 176). Studies have shown that African American youth tend only to have athlete role models of their own race. They also place a higher value on athletic achievement than do European American youths (Sailes, 1987, 165).

Harry Edwards cited role models in addition to occupational discrimination in the success of African American athletes (Leonard, 1980, 180). Edwards claimed that minority group members could only excel in the areas open to them. Coakley added to this that professional sports owners, due to the large profits involved, were less concerned about the race of athletes and more intent on their skill and talents (Wiggins, 1989, 177).

Eitzen and Sage added to occupational discrimination the concept of *sports opportunity structure* (Leonard, 1980, 180). They claimed that African Americans tended to excel only in the sports that were readily accessible to them. Facilities, coaching, and competition were more readily available in some sports (basketball, football, track and field, boxing) than in others (golf, tennis). African Americans tended to be over-represented in the former sports and underrepresented in the latter.

Citing the work of H. M. Blalock, sociologist Rodney Stark suggested that dominance of African Americans in athletics suggested: 1) deficiency of other means to social and economic achievement, and 2) overcoming discrimination in fields where quality is most readily measurable (Stark, 1992, 327–329). Stark noted that quality of athletic performance is more readily judged than is quality in academic or other professional performance. He also pointed out that ethnic groups at lower levels of social stratification have always excelled in athletics; for instance, Irish fighters dominated boxing in the late nineteenth century, while Jewish boxers dominated the sport in the early twentieth century. Stark also cited this reason for the success of many African Americans in the entertainment industry.

Sociologist James Leflore acknowledged many factors in the supremacy of African American athletes, but affirmed that the major explanation was "subcultural and informational poolings" (quoted in Wiggins, 1989, 177). Leflore claimed that sports participation of African American athletes depended on their cultural circumstances and the *contingent perceived outcomes* for various activities. African Americans tended to participate in activities (including sports—presumably basketball, football, track and field, boxing, etc.) perceived to bring social rewards, while avoiding activities (including sports—presumably tennis, golf, etc.) that were not perceived to bring social reward or that were perceived to bring social punishment (Wiggins, 1989, 177–178). Other studies also support the notion that social norms affect African American sports participation. One of these studies indicated that African American athletes, relative to European American athletes, prefer sports roles that: 1) accentuated a personal rather than a team orientation, 2) emphasized stylistic performance rather than technical orientation, and 3) produced an individual rather than team power orientation (Sailes, 1987, 165).

Is there a genetic basis for the success of African American athletes? The evidence is unclear at this time. Several lines of data seem to point to genetic factors, but these lines do not fit together, and in some cases they even contradict each other. The issue warrants further study before any conclusions can be made. Particularly, further studies on muscle fiber data and the genetic basis of sports performance would help to resolve the issue. However, researchers working in this area should appreciate the sensitive nature of this issue. First, everyone should acknowledge and appreciate the fact that there is much more variation within so-called races than there is among them; this holds for any trait. Second, Edwards (1971, 39) and others claimed that the idea of African American athletic superiority "opens the door for at least an informal acceptance that whites are *intellectually* superior to blacks." This is a common racial stereotype, as is the notion of African American athletic superiority. Many people may think that the evidence for one of these supports the other—an absolutely false notion. There is no reason to think that athletic excellence correlates with intellectual inferiority. It is true that many, particularly African American youths, may neglect academics to pursue athletic endeavors, but that in no way implies genetic inferiority. Third, many feel that focusing on a genetic basis for African American athletic success undermines the hard work and motivation of African American athletes. Regardless of any genetic advantage, it takes a tremendous amount of work and motivation to become a world-class athlete. This fact should be appreciated by all who investigate this issue. Fourth, many feel that these studies will fuel hopeless dreams for many African American youths, only a few of whom will become world-class athletes. By focusing solely on athletics, African American youth may neglect academics, thereby harming their own personal and professional development. This is a very legitimate concern and should be addressed by all. The chances of becoming a professional athlete, regardless of one's racial affiliation, are extremely small. No one should pursue this dream to the neglect of life's other endeavors.

The issue of African American athletic success has been extremely controversial over the years. Many have claimed that studies of a genetic basis for this success are inherently racist (Edwards, 1971 and 1973; Lapchick, 1989; Davis, 1990; Smith, 1995). However, this is not true. It is possible to be interested in human variation, including racial variation, without adopting the notion that one race is inherently superior to another. Studying these kinds of issues helps to sort out fact from myth in common stereotypes. This, rather than denying that any variation exists, is the proper way to combat racism and bigotry. It is the sincere hope of this author that we are able to acknowledge those differences that do exist among us and, at the same time, live together harmoniously.

Note

The author would like to thank Dr. Gary Sailes of the Department of Kinesiology, Indiana University, and Dr. Karen Rosenberg of the Department of Anthropology, University of Delaware, for their help with this article.

References

Ama, P. F. M., Simoneau, J. A., Boulay, M. R., Serresse, O., Theriault, G., and Bouchard, C. (1986). "Skeletal Muscle Characteristics in Sedentary Black and Caucasian Males." *Journal of Applied Physiology*, 61(5): 1758–1761.

Ashe, A. (1993). *A Hard Road to Glory: A History of the African-American Athlete since 1946.* (Vol. 3). New York: Amistad Press.

Bouchard, C. (1986). "Genetics of Aerobic Power and Capacity." In R. M. Malina and C. Bouchard (eds.), *Sport and Human Genetics*, pp. 59–88. Campaign, IL: Human Kinetics Publishers.

Bouchard, C. (1988). "Genetic Basis of Racial Differences." *Canadian Journal of Sport Sciences* 13(2): 104–108.

Cobb, W. M. (1936). "Race and Runners." *The Journal of Health and Physical Education*, 7: 3–7 and 52–56.

Costill, D. L., Daniels, J., Evans, W., Fink, W., Krahenbuhl, G., and Saltin, B. (1976). "Skeletal Muscle Enzymes and Fiber Composition in Male and Female Track Athletes." *Journal of Applied Physiology*, 40(1): 149–154.

Curtin, P. D. (1992). "The Slavery Hypothesis for Hypertension among African Americans: The Historical Evidence." *American Journal of Public Health*, 82(12): 1681–1686.

Davis, L. (1990). "The Articulation of Difference: White Preoccupation with the Question of Racially Linked Genetic Differences among Athletes." *Sociology of Sport Journal*, 7: 179–187.

Edwards, H. (1971). "The Sources of the Black Athlete's Superiority." *The Black Scholar* 3: 32–41.

———. (1973). *Sociology of Sport.* Homewood, IL: The Dorsey Press.

Herrnstein, R. J., and Murray, C. (1994). *The Bell Curve: Intelligence and Class Structure in American Life.* New York: Free Press.

Himes, J. H. (1988). "Racial Variation in Physique and Body Composition." *Canadian Journal of Sport Sciences*, 13(2): 117–126.

Jordan, J. (1969). "Physiological and Anthropometric Comparisons of Negroes and Whites." *Journal of Health, Physical Education, and Recreation*, 40: 93–99.

Kane, M. (1971). "An Assessment of Black is Best." *Sports Illustrated*, 34 (January 18): 72–83.

Lapchick, R. E. (1989). "Pseudo-Scientific Prattle About Athletes." *New York Times* (April 29): 27.

Leonard, W. M. (1980). *A Sociological Perspective of Sport.* Minneapolis: Burgess Publishing Company.

Lortie, G., Simoneau, J. A., Boulay, M. R., and Bouchard, C. (1986). "Muscle Fiber Type Composition and Enzymatic Activities in Brothers and Monozygotic Twins." In R. M. Malina and C. Bouchard (eds.), *Sport and Human Genetics*, pp. 147–153. Champaign, IL: Human Kinetics Publishers.

Malina, R. M. (1975). *Body Weight, Stature, and Sitting Height in White and Negro Youths 12–17 Years.* U.S. Vital Health Statistics Survey, Series 11, 26. Washington, DC: U.S. Government Printing Office.

————. (1986). "Genetics of Motor Development and Performance." In R. M. Malina and C. Bouchard (eds.), *Sport and Human Genetics*, pp. 23–58. Champaign, IL: Human Kinetics Publishers.

————. (1988). "Racial/Ethnic Variation in the Motor Development and Performance of American Children." *Canadian Journal of Sports Sciences*, 13(2): 135–143.

Metheny, E. (1939). "Some Differences in Bodily Proportions between American Negro and White Male College Students as Related to Athletic Performance." *Research Quarterly*, 10: 41–53.

Moore, D. L. (1989). "Perpetuating Stereotyping Condemned." *USA Today*, sec. C (April 26): 1–2.

Moore, K. (1990). "Sons of the Wind." *Sports Illustrated*, (72), (February 26): 72–84.

Nature (1995). "Bias-Free Interracial Comparisons," (377): 183–184.

Norde, G. S. (1985). "From Genesis to Phoenix: The Breeding of Slaves During the Domestic Slave Era 1807–1863 and Its Consequences." Unpublished doctoral dissertation, University of Delaware.

Poussaint, A. F. (1972). "Sex and the Black Male." *Ebony* (27): 114–120.

Rowe, J. (April, 1988). "The Greek Chorus: Jimmy the Greek Got It Wrong But So Did His Critics." *Washington Monthly* 20: 31–34.

Sailes, G. (1987). "A Socioeconomic Explanation of Black Sports Participation Patterns." *The Western Journal of Black Studies* 11(4): 164–167.

————. (1991). "The Myth of Black Sports Supremacy." *Journal of Black Studies* 21(4): 480–487.

Sauer, N. J. (1992). "Forensic Anthropology and the Concept of Race: If Race Don't Exist, Why are Forensic Anthropologists So Good at Identifying Them?" *Social Science and Medicine*, 34(2): 107–111.

Simoneau, J. A., and Bouchard, C. (1995). "Genetic Determinism of Fiber Type Proportion in Human Skeletal Muscle." *FASEB Journal*, 9(11): 1091–1095.

Smith, E. (1995). "The Self-Fulfilling Prophecy: Genetically Superior African American Athletes." *Humboldt Journal of Social Relations*, 21(2): 139–163.

Sokolove, M. (1988). "Are Black Athletes Better Than Whites?" *Inquirer: The Philadelphia Inquirer Magazine* (April 24): 16–40.

Stark, R. (1992). *Sociology*. Belmont, California: Wadsworth Publishing Company.

Time. (1977). "Black Dominance," (109), (May 9): 57–60.

White, J. E. (1988). "Of Mandingo and Jimmy 'the Greek.'" *Time*, 70, (February 1).

Wiggins, D. K. (1989). "'Great Speed But Little Stamina': The Historical Debate Over Black Athletic Superiority." *Journal of Sport History*, 16(2): 158–185.

Wilson, T. W., and Grim, C. E. (1991). "Biohistory of Slavery and Blood Pressure Differences in Blacks Today—a Hypothesis." *Hypertension*, 17 (suppl. I): I-122-I-128.

9

An Examination of Basketball Performance Orientations Among African American Males

Gary A. Sailes

Historically, the racial prejudice, discrimination, and social stereotyping practiced by the dominant culture precipitated the construction of social barriers to preserve the culture, status, and privilege of white society. Many whites felt their culture was distinct from and superior to African American society (Hacker, 1992; Bell 1992). Consequently, the distinct negative perceptions and definitions of African American culture precipitated social estrangement from white society. However, this compelled African Americans to develop positive and more accurate images of their culture. The outcomes of that effort are apparent in the diverse contributions of African Americans to North American art, music, literature, and sports. Much of African American culture is rooted in its historical and contemporary response to the racism, discrimination, and social stereotyping practiced by the dominant culture (Staples, 1982; Asante, 1988; Bell, 1992; Hacker, 1992). The inferior status relegated to African Americans emanated from the dominant culture's preoccupation with maintaining its status quo and strengthening its position of status, power, and privilege (Davis, 1990; Hacker, 1992). Inferior status was relegated to African American males, in particular, who symbolically represented the greatest threat to the dominant culture (Staples, 1982, Madhubuti, 1990).

Racism, discrimination, and social stereotyping manifested themselves in sport as in other American social institutions. The dominant culture held negative stereotypical beliefs regarding African American male athletes (Hoose, 1989; Davis, 1990; Sailes, 1993). The utilization of genetic definitions to rationalize African American domination in amateur and professional sports was socially stigmatizing and undermined the efforts of African American athletes to be successful (Worthy & Markle, 1970; Bledsoe, 1973; Jones & Hochner, 1973; Phillips, 1976; Hoose, 1989; Davis, 1990; NBC, 1990). The negative stereotypical beliefs about African American male athletes were manifested through stacking, the practice of racial positioning which was prevalent in professional baseball and football (Coakley, 1994; Eitzen & Sage, 1993; Leonard, 1993). The absence of African Americans in professional and intercollegiate sports ownership, management, administration, and coaching further exemplified the racism, discrimination and stereotyping prevalent in American sports institutions (Coakley, 1994; Eitzen & Sage, 1993; Leonard, 1993).

The African American male response to racism, discrimination, and social stereotyping was socially discernible. This coping skill was developed subliminally through the socialization process and displayed to balance or nullify the negative stigma associated with perceived inferior status (Staples, 1982; Majors, 1990; Steele, 1990). Moreover, responses to racism among African American males were a much valued and unifying component of African American male bonding (Madhubuti, 1990; Majors, 1990; Akbar, 1991;). Some African American athletes reacted to the racism, discrimination, and social stereotyping they experienced through performance on the playing field. The performance orientations among African American athletes were noticeably distinct from their white counterparts (Worthy & Markle, 1970; Axthelm, 1971; Bledsoe, 1973; Jones & Hochner, 1973; Phillips, 1976; Greenfield, 1980; Carlston, 1983; Majors, 1990; NBC, 1990; George, 1992).

Style variations in sports performance orientations among African American athletes, that were distinct from white athletes, had early origins. Historically, African Americans were denied participation in organized American sport. Except for a few token members on predominantly white college athletic teams, African American athletes were barred from participating in professional and amateur sports (Rust & Rust, 1990; Ashe, 1993). In response to the dominant culture's strong inclinations against African American participation in organized sports, African Americans established their own professional and amateur sports leagues. Further, Historically Black Colleges competed against one another in a variety of sports prior to the twentieth century (Rust & Rust, 1990; Ashe, 1993). Distinct individual expression or "style" was important among early African American athletes. Individual style was the norm and was practiced regularly by early Negro athletes (Peterson,

1984; Miller, 1986; PBS, 1988). Style is still evident and an important psycho-social mechanism among contemporary African American athletes (Majors, 1990; NBC, 1990).

Self-expression was an important coping mechanism among African Americans in combating the racial inferiority anxiety that generally accompanied the racial prejudice, discrimination, and social stereotyping experienced through social contact with the dominant culture (Majors, 1990; Steele, 1990). Self-expression manifested itself in the performance of many African American athletes and accounted for the individual orientation over the team orientation found among many African American athletes in team sports, most notably in basketball (Jones & Hochner, 1973; Phillips, 1976; Greenfield, 1980; Miller, 1986). These points were further exemplified by Julius "Dr. J" Erving when he asserted "Style counts among inner-city basketball players" (NBC, 1990). Examples of these phenomena were in-zone displays by athletes after scoring a touchdown in football (currently banned by NFL league rules) and the individual fakes and moves of some African American basketball players.

Some African American basketball players tended to engage in "electric" self-expression, possessed the need to prove oneself, and to overcome obstacles with finesse and body control (Greenfield, 1980). Style and self expression were more important than success, fundamental technique, or performance. The power orientation of the African American athlete was personal and individual, and sometimes, it had more importance than team winning. Moreover, black athletes established personal empowerment, a sense of masculinity, and personal identity through their sports participation and performance on the playing field (Majors, 1990).

Distinct social constraints also accounted for the performance orientations among contemporary African American athletes. Limited facilities in the sports opportunity structure restricting opportunities to participate in a wide variety of sports channeled African Americans into few sports (Carlston, 1983; Sailes, 1984). Moreover, limited facilities created overcrowding and consequently generated a more aggressive competitive performance orientation, particularly in basketball (Carlston, 1983).

The barriers to participation in college and professional basketball eventually fell, creating opportunities for African American athletes (Rust & Rust, 1985). Their participation increased dramatically and their presence literally transformed the game to its present model

(George, 1992). African American participation in college and professional basketball is seven times higher than their current representation in the American census (Sailes, 1984; Coakley, 1994; Leonard, 1993). The fast paced and aggressive style of current American basketball is in stark contrast to the slower, methodical game of past decades. These factors were attributed to the distinct playing style and talent of African American athletes (George, 1992).

Apparent social factors account for the participation and performance orientations among African American athletes. Those distinct performance and participation patterns are discernible in college and professional basketball. The performance orientation of the African American basketball player is the foundation for the creation of American's greatest contemporary African American basketball folk heroes (Julius Erving, Michael Jordan, Magic Johnson). The thrilling performance orientation of African American basketball players is used in the marketing of basketball licensing merchandise and is a highlight in the promotion of the game itself.

Conceptual Model

It was the intent of this inquiry to confirm the specific patterns of play that were evident among African American basketball players. The premise that African American performance orientation might have been created within a sport socialization context distinct from that of white players served as the determining factor in formulating this inquiry, thereby positioning race as the independent variable.

The literature supports the assumption that African American basketball players would be more individually oriented, more aggressive, and more expressive thereby creating more improvisational situations than their white counterparts. Utilizing a multivariate approach, these components were conceptualized in the current investigation, which attempted to quantify and extend the work of Jones and Hochner (1973), Carlston (1983), and George (1992).

Methodology

Upon studying informal (pick-up) basketball play at a large predominantly white midwestern university during the indoor basketball season, it was determined that distinct social norms regulated play. The best players, assessed by preliminary observations of skill orientations, congregated on two specific basketball courts at the primary recreational facility on campus. Varsity basketball players would join in some games when their sport was not in season. Mediocre players generally shied away from occupying the two courts during peak recreational periods.

Play was governed by a fixed set of rules. Games were over when a team scored 15 points and was ahead by two points. A basket was worth one point. Winning teams remained on the floor to play against new challengers. Teams were selected by an individual player who called "winners" on a first-come-first-play basis.

A total of fifty informal (pick-up) basketball games were observed over a period of ten weeks. Only racially isolated (all white or all black) teams were observed to preserve the homogeneity and continuity of the cultural paradigms that governed play among players of the same race. Some games contained two all-white or two all-black teams while other games included an all-black versus an all-white team.

Informal play was preferred over interscholastic, intercollegiate, or professional basketball games to ensure freedom of movement and decision making among the participants. Coaches inculcate restrictions on play through the implementation of coaching philosophy, discipline, and strategy. The success of this inquiry was dependent on the freedom of movement and decision making among the participants.

Observation teams consisted of two individuals who were not visible to the players. Game statistics were recorded by race on the following variables: shooting percentages, three-point attempts, forced shots, assists, number of passes before a shot, defensive rebounds, offensive rebounds, turnovers, steals and improvisational play. Shot charts were utilized to determine patterns of attempts at the basket.

The data recorded under improvisational play were pooled. This category included between the legs dribble, behind the back dribble, reverse pivot dribble, single or double pump before a shot, behind the back pass, between the legs pass, no-look pass, reverse lay-up, shake-and-bake moves, and other miscellaneous fakes and moves as they appeared. Each time a player attempted an improvisational move, a single point was scored.

One factor that could not be controlled by this investigation was the repeated involvement of some players or teams. Some teams were very good, defeated new opponents, and played two or three successive games. On other occasions, individual players would reappear randomly. This lack of control over repeated measures undoubtedly affected the results of the statistical procedures employed in this investigation.

However, it is felt that pick-up basketball games are governed by powerful cultural factors and norms that would confound any different theoretical approach. In retrospect, the intent of this investigation was to support a behavioral orientation among African American men rather than make any initial theoretical assumptions about specific race-based behaviors among African American and white males in informal pick-up basketball games.

Results

Shooting

The data demonstrated that the African American players had lower shooting percentages than their white counterparts. Overall, whites made 54.8% of their shots while African American players made only 43.9% of their shots. The reasons for this disparity were apparent. Even though shooting outside the three-point line scored only one point, African American players made more attempts from beyond the three-point line than white players (AA = 3.70, w= 2.60). In addition, African American players took more forced shots (defender present) than white players (AA = 4.10, w = 2.70).

The African American players averaged fewer assists (AA = 0.56, w = 2.65) and fewer passes before each shot per game than their white counterparts (AA = 1.80, w = 3.40). All of the results in this category were statistically significant (F = 3.90, p < .05).

Rebounding

There was no significant difference between the two groups on the offensive rebounding variable. However, the African American players out-bounded their white counterparts on defensive rebounding by almost two to one (AA = 7.60, w = 3.90). This result was also statistically significant.

Improvisational Play

The African American players engaged in improvisational play (style) almost twice as often as the white players (AA = 6.32, w = 3.36). This finding was statistically significant. Although it was not reflected in the data, it was observed that improvisational play contributed to turn-

TABLE 1
Comparisons of Patterns of Play

	Blacks	Whites
Shooting %	43.90	54.80*
3-Point Attempts	3.70	2.60*
Forced Shots	4.10	2.70*
Assists	0.56	2.65*
# Passes Before a Shot	1.80	3.40*
Defensive Rebounds	7.60	3.90*
Offensive Rebounds	5.20	5.40
Turnovers	3.90	3.89
Steals	2.90	2.80
Improvisational Play	6.32	3.36*

*Statistically significant ($F = 3.90$, $p \leq .05$)

overs for African American players. There was no significant differ-ence between the two groups on the average number of turnovers and steals per game.

Discussion

The literature clearly established that African American males played basketball differently than white males for the most part. This investiga-tion was able to support that assumption. Moreover, the data contained in this investigation suggests the rationalizations of Greenfield (1980), Jones & Hochner (1973), Carlston (1983), and Majors (1990) are valid.

The data suggests African Americans were more concerned about individual play and self-expression than were their white counterparts. The African American players had lower shooting percentages because they took more shots that were more difficult to make (three-point shots, defender present). However, those same shots generated the greatest amount of personal prestige if made. In addition, the African American players had fewer assists per game and passed less often, highlighting that an individual orientation was present. On the other hand, white players had more assists and initiated more passes per shot than their African American counterparts, suggesting a team orientation.

The data also revealed that African American players engaged in improvisational play (style) which was not specifically or directly related to shot making. Moreover, their engagement in improvisation sometimes led to turnovers. These findings further suggest the African American players were more concerned about individual self-expression (style) compared to white players. Consequently, the individual orientation for African Americans versus the team orientation for whites was present.

There were other components of this investigation which suggested that self-expression was more of an important factor to the African American players. The initial data collections in this investigation were made courtside. The recorders were not only visible to the players, but dialogue took place between the recorders and some players. However, only the African American players appeared to be curious about the presence of the recorders. When they learned that game statistics were being recorded on their pick-up games, they insisted the recorders watch closely as they played. Although the white players did make curious glances at the recording team, no verbal discourse took place at any time. It became necessary to discard the original data and to observe the games from a position not visible to the players.

It was anticipated that support for Carlston's (1983) rationalization for aggressive play among African American basketball players would appear in the data. It was forecasted that if this rationalization were valid, the African American players would lead in most or all statistical categories. The raw data validated Carlston's claim that African American players were more aggressive than white players. The African American players in this investigation took more three-point shots, took more forced shots, had more defensive rebounds, and averaged slightly more turnovers and steals per game. It would appear that Carlston's (1983) rationalizations are valid. In addition, it is plausible that African Americans play harder at sports, and basketball in particular, because it is a more important component of masculine role identity for African American males (Majors, 1990, Sailes, 1993).

Summary

It was the intent of this investigation to examine distinct patterns of play among African American athletes in basketball, a topic which is the focus of much discussion in popular sports culture, and to dispel some of the myths that permeate sport. It was not the intent of this investigation to determine one race's intellectual or physical superiority over the other. In fact, this investigation was able to support the contention that social and cultural variables were probably the primary reasons for the performance orientations of African American athletes. Current trends in sports commercialism suggest that African American performance orientations are the accepted norm for play among contemporary amateur and professional athletes. As such, they serve as the model for the development of future basketball players irrespective of race or gender.

Distinct patterns of play were evident in this investigation. While it is sometimes the popular belief that stellar performances by African Americans in sport can be attributed to genetic or physical differences from whites, this investigation was able to support the social rationalization that different environmental variables led to the development of divergent norms for sports performance orientations. More specifically, the sport socialization process generally has a greater impact in formulating athletic performance orientations than genetic or physical differences between African Americans and whites (Sailes, 1984).

While this investigation focused on the sport of basketball, its implications are far-reaching and have tangible meaning for other sports. There is clearly a need for more empirical research to understand and objectively interpret the relationship between race, culture, and sport participation.

References

Akbar, N. (1991). *Visions for Black Men.* Nashville: Winston-Derek Publishers.

Asante, M. (1988). *Afrocentricity.* Trenton, NJ: Africa World Press.

Ashe, A. (1993). *A Hard Road to Glory: A History of the African American Athlete.* New York: Amistad Press.

Axthelm, P. (1971). *The City Game.* New York: Simon & Schuster.

Bell, D. (1992). *Faces at the Bottom of the Well: The Permanence of Racism.* New York: Basic Books.

Bledsoe, T. (1973). "Black Dominance of Sports: Strictly from Hunger." *Progressive* (June), 16–19.

Carlston, D. (1983). "An Environmental Explanation for Race Differences in Basketball Performance." *Journal of Sport and Social Issues*, 7, 30–51.

Coakley, J. (1994). *Sport in Society: Issues and Controversies.* St. Louis: Times Mirror/Mosby.

Davis, L. (1990). "The Articulation of Difference: White Preoccupation with the Question of Racially Linked Genetic Differences among Athletes." *Sociology of Sport Journal*, 7, 179–187.

Eitzen, S., and Sage, G. (1993). *Sociology of North American Sport.* Indianapolis: Brown & Benchmark.

George, N. (1992). *Elevating the Game: Black Men and Basketball.* New York: Harper/Collins.

Greenfield, J. (1980). "The Black and White Truth about Basketball: A Skin-Deep

Theory of Style." In Stubbs and Barnet (eds.), *The Little, Brown Reader* (2nd ed.). Boston: Little, Brown.

Hacker, A. (1992). *Two Nations: Black and White, Separate, Hostile, Unequal.* New York: Charles Scribner & Sons.

Hoose, P. (1989). *Necessities: Racial Barriers in American Sports.* New York: Random House.

Jones, J., and Hochner, A. (1973). "Racial Differences in Sports Activities: A Look at the Self-Paced versus Reactive Hypothesis." *Journal of Personality and Social Psychology*, 27, 86–95.

Leonard, W. (1993). *A Sociological Perspective of Sport.* New York: Macmillan Publishers.

MacDonald, W. (1981). "The Black Athlete in American Sports." In W. Baker and J. Carroll (Eds.), *Sports in Modern America* (88–98). St. Louis: River City Publishers.

Madhubuti, H. (1990). *Black Men: Obsolete, Single, Dangerous.* Chicago: Third World Press.

Majors, R. (1990). "Cool Pose: Black Masculinity and Sports." In M. Messner and D. Sabo (Eds.). *Sport, Men, and the Gender Order: Critical Feminist Perspectives* (109–114). Champaign, IL: Human Kinetics.

Miller, P. (1986). "The Early Afro-American Experience in Sports." *Proteus*, 3, 60–66.

NBC Special Documentary Program. (1990, Spring). *The Black Athlete: Fact or Fiction.*

Peterson, R. (1984). *Only the Ball was White.* New York: McGraw-Hill.

Phillips, J. (1976). "Toward an Explanation of Racial Variations in Top-Level Sports Participation." *International Review of Sport Sociology*, II, 39–55.

Public Broadcasting System Documentary Film (1988, Fall). *Black Champions: A History of the Black Athlete.*

Rust, E., and Rust, A. (1990). *Art Rust's Illustrated History of the Black Athlete.* Garden City, New York: Doubleday & Company.

Sailes, G. (1984). "Sport Socialization Comparisons among Black and White Adult Male Athletes and Non-athletes." Unpublished doctoral dissertation, University of Minnesota.

———. (1993). "An Investigation of Campus Stereotypes: The Myth of Black Athletic Superiority and the Dumb Jock Stereotype." *Sport Sociology Journal*, 10, 88–97.

Staples, R. (1982). *Black Masculinity: The Black Male's Role in American Society.* San Francisco: Black Scholar Press.

Steele, S. (1990). *The Content of Our Character.* New York: St. Martin's Press.

Worthy, M., and Markle, A. (1970). "Racial Differences in Reactive versus Self-Paced Sports Activities." *Journal of Personality and Social Psychology*, 16, 439–443.

IV

College Sports:
Opportunity or Exploitation?

10

The Case Against NCAA Proposition 48

Gary A. Sailes

Sidney Prince, a black all-star high school football player, lay on his bed at 12:08 A.M. unable to sleep. His mind was filled with thoughts about the English exam he had the next day. A smile appeared on his face as the confidence he felt came to the surface; he was prepared to "ace" an exam in a subject he enjoyed very much. One of the brightest students in his senior class, he was totally unaware that he would graduate number two in his class in the spring. He was also unaware that he would be labeled "not good enough" by a system he was about to enter, the college sports system.

Sidney Prince was one of the most sought-after high school football players in Oklahoma in 1986. He was recruited by and signed a letter of intent to play football at the University of Oklahoma. The high school scouting reports listed him as an honor student, a top football prospect, a bona fide "Blue Chipper"—a college coach's dream. But Sidney Prince did not play football in his first year of college. He failed to meet the minimum academic standards set by the NCAA that year for incoming freshman student athletes. His score on the math portion of the SAT exam was too low. Sidney Prince was a sacrificial lamb in a college sports system much bigger than his school, his teachers, his family, and himself. He was a Proposition 48 casualty, another statistic in a seemingly cold and insensitive institution whose harsh rules and hypocritical ethical code altered his life. He was victimized before he ever had a chance to play the big game, and his dream had to be postponed for at least a year.

Background Information

In January 1983, at its annual meeting, the National Collegiate Athletic Association (NCAA) enacted Rule 5–1–(j), better known as Proposition 48. In an attempt to tighten admissions standards for incoming freshmen student athletes, the rule stipulated that, to participate in varsity competition at an NCAA-affiliated college or university, new recruits must graduate from high school with a minimum grade point average of 2.0 on a core curriculum of eleven courses, including three years of English, two years of social science, two years of mathematics, and two years of a natural or physical science. In addition, they had to score at least 700 points out of a possible 1600 on the Scholastic Aptitude Test or a minimum of 15 points out of a possible 36 on the American College Test.

A supplemental proposition, Rule 49–b, stated that Proposition 48 would go into effect at the beginning of the 1986–87 school year and would only affect the 277 institutions competing at the Division I level. Students who did not qualify could be admitted and attend class but could not participate in either varsity practices or competition. Nonqualifiers could compete as sophomores after demonstrating satisfactory academic progress, and they would receive four years of varsity eligibility if they continued to maintain satisfactory academic progress. Partial qualifiers (those who met one but not both of the requirements) could receive an athletic scholarship, but they would thereby forfeit or year of varsity eligibility.

Public Reaction

Proposition 48 initiated an outcry from black university presidents, educators, and coaches and from the civil rights establishment. They claimed the rule was biased against blacks, that standardized tests like the ACT and SAT favored whites and would adversely effect the eligibility of black freshmen student athletes and the recruitment efforts of athletic coaches at historically black colleges and universities.

A *USA Today* report ("Fewer Athletes" 1987) revealed that black student athletes and black colleges and universities in the United States had, in fact been most adversely affected by NCAA Proposition 48. The American Institutes for Research (1988) reported that in its first year, 65 percent of all Proposition 48 casualties were black. Moreover, they reported, blacks accounted for an alarming 91 percent of the Propo-

sition 48 casualties among recruits for Division I basketball. The so-
called emotional response from the African American establishment
served as an early warning to the NCAA. As predicted, black athletes
were more adversely affected by the new rule than were white athletes.

As mentioned earlier, partial qualifiers could receive an athletic scholarship but were not allowed to compete in their freshman year and
would lose one year of varsity eligibility. That door was slammed shut
in January, 1989. At its annual conference, the NCAA passed another
rule called Proposition 42. This new rule denied first-year eligibility,
an athletic scholarship, and school financial aid of any kind to entering
college freshmen student athletes not showing both the minimum grade
point average and the minimum SAT/ACT score upon graduation from
high school.

The implementation of Proposition 42 outraged the black establishment. Georgetown University basketball coach John Thompson and
Temple University basketball coach John Chancy, outspoken critics of
Proposition 48, publicly protested its enactment. The NAACP and the
National Urban League publicly took a hard stand against Proposition
42, arguing the new rule could keep many black athletes from attending college. Joseph Johnson, president of Grambling State University
and chairman of the National Association for Equal Opportunity in
Higher Education, strongly opposed Proposition 42, arguing it was discriminatory against blacks and economically disadvantaged Americans
in particular. He maintained most black athletes would not be able to
attend college without an athletic scholarship. In support of his conten-
tions, the American. Council on Education (1989) has reported that
approximately 87 percent of African Americans attending college require financial aid. These findings support the assertion that Proposition 42 was blatantly discriminatory and partially blocked black high
school students' access to higher education.

The academic establishment also supported black college presidents,
educators, and coaches, asserting that the NCAA had stepped out of
bounds with rules regulating who could and could not receive financial
assistance at their respective institutions. The academics were incensed
by the NCAA's seemingly outrageous arrogance and ill-founded claim
of authority. Intense pressure from the public and academic arenas influenced the NCAA to amend Proposition 42; now partial qualifiers
could receive school financial aid but not athletic scholarships. However, partial qualifiers lost one year of eligibility, having to sit out both
practice and competition during their first year.

Implications of Proposition 48

The discussion surrounding Proposition 48 seemed extremely one-sided. The arguments against the rule are far more extensive and consequential than those arguments for it. At the time of the rule's inception, approximately 43.5 percent of all senior student athletes participating in football and basketball at Division I institutions were graduating, but only 38 percent of black athletes were graduating. The NCAA felt that if tighter academic requirements were implemented, more disciplined and capable student athletes would enter college as freshmen, and so national graduation rates would increase. Such an improvement would help to decrease public criticism, diminish congressional scrutiny, and perhaps ameliorate the tarnished image of the NCAA. At best, this notion was ill-founded and embarrassingly naive.

Establishing academic eligibility requirements for incoming freshmen student athletes would never resolve the serious problem of low graduation rates among college athletes. The variables affecting the academic performance of the student athlete are diverse and complex, and they require considerably more than a quick fix. The academic and athletic demands on the typical student athlete at a Division I school are immense, requiring more than sixty-five hours per week of the athlete's time. The rule served as nothing more than a pathetic attempt on the part of the NCAA to restore some degree of academic integrity to college athletics, to eliminate media pressure, and to influence public opinion about the internal operations and state of affairs of college athletics in the United States.

Most of the freshmen student athletes who failed to meet Proposition 48 eligibility requirements were blocked by low standardized test scores. Yet, the admissions network at American colleges and universities believes standardized tests have cultural biases that favor middle- and upper-income whites. Thus, the SAT and ACT are unfair to minorities and the economically disadvantaged. Appropriately, admissions offices do not base their entire decisions on standardized test scores; they also look at high school grade point averages, letters of recommendation, class rank, national origin, gender, race, declared major, and other factors. The experts in college admissions do not feel that high school grades and standardized test scores alone adequately determine the typical high school student's capability to successfully manage college academics.

The NCAA stands alone basing academic eligibility requirements solely on grade point average and SAT/ACT scores. After reviewing the literature, I can only conclude that the NCAA's hard stand is unjustified and unethical. For example, a 1987 University of Michigan (Walter, et al. 1987) study of more than seven hundred football players between 1974 and 1933 found no relationship between GPA in high school or the first year of college and SAT scores. Further, only high school GPA sewed as an accurate predictor for GPA during the first year of college. Furthermore, 86 percent of players who would have been ruled out by Proposition 48 because of low test scores actually graduated from college. In support of the Michigan study, (Walter et al. 1987) the American Institutes for Research (1989c) reported that 79 percent of all 1986 and 1987 Proposition 48 casualties playing Division I basketball and football were still in college making normal progress towards a degree. Over 60 percent of those student athletes did not meet Proposition 48 eligibility requirements because of deficient standardized test scores.

Further evidence against employing standardized test scores as valid admissions criteria is provided by Crouse and Trusheim (1988), authors of *The Case against the SAT*. They not only found that SAT scores do not correlate well with college grades, but they also uncovered an economic bias in the SAT: for every $18,000 increase in family income, SAT scores increased by an average of 200 points. This is particularly significant in view of the fact that African Americans at the time of the study earned half the income ($18,000) of white Americans; 33 percent of black Americans lived in poverty, and 16 percent in extreme poverty. Moreover, the American Institutes for Research (1989b) reported that approximately 50 percent of the black student athletes who play Division I football and basketball emanate from impoverished backgrounds, compared with 13 percent for whites. It seems clear that black high school student athletes are more adversely effected by Proposition 48 than are their white counterparts.

An examination of recent national test score norms from the Educational Testing Service appear to support the assertion that African Americans were' targeted by the NCAA's new rule. Black high school students had average scores of 712 and 13.0 on the SAT and ACT respectively in 1987. Their average ACT score was two points below the minimum requirements established by the NCAA, and their average SAT score barely met the minimum. In 1990, the NCAA raised the ACT requirement to 18, making it even more difficult for African Americans to comply with the rule. The 1987 averages for white high school students on the SAT and ACT were 890 and 19.7 respectively, well above the minimum requirements established by the NCAA.

While the desire of the NCAA to eventually graduate more student athletes is noble, its current method of pursuing this goal is not only discriminatory but victimizes black and economically disadvantaged student athletes. For that reason alone, the rule should be amended or abandoned altogether.

The element most universally damaging to the scholarship and graduation rates of student athletes is the business mentality of the college sports system. College sports in fact constitute a thriving business generating hundreds of millions of dollars in income every year. College sports observe all the unwritten rules of corporate businesses: they perpetuate the philosophy of capitalism and profit; establish marketing and promotion strategies based on product demands and consumption; sabotage, control, and/or eliminate competitors; bend or circumvent the rules of fair trade to gain a market edge; strive to win at all costs; and acknowledge expendable commodities (coaches and student athletes) in the name of profit.

However, only about 13 percent of NCAA Division I schools project a profit on their own. Coming to the rescue, the NCAA offers huge sums (over $2 million to the basketball national champion and a $16 million split at the Rose Bowl) to winning schools and/or conferences at national championships. CBS's recent agreement to pay the NCAA $100 billion over seven years to broadcast the National Basketball Championship will only magnify the problems permeating college athletics. The drive for the great financial rewards made available by the NCAA and its sponsors creates more competition between athletic programs and places more pressure on coaches to win, encouraging cheating in the system. This system also increases the time-consuming demands and pressures on student athletes, encouraging them to believe that athletics are more important than academics.

The research supports this contention. The Women's Sports Foundation (1989) released a study entitled *Minorities in Sports.* It was reported that student athletes had higher GPAs coming out of high school than they earned in college. Also, the American Institutes for Research, (1989a) reported student athletes cited lack of time to pursue their academic studies as the chief problem Acing them during their college experience. Division I student athletes also reported that approximately two-thirds to three-quarters of their time was monopolized by athletics, leaving them little time to attend class or to manage their studies.

Discussion

Most black college presidents and educators and the civil rights establishment feel Proposition 48 is not a fair rule. Many arguments have surfaced regarding the rule's ethical and philosophical implications. Some argue that the eligibility standards established by Proposition 48 are so minimal that anyone not able to meet them does not belong in college. That assumption is elitist and demonstrates a lack of awareness of and sensitivity to the mission of historically black colleges and universities. The literature has demonstrated on numerous occasions that standardized test scores do not accurately predict an individual's ability to manage college course work. Yet, it is the standardized test scores that are preventing over 66 percent of Proposition 48 casualties from obtaining freshman eligibility and athletic scholarships to attend college. Moreover, the literature has also shown that over 80 percent of Proposition 48 casualties probably will graduate from college. Further, among historically black colleges and universities there is the conviction that all persons have the right to pursue an education, and no one who chooses to attend one of these schools shall be discriminated against. Denying anyone access to higher education because of elitist philosophies based on the results of culturally biased standardized tests violates the principles of freedom that are the foundation of this country's Constitution which guarantees the rights of its citizens.

Still, some argue that "anyone against Proposition 48 is against academic excellence!" That assumption is terribly naive. In fact, Proposition 48 bars student athletes from demonstrating their capacity for academic excellence. Not all students who earn low scores on standardized tests are poor or marginal students. It is well known to educators that the quality of instruction in American inner-city public high schools is not consistent with the instruction taking place in financially better off private, rural, or suburban schools. Quality of high school instruction has an impact on how well the student scores on standardize tests. The ACT and SAT standardized tests reveal more about the disparities in the American educational process than about the capability of students to handle college course work.

The following question was raised: "Were the architects of Proposition 48 motivated by prejudice or bigotry?" It is apparent that the rule was not clearly thought out, its consequences were not thoroughly investigated, and its implementation demonstrated a lack of racial and cultural awareness and sensitivity. The NCAA's biggest mistake was to exclude officials representing historically black colleges and universities from the committee that conceptualized Proposition 48. Had such officials been included, the NCAA could have avoided controversy and bad press.

Proposition 48 should be abandoned primarily because it serves no viable purpose and survives only on principle. Proposition 48 demonstrates a power play on the part of the NCAA and has created distance between the NCAA and academia, black educators, and the civil rights establishments. The NCAA has overextended its authority by implementing a rule that undermines and attempts to regulate the admissions and financial aid policies of American college and universities. It simply does not have that right nor is it qualified to do so. Proposition 48 prevents deserving and capable young student athletes from receiving their only possible means of financial aid to attend college. From an educational standpoint, that is totally unacceptable.

Common knowledge dictates that the problem with college sports isn't the type of student athlete who is being recruited; the problem is the system within which the athlete must compete. Student athletes are not given adequate time to pursue their college studies leading to the degree. The business mentality of athletic programs is in direct conflict with the philosophy of amateurism and scholarship the NCAA is so nobly trying to reestablish in college sports. That the two ideologies are not compatible is especially clear in view of the current state of affairs in college sports. Unless the NCAA exercises more control over its governing institutions, it will continue to experience its current problems, drawing unwanted negative media exposure and pressure from the general public.

Recommendations

The NCAA will probably never control the business side of college sports. It can, however, recapture part of their integrity and reestablish scholarship among student athletes by implementing and enforcing sweeping reforms to protect the rights of student athletes. Many reforms have been proposed by the NCAA University Presidents Committee and by a Congressional committee called the Knight Commission (1991). Many of the proposed reforms have met extreme resistance and criticism from the body of Division I athletic directors and coaches. They maintain that the proposed reforms would diminish their capacity to generate revenues which would in turn reduce the competitiveness of their athletic programs, most notably in football and basketball, the two major revenue-producing sports at most schools.

The primary focus of the two reform committees was to protect the rights of student athletes to pursue an education and to graduate with their classmates. To accomplish this, they concluded, the pressures associated with intercollegiate competition would have to be reduced, freeing more time for student athletes to pursue their academic studies. The proposal generating the most criticism from coaches was to reduce weekly practices to twenty hours per week. Currently, most Division I football and basketball teams practices between thirty and forty hours per week (Knight Commission, 1991). Other reforms included eliminating spring football practice, reducing the number of contests played in a given season, and having later starting dates for intercollegiate seasons. On the average, Division I basketball teams play thirty contests per year, more if they make it to the NCAA tournament. Intercollegiate baseball teams play an average of sixty contests per year. On average, Division I basketball and football players miss approximately six classes per semester. In many cases, professors are either required or encouraged to make bothersome arrangements to allow student athletes to take make-up examinations. Implementing restrictions on the number of allowable contact hours in athletics for student athletes would greatly reduce the pressures and demands they experience and allow them more opportunity to pursue academic work leading to a degree.

Another proposal submitted by the NCAA Presidents Committee was to eliminate athletic dormitories (Knight Commission, 1991). This recommendation would have two major benefits. First, it would eliminate the athletic department's expense of maintaining housing for student athletes, turning over this responsibility to the campus housing office. Second, "mainstreaming" student athletes would help to dispel the traditional jock mentality, increase the student athlete's competitiveness in the classroom, and expose athletes to a more balanced social experience. In fact, studies have demonstrated that students who involve themselves in the social environment of college and university campuses do better academically and have a greater chance of graduating. Living in a restricted environment centered around athletics diminishes that possibility.

The Knight Commission (1991) proposed that academic safety nets be developed and maintained for student athletes. Tutoring, counseling, and academic monitoring programs would help to ensure the academic success of student athletes. Studies have demonstrated that many student athletes require some type of counseling or tutorial assistance to balance the demands of being both a student and an athlete.

It was recommended that individual schools as well as the NCAA establish scholarship funds to pay the educational expenses of student athletes who exhaust their eligibility before graduating (Knight Commission, 1991). Currently, only 43.5 percent of student athletes actually complete their major course requirements to earn their bachelors degree in four years. For all students, studies have demonstrated, an average of five years is required to obtain a bachelor's degree; however, most athletic scholarships are awarded for only four years. Since the majority of black athletes come from families who are unable to pay their college expenses, establishing and maintaining posteligibility or five year athletic scholarships become very important issues.

Athletes should receive a monetary stipend in addition to their athletic scholarships. Currently, the NCAA does not allow student athletes to hold jobs or to receive funds in addition to their athletic scholarships (Knight Commission, 1991). Generally, it has been reported, athletic scholarships do not cover normal expenses. The monetary restrictions imposed by the NCAA limit the activity and sociability of student athletes to an extent that can adversely affect their adjustment to the college environment. Studies have shown that becoming involved in normal social activities on the college campus contributes to the student's identification with the school and to academic achievement leading to graduation (Fleming, 1988).

First-year student athletes should not be allowed to compete in varsity athletics. The NCAA enforced this rule until the late 1970s. Eliminating the first year of eligibility would give the student athlete the opportunity to mature to become socially and educationally adjusted to the university, to focus on and become serious about their studies. These developments would increase the chances of earning a degree. To maintain four years of eligibility, they would need five-year scholarships. Granting them would demonstrate the institution and the NCAA's commitment to the educational attainment of the athletes.

The NCAA should mace coaches more accountable for graduating the.. athletes and placing them in degree-granting curriculums. For failing to graduate their student athletes, coaches should be penalized (fewer scholarships, no postseason play, fewer recruitment visitations). The NCAA should also encourage college and university presidents and chancellors to exercise more control over their athletic programs, including those academic programs that service student athletes. If academically marginal student athletes are recruited, remedial programs, such as the one at the University of Georgia, should be established to provide such student athletes with the opportunity to develop those skills and to become competent and competitive in the classroom.

There should be widespread support for current legislation, recommended by the Knight Commission, requiring colleges and universities to publicize the graduate rates of their student athletes. Prospective student athletes can then make informed decisions about the schools they will attend and avoid programs that are not graduating their athletes.

Summary

Proposition 48 discriminates against blacks, and the research confirms that it does. An overwhelming majority of Proposition 48 casualties are African American. If parity existed in the educational system and if Proposition 48 were a fair rule, only 12 percent of the casualties would be black, since African Americans represent 12 percent of the American population. However, cultural and socioeconomic biases are built into the rule; they emanate from the biases built into the SAT and ACT tests. As long as standardized test scores are utilized to establish eligibility requirements for college athletic participation, discrimination will continue.

The implementation of Propositions 48 demonstrated a lack of foresight and poor judgment on the part of the NCAA. Student athletes are not the problem in college sports; given the chance, they could succeed in the classroom. Integrity can be restored to intercollegiate athletics by implementing policies that protect the rights of the student athlete to receive a college athletic scholarship and a college education. The number of athletes who exploit the college system so as to enter professional sports is minimal. Implementing a rule that attempts to exempt them from the college sports system at the expense of denying access to deserving student athletes is unfair and unethical. The implementation of sweeping reforms in the college sports system, and not a quick fix, is the only logical alternative for the NCAA. Only then will the Sidney Princes in our high schools get the opportunities they deserve.

References

American Council on Education. (1989). *Minorities on Campus.* Washington, D.C.

American Institutes for Research. (1988). *Report No. 1: Results from the 1987–88 National Study of Intercollegiate Athletes.* Washington, D.C.

———. (1989a). *Report No. 6: Comments from Students in the 1987–88 National Study of Intercollegiate Athletics.* Washington, D.C.

———. (1989b). *Report No. 3: The Experience of Black Intercollegiate Athletes at NCAA Division I Institutions.* Washington, D.C.

———. (1989c). *Report No 5: Analysis of Academic Transcripts of Intercollegiate Athletics at NCAA Division I Institutions.* Washington, D.C.

Crouse, J., and Trusheim, D. (1988). *The Case Against the SAT.* Chicago: University of Chicago Press.

Fleming, J. (1988). *Blacks in College.* San Francisco: Jossey-Bass.

Knight Commission on Intercollegiate Athletics. (1991). *Keeping Faith with the Student Athlete: A New Model for Intercollegiate Athletics.* Miami.

Walter, T., Smith, D., Hoey, G., Wilhelm, R., and Miller, S. (1987). "Predicting the Academic Success of College Athletes." *Research Quarterly for Exercise and Sport*, 58(2): 273–279.

Women's Sports Foundation. (1989). *Minorities in Sports.* New York.

Fewer Athletes are Getting Benched by Proposal 48. (1987, September 8). *USA Today*, p. C1.

11

African American Player Codes on Celebration, Taunting, and Sportsmanlike Conduct

Vernon L. Andrews

The color line in sports has gradually shifted in America in the twentieth century. As more African Americans have taken the field—first in leagues of their own, and more recently with whites—they have brought with them the expressive improvisational behaviors and attitudes from ghettos in Oakland to Saint Louis; the verbal "talk" and physical survival skills of the projects from Chicago to Coney Island; and the cool calculated confidence of rural and suburban environments from Texas to Ohio. These adaptive patterns of behavior have often clashed with white behaviors and attitudes in college classrooms. Acts by black children and adolescents are misunderstood and reprimanded because they are not quite right—not quite "white" (see also Foster, 1995; Fordham, 1993; Kochman, 1981). Likewise "coolness" and stylistic improvisation in speech or movement—among other black masculine responses to harsh living conditions—have been misinterpreted not only in our classrooms but in the work place, on city streets, and even on the sporting field (see Andrews, 1996a, 1991; Dyson, 1993; Fiske, 1993; George, 1992; Majors and Billson, 1992; Jones, 1986; Holt, 1972). This research is thus part of the broader study of the racial conflict over behavioral and verbal style in social settings and social institutions in America.

This article, specifically, focuses on African American college football player codes of behavior and the white normative construction of sportsmanlike conduct. Previous research has focused on NFL football rules about what is and is not "sportsmanlike," and how cultural environment plays a pivotal role in shaping attitudes and behaviors of athletes and mainstream media (Andrews, 1996a).[1] In this article I review interviews with African American student athletes on the 1995–96 University of Wisconsin football team to determine on-field behavior patterns, attitudes about expression of others, how athletes learn appropriate behaviors from mentors, role models, and coaches, and player thoughts on National Collegiate Athletic Association (NCAA) sportsmanlike conduct rules.[2] How do players gain knowledge of appropriate sports conduct? How is this knowledge negotiated on the field? Do player codes of conduct converge or diverge with NCAA views of sportsmanship? How might the NCAA have come about its knowledge of sportsmanship? The college football "anticelebration rule"—a subset of the broader area of sportsmanlike conduct—appears extremely strict and unwarranted, in addition to being centered around white middle-class behavioral norms. It appears also that the NCAA has little intention of shifting its attitudes about what behaviors are "unsportsmanlike." I contend that player's codes of conduct are ways in which athletes acknowledge, reward, or reprimand extreme forms of behavior which are considered "out of bounds." The interviews shed light on player codes, learned behaviors, and the convergence with the NCAA, while the literature below grapples with the last question: NCAA knowledge. I review theory on the roots of sportsmanship in English society, parallel issues of appropriate public behavior ("manners"), and the development of attitudes on public "civility." These ideas are juxtaposed with theory on the uses of power, control, and rules on behavioral constraint as ways in which the NCAA bureaucratic elite attempt to maintain the status quo of whiteness in the social institution of sport.[3]

Theory

White Manners and Civility

In *The History of Manners* (1978) and *Power and Civility* (1982), Norbert Elias traces the development of manners and social behavior of the Middle Ages in Germany, France, and England. Elias in painstaking detail notes the sociogenesis of rules of conduct at, among other places, the dinner table and the bedroom. One goal of Elias's research is to discover the process of changes in habits and customs of people over time, and to ac-knowledge that human habits and culture—"good manners" and "civil" social behavior—are all part of long-term processes of development that are dependent on a variety of social factors. He claims that there is no "zero point in civility," such that France or England went from being uncivilized to civilized, but, based upon specific indices, societies go from a lower to a higher level of civilization.[4] Further, he notes that if members of present-day Western society were suddenly transported into a past epoch of their own society, they would find that what was determined as civilized or well-mannered social behavior two hundred years ago in the court societies of Paris, would be considered the poor-est of manners today, even by lower class standards.[5] The central elements in the process of civilization for Elias are:

> An elaboration and refinement of social standards regarding the control of "natural" functions and the conduct of social relations generally; a concomitant increase in the social pressure on people to exercise self-control; and, at the level of personality, an increase in the importance of "conscience" as a regulator of behavior. In the course of this process, external restraints grew more subtle and all-pervasive, and the use of direct force was pushed increasingly behind the scenes. (Dunning and Sheard, 1979, p. 8)

Elias notes that the concept of civilization sums up the early belief that Western society thought itself superior to earlier, "more primitive" cultures, and further that the concept of civilization merely emphasized "what is common to all human beings—or in the view of its bearers—should be" (Elias, 1978: 5). Elias moves his research on society eventually into the world of sport. One of the questions he seeks to answer concerns the parallel rise in vio-lence and control in society, and the similar rise in violence and control in sport, a topic taken up later in this article (Dunning and Sheard, 1979, 9).

According to the civilizing processes outlined above, social stan-dards are refined, self-control is requested, conscience becomes our guide, and, when all else fails, external restraints and (invisible) power and force are used to control behavior. And though manners are much more specific and micro-level, the concept of civilization refers to a wide array of controllable factors, like technology, the development of scientific knowledge, religious ideas, customs, the attitudes or behav-iors of people, right down to the "type of dwelling or the manner in which men and women live together" and to the "way in which food is prepared. Strictly speaking, there is almost nothing which cannot be done in a civilized or an uncivilized way" (Elias 1978: 3, 5).[6] In a similar sense, it seems almost anything on the field of play in sport can be classified as sporting or unsporting, fair or unfair. And it is not a coincidence that those who make the rules get to choose what is and what is not right, based upon their histories and perceptions and ends.

On Sport, Work, and Play

Theorists have commented on critical intersections of sport behavior and social influences, including Huizinga (1949), who wrote on the move from "play" to "seriousness" in sport paralleling industrialization in America. Stone (1971) commented on the polarization of "work" and "play" in the U.S.—and thus professional versus amateur dichotomy—as stemming from the dominant ideology of the Protestant ethic in North America. Another researcher, applying a Marxist approach, sees a growing structural similarity between sport and work in society. Rigauer (1981) sees the "real" function of sport in modern society as reinforcing an ethic of hard work, achievement, and group loyalty—all functions necessary for the operation of an advanced society. He cites the top levels of both professional and amateur team sports as dehumanizing and characterized by the goal to break records and achievement striving. In addition, he sees modern sport as a bourgeois produce, with an end result of maintaining the status quo and bolstering ruling class dominance. In a final swipe at those in power, Rigauer notes that sport administration boards control the making of sport rules, and that full-time officials—who are not sportsmen themselves—decide matters of policy. The result, Rigauer says, is private decision-making and dominance over the majority by the bureaucratic elite.

Sportsmanship, Fair Play, and the English Tradition

The NCAA is very specific in how it constructs sportsmanlike conduct. These images, as noted in their rules book statement about sportsmanlike conduct, draw on past European knowledge:

> The playing rules are very clear in their prohibition of actions that are unsportsmanlike or demeaning to opponents. Players will express excitement over a great play but must

never address remarks or gestures to opponents or spectators, nor may they spike the ball or throw it into the air. Choreographed or delayed spectacles have no validity in football and detract from its honored traditions. Continued dedicated efforts by players, coaches, officials and administrators are essential to reversing all negative trends in sportsmanship. Enthusiasm without exhibitionism must be the goal for the 1995 season.... The NCAA Presidents Commission has expressed concern regarding the linguistic behavior and attitude of coaches and players. Therefore, coaches and student-athletes are required to observe well-defined football rules concerning verbal behavior and illegal demonstrations. (NCAA 10)

"Choreographed or delayed spectacles" and "linguistic behavior" are NCAA shorthand for celebratory (or end zone) expression and "taunting," and is conduct deemed outside the "honored traditions" and "well-defined" goals for 1995. Whose traditions? Whose goals? A closer look at past constructions and mutations in "sportsmanship" sheds light on whose knowledge is at work.

Ikuo Abe, in a study of the history of sportsmanship, traces the roots of the word *sportsman* back to England in 1677, where he notes Nicholas Cox's first usage in *The Gentleman's Recreation*. The first usage here was "sports-man" and was referring to a "man of pleasure," and later, in *The History of Tom Jones* (1749), sportsmanship was synonymous with skills on the field of play (Abe, 1988, p. 1). Early uses of the word did not refer to ethical behavior on the field or a player's code of appropriate conduct. The use of the term in an ethical context was first observed in 1949 in P. Cummings's book, *The Dictionary of Sports*. This modern usage is the one echoed in current discourse on behavior in sport, and the definition the NCAA appear to reference when noting "tradition": "Sportsmanship: The ethical code embodied in sport at its best. It includes fairness in action and attitude, abiding by the rules, refusing to take an unfair advantage, courtesy toward the opponent, modesty in victory, graciousness in defeat" (Cummings, 420).

The above ethical definition arose at the turn of the twentieth century, as Abe estimates there is a fifty-year time lag between first word usage and placement in the dictionary. The usage of the word thus underwent a change over a couple of hundred years from referring to sportsmen as generally a person "fond of hunting" and such sports or "skill" in sport, to the current usage of sportsmanship as "a person who behaves generously in defeat or victory," or generous behavior befitting a good sportsman (Abe, 1988, 9). There is also a brief mention of the concept of *amateur*, first used in 1784 as "one who has a taste for anything," or "one who cultivates anything as a pastime," to the usage in England of the word *amateur* in the late eighteenth century and then to the word *amateurism* in the late nineteenth century. The current usage of amateur has its roots in the 1901 definition: "One who cultivates a particular study or art for the love of it, and not professionally: in general terms, one who plays for money—nearly every game has its special definition to meet its own requirements" (Abe 1988, 9).

The connection of sportsmanship to the ethical nuances of sport thus came about in the 1890s, and at the same time the concept of amateurism began to be tied to sporting activities. In a cross-cultural note, Abe cites English-Japanese dictionaries as responsible for infusion of and acceptance of the term *sportsmanship* in Japan, though Japan had a different understanding of modern sport and therefore adapted the term to fit Japanese traditional culture and attitude. The note about Japan is relevant because it points to the English beginnings of the ideology of modern sportmanship and, therefore, the English definitions of what is sportsmanlike and what is not. Abe ends with a note on the English influence:

> However, it is not deniable that some time after the second half of the nineteenth century, a "sportsmanship" movement arose as a world-wide ideological movement, diffusing the "game ethic." In other words, the conceptual changes of "sportsman" and "sportsmanship" reflect not only the export of English public-school game ethic from the second half of the nineteenth century, but also the international diffusion of Pierre de Coubertin's "Olympism" from the end of the nineteenth century. (Abe, 1988, 25)

Indeed, Jan Cameron addressed the International Olympic Academy in July 1993 and commented that the ethic of sport has a gendered and English background, noting that: "The form of sport which was considered legitimate was determined by those in control, usually dominant men and, in the case of the British colonial sport, the English 'mother country.' So it was clearly their ethics and values which determined fair play" (Cameron, 1993, 4). Cameron says further that politics, ideology, power, and sports are often bedfellows, and that neither the beginnings of the notion of how sport should be played or current ideas about fair play are random or condoned by all. She notes that: "sports, and their rules, are controlled by a very small elite. As such, sport is a very useful, and increasingly important vehicle, for conveying the ideas and values of those in power" (Cameron, 1993, 5). She later states that sport is infused with dominating ruling class ideas for fair play and good manners, in the end representing "hegemony in action"

(Cameron, 1993, 6). Cameron says fair play is cultural and contextual, and that officials need to look more at the circumstances or intent of actions versus whether or not one ideological knowledge considers it "unfair." She also suggests consulting athletes about fair play, allowing those who engage in sport to enter the hegemonic debate.

Research Design and Methods

What do college athletes think about expression—their own and the expression of others? What do they think about concepts like sportsmanship and players' codes? I conducted intensive interviews with six black athletes who were starters in the 1995 NCAA season for the University of Wisconsin-Madison football team. With such a small sample, I wanted to insure that I captured as much as possible the range of expression and a representation of offensive and defensive players. Randomly sampling the starting lineup, there was the possibility that I would end up with six players who represented the high or low end of the expressive spectrum, and possibly all defensive and nonscoring players. I thus ended with a good representation of the range of on-field expression by Wisconsin players who were considered the highest and lowest expressive black athletes as assessed by independent judges.

Choosing the Athletes

To select the six black athletes interviewed for the study, I obtained the list of UW football players who started the first game of the year against the University of Colorado in September 1995. I decided to select players for interviews who appeared in the starting lineup rather than choosing from the entire roster to insure I had players who had been in game situations where they had the opportunity to express themselves. I next needed to find qualified judges to rank the expressiveness level of athletes on the field; the main goal was to insure that I was interviewing a range of expressive athletes and not just those with low or high levels of expression. Judges needed to be people who primarily knew the athletes as on-field players. Therefore coaches, the athletic department, and friends of players were not considered appropriate for selecting the expressive range of athletes as they all spent many hours with athletes off the field and therefore might converge the two contexts. I selected two sports writers from the campus newspaper, *The Daily Cardinal*, who followed the sports program but who were also not too close to the athletes to accidentally merge their on-field and off-field personalities. One judge was the sports editor, Jonathan Babalola (fall 1995), and the other judge was the former sports editor (1994–95) and editor-in-chief (1995–96), Valerie Panou. Both writers had between them seen virtually every game—and also the training camps—over the past four years and thus would be good judges of the on-field expression of the athletes. I gave them the list of black (and white) players and suggested they divide them into offense and defense, and rank the players from highest to lowest in expression. They had to agree on all rankings and discuss out loud their decision-rules. The players chosen to be interviewed were Tony Simmons, Daryl Carter, and Michael London—ranked the highest in expression among African Americans—and Reggie Torian, Kevin Huntley, and Carl McCullough, ranked the lowest among the eleven African Americans in the starting lineup. This insured that I captured the extreme ranges of black expression on the team.

The Interview

The method of research was intensive, open-ended interviews. Questions were formulated to probe four major areas of concern: (1) athlete's self-expression; (2) opinions on the expression of other athletes, sportsmanlike conduct, and conduct rules; (3) athlete's expressive socialization from mentors and role models; and (4) athlete demographic information. More specifically, the first section of questions on self-expression were intended to find out how the interviewee expressed himself in sports on the field verbally and physically. The second section was intended to probe their specific feelings about celebration rules, celebratory expression, and "talk" on the field. I also wanted to know if there were unwritten rules, or a "players' code" that might act as a mechanism to promote desired sports conduct apart from written rules. Thematic coding was used to analyze the data from the six interviews.

The Data

Athlete Families

The first item of note on the black athletes who rated lower in on-field expression is that their families are small. Both Kevin Huntley and Car McCullough were raised as single children. Huntley was raised in a two-parent home and McCullough was raised by his single mother. Reggie Torian was also raised by a single mom, in a hostile area of Chicago, but he had a sister and constant contact with his father. Both of Huntley's parents were white-collar workers: his mother is a city editor of the town newspaper and his father is a plant supervisor at the local Martin Marietta factory. He was raised in Fremont, Ohio (population 22,000), in a predominantly white neighborhood and attended all-white elementary, junior high and high schools (though his cousin did join him in high school and he recalls there was a black freshman who enrolled in the Catholic school he attended in his last year).

McCullough grew up in Texas with his single mom, who had Carl when she was sixteen years old, forcing her to drop out of high school. His father was murdered when he was very young. He grew up in a rough neighborhood with a lot of love, but little supervision from mom, as she was away doing small cleaning or assembly-line jobs. She had a growing concern for his safety, and felt he needed a male role model so she sent him to St. Paul to live with an older uncle (who is now thirty-five years old). He attended a high school with an 80% white enrollment. Reggie Torian also grew up in a very rough neighborhood in Harvey, Illinois. His parents divorced the year he was born, 1975, and thus he and his sister (five years older) were raised by their single mother. He spent a year and a half in high school in Pasadena, California, before returning to Harvey and Thornwood high school, where he ran track and played football. Thornwood high school was 65% white and 35% black, and the football team was 50% black.

Religiosity

All six athletes at some point in their lives had been "religious" to some degree and referenced some form of "faith" during interviews. Huntley attended Catholic Church his whole life and considers himself a Catholic. Although Carl McCullough attended a Catholic high school in St. Paul on a scholarship, he maintains that he was and remains Baptist by faith, even though he does not attend church as much as before. Carter attended his grandfather's Baptist Church in Gary, Indiana, for a few summers while growing up, but stopped when he was thirteen and has not attended church regularly since. London, likewise, was a Baptist and attended church with his family while growing up. Simmons was raised in the Catholic school system in Chicago and considers himself to be Catholic. Torian, like McCullough, was raised as a Baptist. Athletes comment on religion within the sporting context in interviews, and I interweave these comments into the text as they relate to issues of expression and attitudes about expression. Below is the first of five sections that review the six athletes' behaviors and attitudes in five areas: (1) self-expression; (2) attitudes about other-expression and sportsmanlike conduct; (3) mentors and role models; (4) football rules; and (5) race and celebratory expression.

Attention and Recognition on the Field

As of the 1995 season, taking off one's helmet on the field of play means the player gets penalized 15 yards. The NCAA made it clear that this form of individual recognition will not be tolerated. But for Tony Simmons, the ultimate form of recognition is for people to be able to see who you are as an individual on the playing field, not as a faceless, mask-hidden, number marching up and down the gridiron. This is key to why his ultimate football "dream" is to take his helmet off after scoring a touchdown, to be recognized by the fans:

> In football no one notices your face, all they see is numbers...once in a while you...want somebody to see; I actually want them to see my face...people always see numbers up and down the field but they never see faces...when they used to play with leather helmets...you always see the face. You see the face...everybody in football is considered a masked person...you see the number, the body shape, but you never see the face...the only way to see the face is through media guides. (Simmons, 1996, 11–12)

He wants his fellow students to notice he's in their class, that he was the guy walking up State Street when they said "hey, he looks like Tony Simmons," and that he is the face they can match with the name. He sums up his desire for both recognition and individuality by commenting that he's "the only Tony Simmons on this earth, and I hope if there is another...he doesn't look like me" (Simmons, 1996, 13). He notes that there are 11 people on the field, each with different aspirations. His happens to be the wish to be noticed as an individual, to "take off my helmet and run around. That's the way I am...probably run it towards the fans, take off my helmet, clap some hands, [run] back to my teammates—that would probably be me" (Simmons, 1996, 9).

The expression Simmons is *allowed* to exhibit is "enthusiasm" after a touchdown. He will jump around, slap hands, pick up other players—"the person I like to see most is Michael London"—and jump into an on-rushing lineman's arms, being sure to "watch out for the linemen...it's tradition for the linemen to come down and beat you up...some people hit you while you're down...the kid stuff, you know" (Simmons, 1996, 28, 29). London, on the other hand, is quite the opposite when it comes to seeking attention, preferring the shadows. London is workmanlike in his attitude toward his role on the field, opting to "score, give the ball to the ref, or set the ball down and go back to the huddle...I would rather just go about my business" (London, 1996, 9). He considers this attitude part of his reserved personality, a personality that does not want attention, that does not want to be on a pedestal, that is "not really a celebrator. I'm not one that will throw the ball in the air. I like to just do what I have to do, turn around, look for my teammates" (London, 1996, 8). Huntley says individuality is the primary objective in keeping on the helmet, the same reason Simmons says he wants to take it off:

> I kind of see it [in] a different way than he does...when I'm on the field, I want to be seen as an individual, not as a football player. Especially on this campus, you tend to get stereotyped. "Oh, he's a football player," instead of just "Oh, he's Kevin Huntley, a student attending this University"...I've had negative responses from some [instructors], and had no problems with others. (Huntley, 1996, 17)[7]

Daryl Carter has at times in the 1996 season awakened his coaches with his "spontaneous, not preplanned" reactions to big games. Once, after a sack of the quarterback during a game against Penn State, he says he, "just kind of got up and stomped my feet real hard and looked around," and another time "[I] jumped as high as I could in the air and got to pumping my arms...sort of spontaneous" (Carter, 1996, 5). He mentioned the word spontaneous three times in his discussion of his own expression, along with five combined mentions of the words excitement, emotion, and fun.

Reggie Torian wants to be known as the athlete who crossed the finish line, and was modest about it. He considers the perfect show of his modesty to be scoring a TD (he has never scored in college), giving teammates high-fives, going to the bench, taking helmet off, talking to his coach, and then sitting down, noting there would be no "extracurricular activity" like high-stepping or dancing. His overarching paradigm for behavior is, as he puts it, "to be humble in victory and gracious in defeat." These are nearly the exact words the NCAA uses in their paradigm of sportsmanship expressed earlier in the introduction to this article, and also the words Torian notes later in the article that he learned from his father. This points up not only the pervasiveness of the "humble-gracious" paradigm in sports discourse, but also the variance in black athletic approaches to expression after on-field successes (or defeats).

Talk and Taunting are Part of the Game of Football

A major theme among black athletes when discussing their expressive behavior dealt with talk and taunting on the field of play. Michael London says right up front that he is not a talker, and that the only time he will talk on the field is when someone does something to him. London situates his talk by saying that many times in his position as receiver he engages in one-on-one battles with defensive backs that get intense during the course of the game. One of the reasons he talks is to either reply to an earlier taunt, or to verbally comment on his opponent being overphysically aggressive and breaking the players' code. The specific part of the code is that of "not attempting to injure another player" in this case via a "cheap shot." This is a capital offense in London's sportsmanlike conduct book. He says, "Sometimes I won't say anything to anybody the whole game," but when he does start to talk, it is because:

> They hit you in the back or do something dirty to you...you know what they were trying to do...you have a different feeling towards that player...you take a whole 'nother attitude: "I don't trust you. You know you're dirty."...when you get a chance to, you let him know—because you understand the type of person he is. "Okay, alright, I see what you did. I'll be back...you have to see me again." (London, 1996, 6)

The talk goes back and forth. The player in this case has already hit London in the back slightly before the whistle has blown the play dead. It appears as though another player's code is not to aggress when there is no situational advantage, which may happen when players are already piled up and no more yardage will be gained or lost, and only the academic task of blowing the whistle remains. London thus comments on one such incident:

The whistle was about to blow and somebody came and hit [me] from the blind side…it was a pretty good shot but it was a cheap shot…after the whistle you turn around and you'll see that person and they maybe standing over [you] talking to you like "yeah, I got you, I got you" even though it was dirty…[I] say, "Okay, I see the type of player you are, so I'm going to have to watch you and I'm also not going to have any lenience on you either, because I see if you get a chance you're going to try to hurt me." (London, 1996, 6)

In London's case the psychological warfare is primarily that—psychological. He says the above response to the over-verbal and physical opponent is a verbal dialogue in his mind—"that's what I say to myself" (London, 1996, 6). His reply after the hit might be just to "say to him, you know, I may turn around and be like 'Okay, you want to play dirty? We can play dirty'" (London, 1996, 6). There are other instances where he confesses to talking, but again in response to the behavior directed at him, for his philosophy is that you have to expect repercussions when you taunt, because "if a person has any type of self-pride they're not going to let you get away with that [taunting]" (London, 1996, 6). He says still that he won't initiate talk until he feels it is warranted. But he will: "Look at them, [keep] real close eye contact—stare him dead in his eyes so he knows…sometimes they just talk, talk, talk, and then [a big play] happens and I just turn around like 'you was runnin' your mouth before. What's going on now?'" (London, 1996, 5).

Tony Simmons admits to taunting fans during road games. He says road fans have little respect sometimes for the visiting team and his goal is to earn that respect. So after a big play touchdown, before teammates arrive in the end zone, he might stand there and talk to fans, saying "what's up, what's up?" (Simmons, 1996, 11). The immediate goal is to quiet the fans down by doing well and "letting them know that you're here to play, that's all…as soon as you get there, people automatically think you've lost." He confesses that in his mind this is somewhat unsportsmanlike, but that the fans cannot understand exactly what he is doing anyway: "You talk to fans but they can't hear you. They just see you. They don't understand what you're saying. They can't even see your face. It doesn't last long—five seconds—you turn around and there are your boys, all your teammates grabbing you, 'ah, here I go!'" (Simmons, 1996, 11).

Some athletes feel that psychological warfare is a means to an end. Michael London played defense as a cornerback for a couple of years before switching back to offense, and so is also aware of talk, hard hitting and defensive aggression. London says he has too many things to think about, though, in his new position as receiver, to worry about talk—which happens primarily on the way back to the huddle after the play is over. Carter, though, implies that talk is almost inevitable, and that the goal is rather to: "Try to keep things respectful...prevent confrontations...a little pushing and shoving out there...talking a little trash...we keep it on a level where it won't get out of control" (Carter, 1996, 16).

Probably the only place talk and taunting are allowed without repercussion is on the practice field or in the training camp, where the Badgers engage in play and camaraderie. Simmons notes that "in training camp we spike the ball in front of their face...the defensive back, if they catch an interception, they'll throw the ball back to us. I'll say, 'Oh, so its like that now.' We have that type of camaraderie on our team—but it's the only time you get to do stuff like that, like showboat and stuff...just do it once in awhile, here or there" (Simmons, 1996, 14). In high school, though, Simmons went far enough to warrant a penalty for taunting for throwing a ball after a touchdown into the defensive back's face. For Simmons, it was a "reap what you've sown" taunt, getting back at the defender for a past offense: "I [dove into] the end zone and caught a pass...had the ball in my hand and threw it back to the DB [defensive back], threw it dead in his face cuz all year [he was] talkin' about how he was going to stop me and he never stopped me the whole game and I got mad and I threw my football in his face" (Simmons, 1996, 30).

McCullough is opposed to talk, taunting, and fighting on the field. He is often commenting in his interview about players "talking, yapping back and forth, fighting," and generally concluding many time over that this behavior was both unnecessary and unsportsmanlike. He says, "just play football," minus the bickering, punches, fighting, and pushing often engaged in after plays (McCullough, 1996, 31). He does not believe in fighting on the field or other-than-above-board tactics to retaliate when aggressed against. Even if another player is in his face taunting him, he will resist striking the other player, even though this type of behavior is to him the most bothersome. His retaliation is harder play, because "that's how you get your respect.... There's always someone who is going to disrespect you on the field until you show them that you're not going to have it" (McCullough, 1996, 14).

Talk, counter-talk; actions, counter-actions; aggression, counter-aggression. Black athletes have not spoken about the banning of talk or trash or taunting during games, but have spoken about on-field control and on-field repercussions for actions. The player's code of conduct by black athletes is that psychological warfare must at some level be countered on the field. The counter seems to depend on personal motivation that appears to be manifested either psychologically, verbally, or in Simmons's case, physically. Simmons's motivation seems to be maintaining respectability. He achieves this by countering physicality with "in your face" behavior, either toward the defender or the fans. London's motivation appears to be to promote fair warning. Carter's motivation is to contain—not prevent—talk and banter, with the general goal of not letting things get "out of control" in an otherwise hectic arena of warfare. These players' codes for conduct are examples of how athletes manage the boundaries of acceptable and unacceptable on-field behavior, each in accordance with past notions of what is beyond and within the boundaries.

Individuality is Fine—to a Point

Daryl Carter believes there is a strong place for individuality within the construct of sportsmanlike conduct. He does not agree with the regulation of self-excitement, instead opting for expressing one's uniqueness on the field of play. Carter says sportsmanlike conduct is "bringing something unique about yourself to the field.... Everybody had something unique about themselves, so I think it is key to be able to express that to a certain extent—to where it wouldn't get out of control" (Carter, 1996, 3). Carter is all for individual expression on the field, saying that expression without the possibility of being judged as unsportsmanlike is key when a player's intent is not to single himself out for attention. Carter echoes the earlier sentiment Simmons voiced about anonymity underneath the helmet by noting that players all have the same uniforms and thus have no uniqueness, unless you are "bringing something unique about yourself to the field" (Carter, 1996, 3). His cautionary note about player self-control is echoed later in his interview when he notes that some players are greedy and seek glory and "want everyone to see them" (Carter, 1996, 17).

He says that type of behavior is out of bounds, and that "out of respect for your teammates" players should not behave too individually. Furthermore, it is the responsibility, he feels, of coaches to not recruit such athletes.

London does not go as far as Carter, but he does say that celebration must be kept in moderation, and that if a big play benefits the whole team, then team celebration is warranted. But if the game situation does not warrant celebration—a big stop on a second down play when there are two downs left—players should maintain and not engage in attention-seeking: "There is a time and a place for celebrating and the extent it should go to" (London, 1996, 22). He sides with Carter also in his view that spontaneous celebration is fine, and also the sentiment that the NCAA has gone too far in its attempt to control players, saying that:

> Almost anything flamboyant they put a regulation [on it] or flag you for it.... I think it takes away from the excitement of the game.... It's just spontaneous and you make a big play...of course you're going to be happy and celebrate...but you almost feel like you have to look over your shoulder when you celebrate. You can't really get your true expression. It's good they put some regulations [in] but I think they might have come a little strong—[they] really nit pick. (London, 1996, 11)

Tony Simmons feels celebratory expression can add to the team concept, specifically because it can be contagious, one big play leading into the next: "like a chain reaction, one good play starts another good play...it makes it better for the team" (Simmons, 1996, 18). The often brutal sport becomes more fun and play becomes more exciting. The point at which Simmons stops is with extreme individual celebration, but not for previously stated reasons. Simmons says embarrassment, ridicule, and teasing is the punishment for failure to properly execute extreme attempts at end zone expression. The worse fate is that the failed act is never forgotten. Simmons creates a humorous "expression gone wrong" episode below:

> What if you did a back flip but didn't land on your feet? Now, you've scored but [you've embarrassed] yourself at the same time. Because I've seen people score. They score, they run around—boom!—they fall. They embarrass themselves right there, and that's what you get for trying to showboat, do you know what I'm saying? Yeah, everything has a drawback, because you can do a back flip and not land on your feet. Now you've just embarrassed yourself. People are looking at you, and now they're laughing at you, and you hope to get up from there...I would say, "hey, you landed on your head—at least you could land on your feet."...People remember stuff like that: "hey, it was a nice play and all, but you still fell on your head." Some people don't remember the stuff you did before that. They remember the stuff you did after. (Simmons, 1996, 41)

This teasing appears to serve the purpose of easing any obvious embarrassment the player may have had initially, to bond teammates, and to replace a burst of player ego with a dose of humility. Here humor can ease pain and also serve as either a deterrent for future botched expression or as a warning to practice in advance. The point here is that expression *to a point* is okay, but overstepping those bounds in the eyes of these players is unsportsmanlike, not a good show of respect for team, and can be embarrassing for not only the opposition, but for teammates and in some cases, the individual who fails in the expressive act. It appears the range of acceptable behaviors among these black athletes is much broader than NCAA parameters, and "honored traditions" are not significant when compared to self- and team respect. There also appear to be situational subtleties and a general attitude of acceptance of expression outside what individuals might perform themselves. In these cases, athletes justify high expression of "others" by noting that it may be the player's own "personality," or because the celebratory behavior can possibly motivate other players and "add to the team."

Kevin Huntley likewise feels that individual celebration can add to the team by bringing an overall excitement to the game of football, drawing attention to the team on the field, and on a player-by-player basis spreading enthusiasm and emotion. He see nothing wrong with players high-stepping down the field and then doing end zone dances. Players taking off their helmets in the end zone "like the Florida State guys" is even fine, though he would not do it himself (Huntley, 1996, 10). Pointing to the crowd, cause for penalty as of the 1995 season, is also fine with Huntley. In fact, he suggests that fans enjoy expression and suggests that the college game has gotten a little stiff: "Like the pro game, it's cool, the crowd likes it and everything. They're usually real quick, they give a little jiggle, a little shake, a little point to the crowd. Which is all cool if you made a touchdown. The college game—I think they should bring it back" (Huntley, 1996, 8).

Huntley draws the line at the length of the celebration, saying that when players like Deion Sanders, celebrate for more than a couple of seconds, then "he tends to draw it out" a little too long. His recommendation if he were Deion's coach? "Settle down afterwards a little bit. It's not necessary" (Huntley, 1996, 9). Other than "the long dance and all that jazz afterwards," Deion is no problem, and expression by other players he feels is fine.[8] McCullough draws a harder line on expression, he says, because of his Texas upbringing. He feels that people in the midwest, or "up north," are more individually expressive. He does not mind a player celebrating or showboating because it does not take anything away from football. Some players, he says, "thrive off that kind of thing. They like a lot of attention" as long as the act is not prolonged and players get off the field, because "it's not like they're sitting in the end zone for 15–20 minutes celebrating, you know" (McCullough, 1996, 31). He does take issue, though, with players taking too much time either dancing or "messing with the crowd," which he feels can border on being unsportsmanlike. The key attitudinal distinction is on his Texas childhood that emphasized team—not individual—celebration, and the time allotted to acknowledgment of his accomplishment:

> Down south we don't celebrate. Like I said, everything's a team effort. It's okay to celebrate as a team but as an individual that's a different story...you won't ever see a dude in the end zone doing something, you know, running through a crowd, whatever. It's a big difference down south than it is up north. When I moved north to Minnesota I noticed that. How much difference [there] was in the attitudes and everything. (McCullough, 1996, 18)

He says if he made a fumble and an opposing player scored a touchdown and did an end zone dance and celebrated wildly, it would not be the celebrating that bothered him, but the fumble. He emphasizes that his focus is always on the game, and that he sees jumping around and crowd involvement as a "waste of energy...that's just not me at all" (McCullough, 1996, 13).

Torian, from the "north"—and a roommate (1996) of McCullough's—is very low in expression himself, and is situated somewhere between the other two players in his tolerance of the expression of others. He only comments on the subject lightly in his interview, though, most notably about reprimanding either Simmons or London if they expressed too much and drew a penalty. Torian says, first, of London, whom he characterizes as a very calm and quiet athlete much like himself, "If he scored a TD he'd put the ball on the ground or give it to the referee" (p. 17). Simmons, who he implies would be much more likely to express in the end zone, would be verbally reprimanded by Torian, his friend. Torian also makes note of Simmons's dancing abilities in his statement: "You, of all people, should know that you shouldn't do that on the field, because if you would have [gotten] penalized, all of us would have [gotten] in trouble—the whole team. But first of all, Tony really doesn't know how to dance" (Torian, 1996, 17).

While Torian would monitor his Badger teammate's on-field behavior, he would not have words for Deion Sanders if they played together. That is primarily because Sanders is a good athlete, he has self-confidence, self-control, and that not only can he do anything on the field—but he can look good doing it. His behavior would be acceptable because Deion would be "making more money" than Torian, and because "He's all that. Everybody knows he's all that" (Torian, 1996, 21, 22).[9]

Respect Your Teammates and the Opposition

Simmons stresses that individuals need to respect and acknowledge other teammates for helping them score touchdowns, because without others "you're nothing...it's always 11 on 11." Simmons, probably the most expressive of the black student-athletes, says that some players take away from the team by running away from teammates in order to separate themselves, as if to say "I'm the man, I'm number one" (Simmons, 1996, 16). There are repercussions for this type of disrespect, he notices: "You put every ounce of attention on yourself and when you come back to the huddle...some of your teammates might look at you wrong...like you didn't do all that...that wasn't called for...that's taking away from the team (Simmons, 1996, 16, 17). Playing a clean game of football earns respect on the field from these athletes, specifically, playing within the rules. Hard play is condoned, hard shots are "part of the game," but dirty shots—"like slamming somebody out of bounds"—are unwarranted and unsportsmanlike (Huntley, 1996, 7). Players should not commit any flagrant fouls, but keep their intensity "within the content of the game" and "within the rules. You know, play a clean game...sportsmanship" (Huntley, 1996, 7).

As a running back, McCullough is more often aggressed against in the pile-up after a play than receivers or, like Huntley, defensive backs. It is the running-back who is supposed to be the most rugged and durable offensive ball-handler, and thus is the player who most often is the target of defensive player aggression after tackles: "there's many times I'm on the bottom of the pile where someone is jabbing me in the ribs or trying to poke my eyes out, stuff like that. Or players just...[throw] me down on the ground or whatever" (McCullough, 1996, 14). His goal is to get the player's jersey number, if possible, and "get him back" (McCullough, 1996, 14). But not in a vindictive manner, but a hard-nosed, sportsmanlike "Texas" manner: "I'm not out there to hurt him.... When I say 'get him back,' I mean next time this guy's coming at me, I'm going to juke him next or...I'm just going to lower my shoulders and go through him" (McCullough, 1996, 14). McCullough's key goal is to earn the opposition's respect with clean, hard play—his counter to unsportsmanlike aggression.

Mentors, Role Models, and Expressive Socialization

In the first theme, "lessons from the neighborhood," environmental factors helped form ways of playing football and an appreciation for life. McCullough, Carter, Simmons, and Torian grew up in starkly different environments than did Huntley and London. I will discuss Carter, London, and Simmons's neighborhood environments in the second thematic area on their parental relationships.

Lessons from the Neighborhood

Huntley's neighborhood was peaceful, had a racial mix of black and white families, and was in a middle-class neighborhood of what appears a middle-class city, Fremont, Ohio. His parents were both employed and able to afford what was necessary to raise a single child, Kevin. Huntley would often play sports with fifteen neighborhood kids, four of whom were black. He and the others would engage in playful talk during their contests, and often get into good-natured taunting, like "I'm going to get you on this play...check this out" (Huntley, 1996, 13). They would often spike the ball when they scored touchdowns and yell "burned you!" (Huntley, 1996, 13).

McCullough grew up playing sports in his neighborhood—basketball, baseball, and football—but also found plenty of time to "do his own thing," which usually involved getting into trouble. He believes that his mother wanted him to move to Minneapolis for at least two reasons. One was because she was not able to spend enough quality time raising him on her own, and the other was that he needed a male role model:

> I'm [from] a rough neighborhood in Texas. You know, typical ghetto. I was always into stuff, doing something [wrong], and so that's one of the reasons why my mother sent me to live with my uncle, 'cause I was getting into so much trouble. They talked, and he said I needed a male role model in my life and he figured that would change everything...That was what I needed. I'm not saying that my mother couldn't do the job. It's just that it was her and me...she was gone all the time...she wasn't around to see what I was doing...to mother me and all.... I needed a change. (McCullough, 1996, 22)

Torian was not raised in the nicest of neighborhoods but attributes his strong family—primarily mom—for keeping him out of trouble. Compared to his family, other neighborhood families were not as stable. With little control over peer pressures, parents "let their children run wild in the streets," where they would often engage in the urban traps of "trouble: shooting...fights...drugs...and I saw that" (Torian, 1996, 27). One of the sad aspects—from his sporting view—was that many athletes, better than himself, never got the opportunity to achieve their potential: they often ended up in jail. He reasons that the difference between him and them was that they didn't have that "guidance to lead them in the right direction...no young person knows how to go about things unless the right individual tells you and shows you...somebody you look up to...to let you know the way to success...some kids out there just [didn't] have a clue" (Torian, 1996, 27). So, while Huntley had a relatively ideal setting, McCullough left a dangerous situation, and Torian was mentored through his scenario by his mother.

Parents as Role Models

In two instances the single mother was the most dominant parental role model, and in the case of Michael London, his father was the dominant model. London's father was not only a role model to his son, but to many kids who played on various teams London senior coached. London describes his father as not only a positive figure in the community, but a "man who would do anything for anybody...he went the extra yard, mile" and often did, once even agreeing to sell the family car to buy a mini van so he could drive other kids to practice (London, 1996, 39). London's father wanted to keep kids out of trouble and went out of his way to help, sometimes paying for kids who could not afford to participate on his teams. The affection was returned, as kids would stop by the house to talk with London senior or call him during the sports off-season.

London describes his family as "not real flashy, we're rather conservative. What we have is good, but we don't have to tell anybody" (London, 1996, 28). Regarding expression, he notes that his family was always very vocally expressive, and he learned early on to verbally express himself to the point where shouting matches, typical between coach and athletes, are not necessary to coach him:

> I can sit down and we can have an intelligent conversation and discuss things rationally...it's from growing up in my household—I feel as though I didn't have to hold back—if there's something wrong I can speak to them and I feel as though I

should be able to speak to anybody.... I respect my parents.... I had a lot of expression. (London, 1996, 37)

It is little wonder, then, that Michael London looked up to his father, a man he resembles almost exactly. He acknowledges his family overall as the group he looks up to, but his father stands out. They were always together, and his father comforted him in good times and bad. If Michael needed to talk, his father was the supportive shoulder he leaned on. "My father and I have a bond that's so tight" summarizes the connection between father and son. And the mentoring and modeling relationship is acknowledged when London says "just from watching my father growing up, I would say he would have to be a role model. He would definitely have to be [my] number one role model" (London, 1996, 38, 39).

London's father, in addition to everything else, was at one time an athlete. Tony Simmons's father and mother were both athletes in high school, but stopped competing when they attended smaller colleges. Simmons describes his family as very humorous, taking the lead from their comedian mother who was always joking. In his house everyone was silly, joking continuously with each other, and getting along very well. There were serious times when chores or other family disruptions would cause mom to get very serious, but she would bounce back to the playful mode after the serious episodes passed. Simmons hints that some of the serious matters may have involved his neighborhood, which he describes as "hectic." Raising four children in this environment no doubt was cause for some concern in his house:

> Around my neighborhood half of them [kids] was either fighting or half of them was playing baseball. That's all we did, play baseball and football and sports all the time...it was Chicago we [were] worried about. When we got to a certain age we [were] worrying about staying out of trouble more than anything, and trying not to be in gangs and stuff...the environment we lived in [our home] was decent, but around our environment was like "why does it have to be so hectic? It ain't gotta be like this all the time." (Simmons, 1996, 27)

Simmons describes the day he left Chicago for Madison, Wisconsin, as the happiest day in the world. He managed to escape with his life, as did some of his close friends, as they acknowledged, "We made it! We're out of here!" (Simmons, 1996, 22). Through it all he admired his mother for her persistence and strength to raise all four children on her own. One thing is for sure, she survives as a role model for his expressive behavior. She has coached him to be expressive after scoring touchdowns. Her emphasis was on the showing of human emotion on the field of play:

> You gotta do something—you can't be quiet...you can't just score a touchdown, hand the ball to the ref and do nothing—just walk back to the sidelines. You're not a robot, you're going to have emotions...you're not a machine. You are human so go out there and show some emotion, that might start something—but you never know unless you do it. If you just go out there and be a robot, that makes everything boring.... I guess you could be having fun but it ain't fun to me. To me it's not fun not showing any emotions. (Simmons, 1996, 29, 34)

These are strong words coming from a parent one sees as a strong model. And the coaching regarding expression did not stop with mom—his high school football coaches also encouraged his end zone expression. Celebratory expression appears to have become Simmons's "normal" mode of behavior, socialized into his persona by mom, possibly his neighborhood pals, and then reinforced by his high school coaches.

Michael London's father—like his mom who suggested he express himself—stresses that Michael be "his own person," that he not be a follower. Thus London says he does his "own thing" and that he strives to be "original" (London, 1996, 39). Daryl Carter speaks only of his mother and a high school coach as people he admired. Mom was a "very expressive" presence in the house, primarily verbally. Carter says that especially when she gets upset, "she expresses. Everybody hears, everybody listens...very verbal" (Carter, 1996, 18). He confesses to taking some things from mom—namely her verbal expression—and quite possibly her intensity. He says he comes from a family "of leaders," and that he was, as is his brother now, a leader in neighborhood "cliques" (Carter, 1996, 19). Verbally, he notes that he was generally quiet, but that if something needed saying, "I said it. People listened to me. I was very straightforward" (Carter, 1996, 19).

He does not comment much on his neighborhood, his family life, or much on the role of mentors, primarily, I believe, because he didn't look up to anyone as a model. He says that as the oldest son, he was on his own, without much guidance or structure to his life. His first role model was a high school coach at Milwaukee-Washington High School, Greg Levin. Levin was the first person who "set parameters on me. Mom let me do what I wanted" (Carter, 1996, 20). Carter says he did not look up to athletes on television because he was a "realist," out to see what he could accomplish himself, though he admits to admiring the money Michael Jordan earned.

Torian had two parents and a sister to look up to and to get his behavioral cues from. Though his parents were divorced the year he was born, discussion of his father strongly suggests active parenting. Torian's father was also an all-state athlete in Illinois. He has worked locally (in the Chicago area) as a professional singer. Reggie considers his father a mental man, a philosopher: "His words have meaning" (Torian, 1996, 24). The words that resonate most are words spoken just as Torian was reaching his all-state potential. These words solidly place the father in the role of mentor. "He sat me down and he just told me one line: be humble in victory and gracious in defeat" (Torian, 1996, 24). These words resonate with Torian, as do the words following the humility tutoring which seem to formulate a way of living and a way of relating to sport: "We all win by losing. You can never win if you never lose every once in a while...keep it modest, keep within yourself...be gratified that you're even out there competing...the Lord giveth and the Lord taketh away" (Torian, 1996, 24).

Torian says he listened to the forewarnings of his father because Torian senior had experience in life and in sport. This respect combined with the mentoring of his parent set forth Torian's way of looking at sport. He was also influenced to think about life outside of sport, to consider what might happen if he did not "make it." This tutoring came from his mother. She would question his dedication to sports and suggested he reverse the order of commitment from sports to the books. He says she "kind of made me think I can hurt myself, I can break my leg, I can pull a hamstring, and I'll be done with athletics" (Torian, 1996, 28).

Huntley, though less verbal, speaks very highly of both parents as his role models. The primary influence on his behavior, he believes, is his parents treating him as an "individual" at a young age (Huntley, 1996, 13). He says his mother specifically treated him as older than he was, giving him many responsibilities and talking to him as an adult rather than as a child. He notes that as he grew older, he "learned to respect that" (Huntley, 1996, 13). In addition to the day-to-day treatment, he stresses that he liked his parents, an assumption often taken for granted and not always true among parents and children, regardless of mentoring. He attributes his low level of excitability to his being an only child—not having anyone his age around the house to share things with. He saw friends at school, but remained "laid back" and continued to keep things in, because it was "just the type of person" he was (Huntley, 1996,

23). It turns out that Carl McCullough also attended a school in Saint Paul that had a high population of white students, but this does not appear to have affected him as much as his mentoring from his uncle and role model, Tim.

Tim was—like Reggie Torian's father—a star athlete (in Texas, not Illinois). McCullough had watched him play football many times and had admired his intensity and competitiveness. Tim liked to serve as not only guardian but also as surrogate football coach, taking McCullough into the back yard each day to school him in football techniques. He was taught drills and coached on his weak spots. Most importantly, Tim coached him on psychological concepts that stuck with Carl. "He'd come home, we'd go outside and play football...Tim was sort of a coach and mentor...'always room for improvement' he said" (McCullough, 1996, 6, 28). Tim was the man who brought McCullough down to earth and taught him to take criticism, to give 110 percent, and not to showboat: "You'll be noticed by your performance" (McCullough, 1996, 5). In the end Tim served the purposes of surrogate father, mentor, role model, and coach. McCullough respected the athletic ability of Tim, who now returns the favor, having missed none of Carl's games in his first two seasons as a Badger.

Carter, Simmons, McCullough, Torian, Huntley, and London thus emerge from their respective environments with a set of circumstances inside and outside the home that have formulated their construction of verbal expression. Physical expression appears to be an outgrowth of attitudes formulated by observing their mentors—their parents (in McCullough's case, his uncle). Hence, Carter states that he would never do anything on the field of play to make self or "the family look bad" (Carter, 1996, 22). These athletes appear to have taken the role of the parent in constructing their physical expression and appropriate and inappropriate ways of behaving. Indeed, Simmons at one point in college has to explain to his mother why he cannot express himself anymore in the end zone: "Mom—they say don't showboat!"

College Football Rules

Celebratory Expression is Part of the Game

All athletes voiced strong opposition to the new celebration rules. London thinks regulations against celebration are drawing attention away from the excitement of the game. He does not feel end zone expression should be banned for it represents the reward for all the hard work put into football—the celebration is the goal:

> If you make a play and you get up and start celebrating—running towards the sidelines—pointing to the sidelines, that's a penalty. I think that is drawing away from the excitement of the game. It makes you almost want to play conservative...you're always looking over your shoulder—are they going to throw a flag if I get excited or not?...When you are out there that's [TDs] your goal, and I think when you get to that goal you should be rewarded—that's the whole object of the game. (London, 1996, 18, 19)

London explains further his point about excitement during the game by pointing to the crowd as an example of exuberance. He feels it is unfair that fans get to celebrate by hugging and jumping up and down, and player expression is contained, it takes some of the "flavor" away from the game: "if you make a spectacular play, you have 80,000 people in there jumping around, but you're supposed to be the only person that stands still...if anything, you have that extra gust because you did it" (London, 1996, 48). Carter sums up his feelings by saying that there are too many other things besides celebration rules to worry about on the football field, and that after big plays—when the adrenaline flows—expressions of happiness and joy should be tolerated.

Simmons acknowledges that the large crowds at Big-10 games and the television cameras affect his expression level, and that if there were no rules in college football, "I probably would dance" (Simmons, 1996, 10). Since he knows the rules, though, he comments that he will control himself. A couple of years ago there was no problem with celebrating, but the rules this year (1995) "changed everything," primarily because "people would celebrate...some people know when to stop and some people just don't" (Simmons, 1996, 15). If he ever does play professional football, where he feels the rules are loosened because of the entertainment factor, he won't stray too far from his current expression, but he will "maybe do a little more...[because there is] not like a rule stopping you from doing what you can...you just wait for the pros" (Simmons, 1996, 8, 9). Players get "excited," explains Kevin Huntley, and "that's what the crowd looks for" (Huntley, 1996, 6).

He understands the intent of the rules, but notes more than once that the rules "were a little drastic" (Huntley, 1996, 6). He says the only good thing was that the NCAA relaxed the rules as the season progressed, but stressed in the end that players were not committing the hard crimes the rule was probably intended to target, such as players extensively pointing to the crowd, posing in front of the camera, and taking their helmets off. His belief, in the end, is that although he would never do anything too expressive himself, that players who score—even on him—should be allowed to express like professional players and do "a little jiggle, a little shake, a little point to the crowd" which would bring more excitement back to the college game (Huntley, 1996, 8).

Torian never says openly that celebratory expression is okay, but he does strongly suggest that attitude by saying that if there were no rules, his fantasy TD would include taking his helmet off in the end zone. Even more so, if he scored a touchdown in a big game like the Rose Bowl, he would take his helmet off because of the large audience watching, especially people he knows:

> If you score a touchdown in a Rose Bowl game, you know your friends at home are watching, you know your mother's watching, you know your high school coach is watching, your pastor, your girlfriend. So I mean you just want to take your helmet off and show your face on national TV. But you can't. You have to be controlled. (Torian, 1996, 13)

Out of Bounds Expression

Daryl Carter voice the strongest opposition to aggressive and personal verbal or physical attacks. His main contention is that there is a difference between celebration and taunting, that the former is an expression of joy and happiness, and the latter, a player who is looking for conflict. Torian suggests that if a teammate does over-express himself and breaks the rules but is not caught, he will be the gatekeeper next time and serve notice. He would comment if friend Daryl Carter over-expressed: "Hey, you got away this time, but I guarantee you next time, DC, they'll be looking at you if score again. So keep it under control" (Torian, 1996, 19). The warning he sounds is based on his knowledge of the process the Big-10 referees go through after each game and in preparing for future games:

> They look over the games as far as how they officiated the game, some of the mistakes they made, some of the things they missed, some of the things they should look for—and certain athletes…they don't necessarily target athletes unless there's a certain athlete that is known for his posing to the crowd, high-stepping…the refs are going to look at you. (Torian, 1996, 18)

Ambiguous Celebration Rules Need Refinement

Huntley explains a scenario early in the 1995 season—the first weekend—when players were being penalized for celebratory expression after big plays. He explains how Terry Glynn of Ohio State caught a pass in the middle of the field and then leaped high into the air in a show of exuberance. He was flagged. Ricky Hayes from Michigan caught a pass the same day and high stepped into the end zone for a touchdown with his hands raised high. No flag. He feels that it created ambiguity among the players in not knowing what the limits of expression were—from a referee stance. From his own stance, both instances were fine, and not only because he thinks so: "That's what the crowd looks for and one got flagged for it and one didn't" (Huntley, 1996, 6).

Carter again leads the charge against celebration rules, noting that referees are too quick to judge "right from wrong" and that there is no discretion in rules, that there is "too much emphasis on what you do instead of how you do it" (Carter, 1996, 4, 11). He gives the example of a player throwing up his hands after a big play as celebration and not taunting, but feels that referees do not exercise situational judgment, and that they "just set rules as if any [expression], regardless of how it's done is unsportsmanlike" (Carter, 1996, 11). He has heard through the player grapevine that ex-football players made the new celebration rules, but finds it hard to believe that a former player would make rules "so tight," given the amount of adrenalin football creates (Carter, 1996, 12). He believes, though, that referees make the rules and should adjust them to account for intent: "I would give the referees a little more ability to judge instead of just setting parameters saying 'if this is done, flag it.' 'If you feel he did it in this way, flag it.' Give the referees a little more lenience as far as calling flags" (Carter, 1996, 22).

London pauses to note that it is good the league put some regulations in, one guesses rules against taunting to curb fighting, but that the current rules are a little too strong, "knit-picking" (London, 1996, 11). He feels players deserve a warning before being penalized. If there was physical contact during the taunting, then a penalty, he feels, is in order. If there was only verbal sparring, then a warning should calm emotions. With the rules as they stand, though, he feels players constantly have to look over their shoulder before and after each action, which, as London stated above, takes away from the game. Simmons echoes London's thoughts regarding worrying about the legality of his on-field behavior. He says he tries to calm down after plays, always aware the referee interprets what is showboating:

> If you just go wild, then you never know...it is his [referee's] interpretation of what he thinks is showboating and you never know...you try to calm down..."alright, if I do this"...you think it through, but [there's only] a split second..."I hope his interpretation of what I just did wasn't a flag or anything." (Simmons, 1996, 13)

While Simmons is concerned with the ambiguity of the interpretation, Carter seems concerned with the rigidity and the fact that there is no "interpretation." London is okay with rules against taunting, but feels that even they need revision to account for contact versus noncontact taunting.

Race and Celebratory Expression

Daryl Carter

Carter is from Milwaukee, which has a black population that totals around 50%. His high school was 60% white and Asian, and 40% black. His high school football team was 80% black and included one or two white kids, a few Hispanic players and an Asian kicker. Carter's comments on race are the closest statements in any interview to my original research question on the factors that might explain the observed differences in celebratory behavior between black and white athletes. While Carter's comments do not speak for all black athletes—either on UW's team or other college teams— I do think he summarizes his specific environmental scenario and subsequent football expression in a sociological way that sheds light on what may be going on with other expressive black athletes. He covers the sociological gamut—from socioeconomic environment to the interpersonal:

> The majority of black kids that are playing are from the inner cities, and I think that expression comes from maybe some of the things that they've experienced. Maybe they're a little more happy to be out of the situation than other kids are. I mean I'm happy that I'm away from the violence, and I don't have to worry about somebody popping their cap [gun] in me. So maybe I'm a little happier when something goes right for me on the field, so that causes me to express myself more than others.... You've come a little longer way than someone else. (Carter, 1996, 23)

Carter next makes the distinction of family differences in behavior norms:

I think it depends on what you were raised to believe is good and what's bad, or what's acceptable in your family or not acceptable. Maybe some families would think it would be outrageous to dance or something. They might think that's embarrassing. But my family wouldn't think that way, they'd say "he's having fun out there. He's doing what he likes to do." (Carter, 1996, 24)

Carter, again, does not claim to speak for all inner-city black athletes, but does, I believe, shed some bright light on why differences might exist: growing up in areas with few rewards for achievement, growing up in fear, higher emotional satisfaction attached to arguably moderate on-field successes, and higher family approval of a wider range of physical behaviors.

Tony Simmons

Simmons notes that the white guys on his Catholic high school football team were expressive—even in the end zone. He says one guy specifically, Bobby Wagner, intercepted a pass, scored a big touchdown, and then proceeded to play the air-guitar in the end zone for two or three seconds. The white receivers also taunted defensive backs after touchdowns. This Chicago high school, Saint Rita, was 60% white, 30% Hispanic, and 10% black when Simmons attended in the early 1990s. His team was 75% white and 20% black, with two or three Asian players on the team. Simmons says the black players would sometimes laugh because the white players were often more expressive—though not as skilled—as their black counterparts at celebration. He remembers saying to one player "what are you doing? Man, you better chill!" (Simmons, 1996, 31). He goes on to summarize the white athletes he observed in high school: "they [white players] looked worse than us...they'd get into the end zone and start playing [imaginary] guitar and stuff...the ref [saw] that stuff but they kind of eased up on us sometimes" (Simmons, 1996, 31).[10]

Michael London

London's primary contribution to the interplay between race and expression is his observation that most of the verbal sparring and taunting that he is engaged in is with other black players. One factor that affects this observation is the fact that most of the defensive backs in the Big 10 are black, with very few white players at the position designated to guard the wide receivers. He describes the white players as "nice," and in the below quote juxtaposes black players with "quiet" white players:

> As far as talk? I usually will have more of a verbal battle with another black player. A lot of times—at least the experiences I've had with the white defenders—they're usually quiet, they really don't say too much. Not in this conference anyway...as a whole, I'm saying the majority of the verbal battles that I had were [with] black opponents. (London, 1996, 8)

There are more black receivers in the league also. One wonders if this is a black-on-black "game-within-a-game" contestation in addition to the overall football game competition, or if black defensive backs go verbally "at it" equally with white receivers.

Reggie Torian

Torian carefully chose his words in describing what he thought were differences not only in how players expressed themselves, but how they approached the game of football. The key word he searches for and finds to describe the phenomena is *style*. Black players and white players express, move, and approach the game with a different style. He says he could remove himself from the playing field and watch the game from the stands and distinguish black players from white players. He cites aggression as a primary way of white expression and physical talent a key factor in black movement.

> You can separate the black athletes from the white athletes as far as their mentality and their emotions...it's hard to explain...it's just the physical appearance and the way they move...It's the style, I'll put it like that. It's the style...the black athletes have a lot of emotion inside them, and white athletes have a lot of aggression...and that's what separates them. (Torian, 1996, 44, 45)

Torian has noted a shift in color and style on the UW team, which he believes will warrant an adjustment in how coaches manage the style and flow of the game. The team, he believes, is becoming more black, much like his high school team underwent a shift when he was there. He notes how the team at Thornwood was predominantly white, and over the years became predominantly black, initiating a black style of play:

> My senior year in high school, all the white players had graduated and the blacks came in and filled those roles...to tell you the truth, it was a different style of team.

It was more talk, more players moving around better and faster, more skilled, and we turned-up our style of the game because we had a different talent out there. (Torian, 1996, 46)

Torian emphasizes the physical while McCullough points up the emotional difference. Black athletes, he feels, make big plays and are very excited about it and show it physically. White athletes make big plays and down-play the result. Where he sees the primary expressive difference is in style of celebratory expression, saying that if he was in the stands—as in Torian's metaphor—he too would be able to identify the black athletes: "The movement is just different...some players you couldn't tell, but for those that showboat, then you can. That's what I'm saying" (McCullough, 1996, 29, 31). Huntley, too, cites a difference. But he attributes the difference to the fact that most skilled positions are filled by black athletes, and that given more opportunities to score, we would see a much wider variety of white expression, though not necessarily a higher level than black athletes.

Conclusion

Through extensive interviews, this study has attempted to capture the richness of African American athletes' experience of sport from their families and neighborhoods through their experience in college with coaches and fellow players. We gain insight into player codes of respectability, individuality, team play, and negotiating differences on the field of play. Knowledge of sport conduct and player codes vary by athlete, the variance dependent on everything from background to individual personality. Athletes vary also in their expression levels, and they vary in what they feel are acceptable levels of "talk" on the field. Athletes also vary in their attitudes about what is and is not appropriate conduct. The bottom line appears to be that there is no one definition of sportsmanlike conduct within this group of athletes sampled from one school. But we do see that black behavior is not irrational nor disconnected from environmental and social considerations. Quite possibly a different sample would yield athlete behaviors even more expansive and with even more meanings: athletes may express on the field for publicity, to acknowledge family members or fraternity membership, or to resist the oppression of white officials and the NCAA. Given these differences in attitudes about everything from length of end zone dancing to the appropriateness of taking off one's helmet on the field, we come to understand that it is problematic to assign one celebratory behavior as either sportsmanlike or unsportsmanlike. But this is exactly what both NFL and—more important for this study—the NCAA have done. If there is no universal agreement within any one race, why would we expect that there would be between racial groups? One thing does appear clear, though: behaviors of these black athletes do differ more than attitudes, and attitudes about celebration rules point in the direction of more reliance on player codes to negotiate disagreement on behavior patterns and less reliance on "extreme" rules that make the games less fun. To this group of athletes, all talk is not trash and all individual celebration is not unsportsmanlike.

The issue is not agreement so much as who has the power to make rules, as Cameron and Rigauer note in their theoretical discussions. An elite few make the rules based primarily on what they see as "appropriate" or "traditional." Elias notes that civility is what "should be" common to all human beings, and it appears the NCAA has similar sentiments about their version of sports conduct. In many ways this dominance is central to Rigauer's hypothesis, where sport is seen as a way to maintain the status quo by sports administrators who decide matters of policy in private. The bureaucratic elite in this "amateur" sport has effectively, in the eyes of the athletes here, taken the human element out of the game. If the NCAA rules committee recognized the fact that their views are not "universal," nor "right," nor everyone's "tradition," they might shift not only the rules but who helps in the production of conduct rules by incorporating players (and even fans) into the process, as Cameron proposes for debates about fair play. As Elias notes in his theory of civility and manners, the process of development of customs and habits shifts over time and is dependent on a variety of social factors. The social factors in the U.S. that often determine group ideas of behavioral customs include power, race, class, and gender. And as the athletes in this study demonstrate, behaviors and attitudes vary within African American culture and more than likely within European American culture also. The power to make all-encompassing rules can be difficult to give away, though. But once NCAA (and NFL) officials realize they work for the players and for the fans—not the other way around—they will shift their policies. Those in charge of the billion dollar college football conglomerate will eventually realize that they are forcing athletes to cling to archaic British traditional norms of "proper social conduct" in today's far less "amateur" college game. I do believe the NCAA will, though, eventually realize that the color of norms must change as has the color of the sport in this century. Then the NCAA will realize that empowering athletes by inviting them into the rule process is, so to speak, a much more civilized use of power.

Notes

I would like to thank Jane Piliavin, John Fiske, Jane Collins, Nina Eliasoph, Ken Harris, Jessica Johnston, Sharon Mazer, Mario Sims, Susanne Painter, Pete Olson, and the UW athletic department and athletes for assistance with this project.

1. I use sportsmanship in quotations for two reasons here. One, because of the exclusion of women from the language and the paradigm, and two, because the word is often used by its constructors to imply something universal. While I will often use the term, it is to critique rather than to promote its usage. I often use the less sexist phrase *sports conduct*, which also connotes the variety of possible definitions of behavior in sport. Unfortunately, though, this study only includes men and their view regarding sports conduct, even though I often say black or African American. These words are used in lieu of the more cumbersome black men or African American males. I want to acknowledge this nonuniversality of my usage, and to say that I have interviewed many women also on their views of sports conduct—both black and white—and will discuss issues of gender in a forthcoming article.

2. The complete dissertation (Andrews, 1996b) includes white athletes, but I only discuss black athletes in this article. A discussion of white versus black behaviors and attitudes is forthcoming.

3. For further reading on professional athletes and expression, see Andrews (1996a), where I review statistical analysis on 50 NFL touchdowns to assess different forms of racial expression and where black culture, family, and media issues are handled in more detail. A complete statistical analysis can be reviewed and duplicated by reviewing the unpublished master's thesis (Andrews, 1991).

4. It is problematic and Eurocentric to represent the world as comprised of societies that are described as less or more *civilized*. That issue will not be taken up here. We need only take note that categories have been devised by those in power and Elias describes the processes therein.

5. Elias cites previously acceptable habits that have shifted in their acceptance level over the years, such as: picking one's ear or nose at the table, dipping a piece of half-eaten meat into the table wine bowl, tossing half-chewed fatty meat against a side-wall in the guest's house, spitting under the dinner table, peeing on the stairwell, farting aloud at the table or other public places (better to be healthy than sick), or, for women specifically, never moving at night in bed lest one awaken or bother the man at her side. All of these things were at one time considered normal behavior (Elias, 1978).

6. Omi and Winant (1986) note the racialized ideological nature of what is socially considered "appropriate" conduct: "In U.S. society, then, a kind of 'racial etiquette' exists, a set of interpretive codes and racial meanings which operate in the interactions of daily life. Rules shaped by our perception of race in a comprehensively racial society determine the 'presentation of self,' distinctions of status, and appropriate modes of conduct" (Omi and Winant, 62).

7. Patricia and Peter Adler note the stereotypes student-athletes endure from professors, echoing Huntley. One player in their study of athletes and academics com-

ments on the "dumb jock" syndrome: "Some try to make it harder on you. They're out to get you 'cause they feel like you living like a king and it shouldn't be that way. With those jerks, it don't matter how hard you try. They gonna flunk you just 'cause you an athlete." (Adler and Adler, 151).

8. The critique here of Deion Sanders was similar to other critiques of Deion by other athletes in the study. Athletes noted that Deion's expression was fine—to a point. Carter likes Deion's "uniqueness" and his physical expression, saying that it may motivate others on his team to do better. Carter laments Deion's drawing too much attention to himself verbally, though. He cited as an example Deion's statement that he could "own any receiver in the league," as an example of individual attention to self rather than to the defensive unit as a whole. London also likes Deion's skills and celebratory behavior, noting that other players feed off of Deion's enthusiasm, that Deion is having fun and involves other players in celebrating, and that Deion wants to win and gets results on the field. London also admires and respects Deion for not putting opponents down, for not debasing them, which in London's eyes is a sign of good sportsmanship. Deion's consistent personality on and off the field gains London's respect, as does the fact that Deion trains hard and plays hard and wants to win despite his huge salary. London cautions, though, that as a player on another team observing Deion, his end zone celebration can bring out comments like "you're getting a little ridiculous" (London, 25). Further, London says another negative about Deion is that he is too flashy, and he predicts this style will diminish with age as his skills diminish. That's when Deion will learn the meaning of the phrase (and why London says he does not celebrate): "what goes around, comes around" (London, 26). Deion might feel the sting of some players he embarrassed early in their careers when he was in his prime. Once in their prime, London says receivers might yell at Deion: "you're on your downswing but you didn't care about it before when you went strutting up the sidelines…when you played us before. But now we're getting you. We're burning you. So now we're going to toast you…[it's] your turn to get some of your own medicine" (London, 27).

9. "He's all that" (or "she's all that") is an African American phrase of recent origin that translates roughly, into "he's all that he's hyped up to be." The phrase is most often used, though, as a negative comment on someone's self-hype, hence the phrase "he's not all that" he hypes—or others—hype him up to be. "He's all that" tends to be the ultimate compliment in black culture in the 1990s. ·

10. When I commented to a white male friend once that I thought the most prevalent occupational fantasy for inner-city black males, including myself, was playing professional sports, he commented that he thought the equivalent fantasy for *all* young white males was playing lead guitar in a rock band.

References

Abe, Ikuo. (1988). "A Study of the Chronology of the Modern Usage of 'Sportsmanship' in English, American and Japanese Dictionaries." *The International Journal of the History of Sport*, 5:1, 3–28.

Adler, Peter, and Adler, Patricia A. (1989). "From Idealism to Pragmatic Detachment: The Academic Performance of College Athletes." In *Sport in Contemporary Society*, D. S. Eitzen (Ed.). New York: St. Martin's Press.

Andrews, Vernon L. (1996a). "Black Bodies-White Control: Race, Celebratory Expression and the Contested Terrain of Sportsmanlike Conduct." *Journal of African American Males*, 3: 2.

———. (1996b). "Race, Celebratory Expression, and the Contested Terrain of Sportsmanlike Conduct: A Case Study of a Big Ten Football Program." Dissertation, University of Wisconsin-Madison.

———. (1991). "Race, Culture, Situation and the Touchdown Dance." Master's thesis. University of Wisconsin-Madison.

Cameron, Jan. (1993). "Fair Play and Playing Fair: The Context of Good Manners." Paper presented at the International Olympic Academy Session for Educators. Olympia, Greece.

Carter, Daryl. (1996). Interview.

Cummings, P. (1949). *The Dictionary of Sports*. Ronald Press Company.

Dunning, Eric, and Sheard, Kenneth Sheard. (1979). *Barbarians, Gentlemen and Players: A Sociological Study of the Development of Rugby and Football*. Oxford, England: Martin Robertson and Co.

Dyson, Michael Eric. (1993). *Reflecting Black: African-American Cultural Criticism*. Minneapolis: University of Minnesota Press.

Elias, Norbert. (1982). *Power and Civility*. Oxford: Blackwell.

———. (1978). *The History of Manners*. Oxford: Blackwell.

Fiske, John. (1993). *Power Plays Power Works*. New York: Verso.

Folb, Edith A. (1990). *Runnin Down Some Lines: The Language and Culture of Black Teenagers*. Cambridge, MA: Harvard University Press.

Foster, Herbert L. (1995). "Educators' and Non-educators' Perceptions of Black Males: A Survey." *Journal of African American Men*, 1:37–67.

———. (1993). *Ribbin', Jivin', and Playin' the Dozens: The Persistent Dilemma in Our Schools*. Cambridge, MA: Ballinger.

Fordham, Signithia. (1993). "Those Loud Black Girls: (Black) Women, Silence, and Gender 'Passing' in the Academy." *Anthropology and Education Quarterly*, 24, 3–32.

George, Nelson. (1992). *Elevating the Game: Black Men and Basketball*. New York: Harper Collins.

Holt, Grace Sims (1972). "Communication in Black Culture: The Other Side of Silence." *Language Research Reports*, 6, 51–84.

Huizinga, Johan. (1971). "The Play Element in Contemporary Sport." (1949). In *The Sociology of Sport, A Selection of Readings*, Eric Dunning (Ed.). London.

Huntley, Kevin. (1996). Interview.

Jones, James M. (1986). "Racism: A Cultural Analysis of the Problem." In *Prejudice, Discrimination and Racism*, John F. Dovidio and Samuel L. Gaertner. (Eds.). San Diego: Academic Press.

Kochman, Thomas. (1981). *Black and White Styles in Conflict*. Chicago: University of Chicago Press.

London, Michael. (1996). Interview.

Majors, Richard G., and Billson, Janet Mancini. (1992). *Cool Pose: The Dilemma of Black Manhood in America*. New York: Lexington Books.

McCullough, Carl. (1996). Interview.

National Football League Digest of Rules. (1990 ed.). "History of NFL Rule Changes." *NCAA Rules Book*. (1995).

Oxford English Dictionary. (1971 ed.). Oxford: Oxford University Press.

Omi, Michael, and Winant, Howard. (1986). *Racial Formation in the United States*. New York: Routledge.

Rigauer, Bero. (1981). *Sport and Work*. Translation, Allen Guttmann. New York: Columbia University Press.

Simmons, Tony. (1996). Interview.

Stone, Gregory P. (1971). "American Sports: Play and Display." In *The Sociology of Sport, a Selection of Readings*, Eric Dunning. (Ed.). London.

Torian, Reggie. (1996). Interview.

V

Racism and Discrimination in Sport

12

The African American Athlete: Social Myths and Stereotypes

Gary A. Sailes

The success and popularity of the African American athlete in the past three decades is unprecedented. African American athletes dominate the popular sports of professional football (60%), baseball (30%), and basketball (85%) in the United States today. African American athletes dominate the headlines of today's sport pages and are at the core of interest in American television sports programming. The accomplishments of the African American athlete have become an accepted facet of American culture. However, in an attempt to explain that athletic success, racial attitudes emerge which further polarize the two dominant ethnic groups in the United States today, African Americans and whites.

The myths and stereotypes which attempt to explain the phenomenal success of the African American athlete are an indication of the deeply rooted divisions that exist in a racially segmented society. Consequently, they also perpetuate the development of structural barriers to entry into management and coaching positions in college and professional sport. This essay will examine the development and perpetuation of racial myths and stereotypes about the African American athlete and present the social conditions that rationalize his rise to prominence in contemporary American sport.American sport is a $200 billion industry with unprecedented interest from fans and active participants in a global market (Coakley, 1994). No social institution in American culture receives the media attention generated by sport. American sport is currently televised worldwide into hundreds of international markets. The most widely and internationally viewed American sport event is the Super Bowl (Coakley, 1994). Millions of viewers worldwide tune into college sports in March to watch the NCAA (National Collegiate Athletic Association) basketball tournament, affectionately coined "March Madness!" The success of the 1996 women's Olympic teams, particularly the basketball team, has spurred the growth of interest in women's athletics. Title IX lawsuits and NCAA enforcement have guaranteed women a place in college athletics. Two women's professional basketball leagues have emerged and Nike has taken the lead in promoting interest in women's athletics through their commercial spots. Sport is big business and there is enormous interest. Virtually no one in the United States today is untouched by sport.

History

Concurrently, American college sport plays a significant role in popularizing sport in the United States. It has gained enormous popularity since the first collegiate event in 1852, a rowing race between Harvard and Yale Universities. Most early college sports were nothing more than extracurricular contests organized and controlled by students (Coakley, 1994). The "Golden Age of Sport," 1919–1930, set the stage for the commercialization and rise of college sport as we know it today. During that period in our history, American technology advanced and, consequently, so did American college sports.

A new invention, the assembly line, created jobs and enabled the mass production of goods which created wealth. As a result, there was a mass migration of Americans from rural areas of the country to major urban centers like New York, Chicago, and Detroit. Inventions like the radio, printing press, and wire service spurred the growth of the mass media. As an outgrowth, the mass media began to write about American sport and sports stars, creating interest among the American public. Huge stadia were built, advances in travel (railroad) allowed schools to travel and compete against other schools, creating rivalries. Consequently, conferences were established, and, finally, the NCAA and other college sports organizations were established to control this tremendous growth (Coakley, 1994).

The media played a major role in the rise of American college sports. Coverage increased, leading to the emergence of sports heroes who later became professional athletes and sports legends. Collegiate rivalries were fueled in the press adding to the popularity of this American pastime. The college All-American was established and today March Madness, the televised presentation of the NCAA basketball tournament, has become the symbol of college basketball's emergence as one of the most popular sports on television (Leonard, 1993).

The Integration of American Sport

American college sport was a "whites only" institution with only a few African American athletes participating on teams at predominantly white colleges and universities until as late as the 1960s. African Americans played college sports at historically black colleges and universities located primarily in the South. By the time Jackie Robinson broke the color barrier in Major League Baseball in 1947, African American athletes were being recruited to play on American college sports teams in relatively small numbers, particularly in football, basketball, and baseball. It was not uncommon for a team to have only one African American player on their college baseball, track and field, basketball or football teams (Ashe, 1993). Today, however, African American athletes account for 67% and 44% of the athletes playing NCAA Division I basketball and football. Moreover, 100% of NCAA Division I football programs and 98% of NCAA Division I basketball programs have integrated teams (Coakley, 1994).

The success of Jackie Robinson in Major League Baseball spurred the recruitment of African American talent from the Negro Baseball Leagues. Professional basketball and football emulated the trend and American colleges followed suit. By the late 1960s, nearly every major American collegiate and professional basketball, football, and baseball team was integrated (Ashe, 1993). As African Americans integrated American sport, they brought their special style of play that distinguished them from their white counterparts. For example, basketball was forever changed in its configuration when African American males began to dominate the sport with their numbers (George, 1992; Sailes, 1996). The "whites only" style of play was slowed down and consisted mostly of ball movement and outside shooting. Individual skills were sometimes sacrificed to augment team-oriented play. However, African American athletes played with a more athletic and aggressive game which highlighted individual skills like improvisational movement to the basket, slam dunking, improvisational dribbling and passing skills, and aggressive rebounding (George, 1992; Sailes, 1996). For a lot of inner-city athletes, these skills were developed in the parks and playgrounds of America's African American ghettoes and have become the standard by which basketball is currently defined.

Racial Stereotypes

African Americans are also breaking ground in sports other than basketball, football, and baseball. African Americans have kept the doors of opportunity open in professional sports like tennis (i.e., Venus Williams, Lori McNeil, Zina Garrison, Chandra Rubin), golf (i.e., Tiger Woods), swimming (i.e., Anthony Nesty), ice skating (i.e., Debbie Thomas), and gymnastics (i.e., Dominique Dawes). Consequently, however, the success of the African American athlete spurred the evolution of specific sports stereotypes and myths in an attempt to explain their success and subsequent attack on the "white status quo." These stereotypes elevated the physical prowess of the African American athlete, but attacked his intellectual capabilities. Simply put, the African American athlete was a spectacular physical phenomenon but still a "dumb jock" (Sailes, 1993b).

The historical origins of the dumb jock stereotype can be traced to 500 B.C. when Greek athletes were criticized for the inordinate amount of time they spent in preparation for competition and for neglecting their intellectual development. Greek athletes were characterized by some philosophers of the period as useless and ignorant citizens with dull minds (Coakley, 1994).

Media attention challenging the scholarship of college athletes, particularly in the revenue-producing sports of basketball and football, has tainted the academic credibility of college student athletes (Sailes, 1993a). Reports of high school student athletes not meeting NCAA minimum academic standards to establish college eligibility, accounts of college student athletes failing their courses, and the particularly low graduation rates among major college basketball and football programs foster the belief that anti-intellectualism exists among college student athletes (Sailes, 1993a, 1996). Unfortunately, Hollywood movies (the character Org in the film *Revenge of the Nerds*) and television situation comedies (the character Coach in the program "Cheers") facilitate the perpetuation of the dumb jock stereotype through the characterizations of unintelligent sports figures.

Sailes (1993b) found that the typical college student felt that college athletes could not compete with them in the classroom. They felt they could earn higher grades and had higher graduation rates when compared to student athletes. It was also felt that college athletes received unearned grades from their professors and took easy courses in order to maintain their athletic eligibility. This, they felt, accounted for any measure of success obtained by student athletes in the classroom.

While these perceptions were disclosed, most traditional college students were reluctant to reveal that they felt that student athletes typified the "dumb jock" stereotype. Moreover, traditional college students felt that African American athletes were least qualified to attend college and probably were admitted chiefly for their athletic talent. In addition, they felt that the typical African American student athlete was not sufficiently prepared to attend college and was least likely to be successful in the classroom. The negative stereotype of academic incompetence was perceived to be higher among African American athletes when compared to their white counterparts. In conclusion, Sailes (1993b) asserted that college students felt that if the typical student athlete was a "dumb jock," the African American athlete was the dumbest of all.

Beezley (1983) studied the development of the dumb jock stereotype traditionally associated with college football players. Although the dumb jock stereotype was prevalent in American sports culture, no substantiation could be generated to confirm its origin or its validity. Similarly, Nixon (1982) found no evidence to support the stereotype of the dumb jock. In a comparison of grade point average, graduation rate, and student perceptions, no significant statistical differences were found between typical college students and student athletes. McMartin and Klay (1983) had similar findings and also reported that positive and favorable attitudes were held about students who were also athletes. Regardless of the low graduation rates of football (53%) and basketball players (46%) that can be attributed to the time demands of these primary revenue-producing sports, the overall graduation rates for college student athletes (58%) were slightly higher than for the ordinary college student (56%) (NCAA, 1996). Although a prevalent stereotype, there appears to be no scientific basis for generalizing that the college student athlete is a "dumb jock."

It is plausible to assume that the retention of unsubstantiated stereotypes about student athletes emanates from a variety of circumstances. It is likely that most college students have very little, if any, contact with college student athletes upon which to draw factual information about student athlete academic competence. Second, if generalizations about student athletes are continually perpetuated by the mass media in fictionalized depictions (television, movies, books), it is likely that those generalizations will continue. In addition, it is doubtful that the general public reads scientific journals which clearly illustrate that student athletes generally hold higher academic grade point averages and graduate in higher percentages then the traditional college student. Sailes (1993a) attributed this to tighter academic restrictions and requirements on student athletes to maintain their eligibility to compete in college athletics.

Steele (1990) argued that one particularly sensitive race-oriented component of white superiority and African American inferiority is intelligence. Support for the physical superiority myth indirectly contributes to the belief that the African American athlete is mentally and intellectually inferior to the white athlete (Davis, 1991; Hoose, 1989; Sailes, 1991, 1993b). Conceptions about the "dumb jock" stereotype targeted at African American athletes are therefore related to racial stereotyping. This racist attitude contributes to the discriminatory practice of channeling African Americans away from the central (leadership and/or decision-making) positions in college and professional sport (Coakley, 1994; Eitzen & Sage, 1996; Leonard, 1993; Schneider & Eitzen, 1986).

Whites are reluctant to hire African Americans into management and head coaching positions in professional and major college sport because they do not have confidence in the intellectual capabilities of African Americans to manage or coach professional or major college ball clubs. Former executive for the Los Angeles Dodgers, Al Campanis, illustrated this practice when he exposed racial stereotyping in sport on national television. He made the assertion that African Americans may not have the "necessities" to be managers in professional baseball (Hoose, 1989). Positional segregation (often referred to as stacking) is prevalent among college baseball, volleyball, and football teams (Coakley, 1994; Jones et al., 1987; Schneider & Eitzen, 1986). African Americans are systematically channeled away from the team leadership positions in favor of white players. Coaches are reluctant to entrust the leadership of the team to African Americans because they believe African Americans are not intelligent enough to be successful team leaders. This is characterized by the dearth of African American pitchers in professional and college baseball and quarterbacks in college and professional football (Coakley, 1994; Leonard, 1993).

Lombardo (1978) noted two distinct stereotypes which emerged regarding African American males. Known as "the brute" and "the sambo" stereotypes, they were developed by whites to maintain their superior position in society and to denigrate African American males, keeping them subordinate. The "brute" stereotype characterized the African American male as primitive, temperamental, over-reactive, uncontrollable, violent, and sexually powerful. This stereotype intentionally separated the African American from intellectualism and mental control. White society placed importance on intellectualism and subsequently removed the African American from equal status by characterizing him with primitive physical attributes. This stereotype has been popularly used to explain the dominance of the African American athlete in football, basketball, baseball, and boxing (Sailes, 1996, 1993b, 1991). Consequently, the belief that intellectualism does not exist among African Americans has kept management and coaching positions in Division I college and professional sports mostly white (Coakley, 1994; Leonard, 1993)

The "sambo" stereotype depicted the African American as benign, childish, immature, exuberant, uninhibited, lazy, comical, impulsive, fun-loving, good-humored, inferior, and lovable. These typecasts about African Americans have historical roots in American slavery. It was felt that these characterizations relegated African American slaves to inferior status. Lombardo criticized the performance of the Harlem Globetrotters for their continued perpetuation of the "sambo" stereotype in sport and for compromising the integrity and positive image of African Americans in general and African American athletes in particular.

Other unsubstantiated race-oriented sports myths have evolved in an attempt to explain the success and over-representation of African American athletes in certain American sports. Most myths attempting to rationalize the apparent dominance of African American athletes in specific sports generally have little scientific credibility. For example, there remains the popular belief that African American athletes are physically superior to white athletes, and that their superior body build is genetically determined, giving them an advantage over their white counterparts. Many believe this advantage accounts for the success among African American athletes in football, basketball, baseball, track and field, and boxing (Coakley, 1994; Leonard, 1993).

A 1988 investigative report by the *Philadelphia Inquirer* sought to answer the question: "Are African Americans better athletes than whites?" (Sokolove, 1988). Similarly, a 1989 NBC special program hosted by Tom Brokaw entitled "The Black Athlete: Fact or Fiction" focused on the question: "What accounts for the success of African American athletes in American sports?" These two reports supported the theory of the physical or genetic superiority of the African American athlete. While some physical differences are apparent between African Americans and whites as a whole, it remains to be demonstrated that anatomical, genetic, and/or physiological differences between African American and white athletes contribute significantly to the dominance of either over the other in sports competition (Coakley, 1994; Eitzen & Sage, 1996; Leonard, 1993; McPherson et al., 1989; Sailes, 1987, 1991, 1993b, 1996; Sokolove, 1988).

Davis (1991) argued that the need to analyze African American success in sport is a racist preoccupation emanating from fear generated within the white status quo. It was felt that white fear of loss of control of American economic, political, and educational institutions was the catalyst for investigating the so-called athletic superiority of the African American athlete. Historically, African Americans were barred from competing against whites in sport for two reasons: (1) the country practiced segregation between whites and African Americans; and (2) it was believed that African Americans were inferior to whites and posed no significant challenge on the athletic field. When African Americans integrated American sport and began to dominate in basketball, football, and baseball, whites precluded that it was the natural physical and/or genetic superiority of the African American that enabled them to dominate those sports. Consequently, the stereotype that African Americans were naturally physically superior to whites precluded the racist notion that they are intellectually inferior and cannot compete with whites in America's corporate boardrooms. This stereotype facilitates the maintaining of white superiority and the white status quo.

Sports Myths

Many of the myths regarding African American athletes suffer from scientifically unacceptable assumptions and are not substantiated by research. Moreover, the variables impacting on the sport socialization and sport participation patterns of African American athletes in American sport emanate from the social constraints placed upon them by the dominant culture and their determination to overcome them (Coakley, 1994; Eitzen & Sage, 1996; Leonard, 1993; McPherson et al., 1989; Sailes, 1987, 1991; Sokolove, 1988).

This author compiled a list of the prevalent myths held by college students about African American college student athletes. While this was informal qualitative research at best, the information gathered was collected every semester over a period of ten years in a university elective course entitled "The African American Athlete in American Sport." Each semester, class enrollment was approximately thirty students with one third African American and two thirds white. Students completed a course assignment which required them to list and explain every myth they heard and/or believed about the African American athlete. The assignments were maintained and organized for inclusion in a book. What follows is a summary of those assignments. It was interesting to note that most of the stereotypes attempted to answer two questions: "Is the African American physically superior to the white athlete?" "Why does the African American athlete dominate American sport?"

Matriarchal Theory

Many students believed that most African American athlete came from a single parent household consisting of an absent father and with the mother as the head of the household. Sailes (1984) found that this was the case for a majority of the African American athletes participating in his socialization study. It was also believed that because of the absent father, the African American athlete was uncontrollable, hostile, and unfocused. He channeled his hostility into the sports area where he excelled. In addition, the absent father caused the African American athlete to seek and establish a bond with the coach. A paternalistic relationship developed and the African American athlete became a better performer as a result of that special relationship. Evans (1978) and Anshel and Sailes (1990) found that most athletes, and the African American athlete in particular, was suspicious and distrusting of the motives of their coaches. At best, the relationship between the head coach and the African American student athlete was distant. The literature refutes the notion that a special relationship exists between the coach and African American athlete because of an absent father at home and that relationship motivated the African American athlete to excel on the athletic field.

Mandingo Theory

Jimmy "The Greek" Snyder popularized this theory with his candid remarks on national television. His remarks led to his termination as an ABC sports analyst. It was believed that the physical superiority of the African American athlete emanated from the days of slavery. This theory holds that slave owners intentionally bred their slaves requiring physically large and muscular male slaves to mate with physically large and muscular female slaves. The offspring were physically superior to the commonly reproduced slave child. This physically superior child, it was felt, would grow up to be a better laborer in the fields.

"The Greek" asserted this type of selective breeding caused the thighs and gluteal muscles in African Americans to become superior. This, he felt, accounted for their superior jumping and sprinting abilities over their white counterparts. Common sense dictates that even if this were true, there is no possible way this could account for the physical development of 34 million African Americans today. White slave owners had slave concubines, slave women were raped by white overseers, free Negroes could choose their own mates, most slaves were unrestricted in their choice of mates (Bennett, 1996; Franklin, 1994), and foreign immigration to the United States probably took their toll on this so-called selectively bred gene pool. Interracial marrying and miscegenation were and are too prevalent in the United States for that gene pool to have survived and eventually account for any physical difference that would predispose itself in the contemporary athletic arena (Sailes, 1991).

History showed that large slaves were used as fighters and heavy gambling took place on those fights by whites. In fact, two slaves, Bill Richmond and Tommy Molineaux, were early fighters who won their owners enough money to earn their freedom (Ashe, 1993). It is quite possible that slaves were used as breeders in isolated instances, but there were too many uncontrollable social variables in early and contemporary American society to give substance to this theory. Additionally, many African Americans lived with Native Americans and intermarried with them. Common sense dictates that in all likelihood, the gene pool from slave breeding was lost prior to the beginning of the twentieth century.

Survival of the Fittest Theory

It was felt that the physical superiority of the African American athlete was incidentally created by the survivors of the "middle passage" of African slaves to the Americas. The trip from Africa to America took several months. During that time, slaves were laid on their backs and chained together by hands and feet. They assumed this position for several days at a time except for brief exercise periods on the deck of the slave ships. They were barely fed, became ill, and sometimes over 65% of the slave cargo was lost to dysentery, suicide, or murder (Bennett, 1996; Franklin, 1994). It was felt that those who survived the middle passage were physically superior beings compared to those who perished.

Today's 34 million African Americans are supposedly the descendants of that superior gene pool and this accounts for their physical superiority on the athletic field. As indicated in the Mandingo Theory, immigration, miscegenation, and interracial marrying between African Americans, whites, and individuals from other ethnic groups, especially after the end of slavery, would most assuredly have caused the dilution of any special gene pool supposedly created by the middle passage.

Genetic Theory

This theory assumed that African Americans had more white fast twitch muscle fibers and whites had more red slow twitch muscle fibers which precluded their potential in athletics. White muscle fibers were power oriented and were better able to liberate greater force over a short period of time. White fast twitch muscle fibers would be most beneficial for sports activities which required agility, speed, quickness, jumping, lifting, and throwing. This explanation was used to justify African American dominance in sports activities like the jumping and sprint events in track and field, basketball, baseball, football, and boxing. One of my white students believed that African Americans were able to run faster and jump higher than whites because African Americans had an extra muscle in their legs. He asserted he was told this by a college professor/athletic trainer who held a Ph.D. from a predominantly white medium-sized midwestern college. There is no available data or research to confirm this belief.

The Genetic Theory also assumed that whites had a preponderance of red muscle fibers which are better suited for endurance events. Red muscle fibers are better able to liberate oxygen from the blood stream to replenish the muscles for long distance activities. This was why whites dominated the middle and long distance endurance sports. Examples are middle and long distance events in track and field, swimming, cross-country skiing, cross-country running, marathons, and skating.

This theory was debunked when West Africans began and continued to dominate the marathons and middle and long distance events in track and field. Olympian Kip Keno of Kenya and others who followed him have won international marathon competitions every year. In addition, no scholar or researcher was willing to step up and confirm through scientific research the claims made by this myth. There is overwhelming evidence which supports the conclusion that social variables such as the sport opportunity structure, social and cultural norms about sport, personal aspirations, economic factors, coaching, and available facilities and programs have a greater impact in explaining the recent success of the African American athlete in American sport. Perceived closed doors to opportunities in mainstream American society and peer pressure not to pursue mainstream opportunities channeled African Americans into the only avenues they felt were open to them, in entertainment, in sports, (Sailes, 1987) or through the underground economy where they engaged in a life of crime (Oliver, 1994).

Psychological Theory

This theory presumed that African Americans were incapable of leadership in positions like quarterback in football, pitcher in baseball, or point guard in basketball. Moreover, as was discussed earlier, Al Campanis reiterated the belief of management in Major League Baseball on national television when he said that African Americans may not have the "necessities" to become managers and field coaches in Major League Baseball.

This theory also claimed that African Americans did poorly under pressure and were not good thinkers which was why they were underrepresented in individual sports such as tennis, golf, skiing, skating, gymnastics, and swimming. However, when given the opportunity, African Americans have excelled in individual sports and in leadership positions in team sports for decades. There are several African Americans participating in professional tennis and golf, and who serve as head coaches in Division I and professional basketball, football, and baseball. Several of these coaches and athletes have won national titles.

The National Brotherhood of Skiers, the American Tennis Association, and the National Golf Association are all African American national organizations. The American Tennis Association is the oldest African American sports organization in the United States today (Ashe, 1993). There are African American swimming and gymnastics programs and clubs across the United States providing programs and instruction and which have produced several national amateur champions (Hoose, 1989).

African American athletes in leadership, management, and coaching positions have won national championships and titles in the United States. For example, John Thompson of Georgetown University and Nolan Richardson of the University of Arkansas have won NCAA basketball titles. Cito Gaston, general manager of the Toronto Blue Jays, and Bob Watson, general manager of the New York Yankees, have both won World Series titles. Doug Williams was a winning quarterback in the NFL's Super Bowl. Tina Sloane Green of Temple University won two NCAA lacrosse championships. However, the Psychological Theory is the primary reason many African Americans are not given management and/or coaching positions in professional and college sports today. White fear of African Americans invading the white status quo and prejudicial attitudes about African American competence are nothing new and continue to create barriers to African American success in the administration of American sports. Given the opportunity, African Americans can excel and have proven themselves worthy of inclusion in the sports market place as on-field leaders, managers, and coaches.

Dumb Jock Theory

A corollary of the Psychological Theory, this theory challenges the academic competence of student athletes. It was generally felt that student athletes could not compete with traditional students in the classroom. In addition, it was felt student athletes took easy jock courses and majored in eligibility (general studies) rather than a legitimate academic subject.

The stereotypes against African American student athletes were even more denigrating. It was generally felt that African American athletes did not belong in college. Students felt it was the African American's athletic talents, and not his intelligence, which provided him admission to college. They felt that if athletic departments did not have special admission policies, most African American athletes could not get into college. While this may have been the practice of athletic departments in isolated instances in the past, this is less possible today. The NCAA has minimum academic requirements for student athletes to establish eligibility to participate in college athletics. Specifically, a graduating high school senior must score a minimum of 900 on the SAT and have a grade point average of 2.5 in order to receive an athletic scholarship and participate in Division I college athletics. Furthermore, the grade point averages and graduation rates of student athletes are slightly higher then their nonathletic counterparts (Sailes, 1993a). The myth of the dumb jock is unfounded and most of the literature indicates that student athletes are doing better in school than traditional college students.

Concluding Discussion

Racial myths and stereotypes are born out of ignorance. Lack of contact with different social and/or ethnic groups create ideologies that are generated from social dissonance and are founded on subjective observations. Our interpretations of other cultures are filtered through our own life experiences. To define others and to derive meaning about others based on our own cultural values, without the benefit of personal contact with those other indigenous cultures, leads to conjecture, myths, stereotypes, and inaccurate depictions of what we see.

In extreme cases, inaccurate depictions can generate fear, prejudice, and misunderstandings which can lead to confrontation. Myths and stereotypes are damaging in that respect. Until we are ready to step up and reintroduce ourselves to one another, social myths and stereotypes will continue to fuel the fires of racial hatred and bigotry that currently polarize American society.

The fears and anxieties of whites in America cause them to subjugate other cultures and ethnic groups within this country to inferior status and to create the caste system of inequities that have kept us apart for decades. It is time to pursue the truth, to interact with one another, and to have meaningful dialogue about who we are. W. E. B. DuBois suggested that the greatest problem that will face America in the twentieth century will be the race problem. Current researchers forecast that this problem will continue into the twenty-first century. It is time to learn to respect one other, to dispel the myths and stereotypes that keep us hanging onto the dark past. We must shield ourselves from the blatant negative media depictions of African American athletes portrayed as mindless physical specimens whose success is predisposed by their genetic and physiological superiority to whites. If we continue on the present journey of distrust, fear, and confrontation which is fueled by our unfounded mythological and stereotypical beliefs about one another, Americans will never reach the peace and harmony that are the rewards of enlightenment.

References

Anshel, M., and Sailes, G. (1990). "Discrepant Attitudes of Intercollegiate Athletes as a Function of Race." *Journal of Sport Behavior,* 13(2), 87–102.

Ashe, A. (1993). *A Hard Road to Glory: A History of the African American Athlete.* New York: Amistad Press.

Beezley, W. H. (1983). "Images of the Student Athlete in College Football." In *The University's Role in the Development of Modern Sport: Past, Present, and Future,* edited by S. Kereliuk. Proceedings of the FISU Conference-Universiade '83 in association with the Tenth HISPA Congress. Edmonton, Canada: University of Alberta, (July 2–4), 447–461.

Bennett, Jr., L. (1996). *Before the Mayflower: A History of Black America.* Chicago: Johnson Publishing.

Coakley, J. J. (1994). *Sport in Society: Issues and Controversies.* Boston: Times Mirror/Mosby.

Davis, Laurel R. (1991). "The Articulation of Difference: White Preoccupation with the Question of Racially Linked Genetic Differences Among Athletes. *Sociology of Sport Journal,* 7(2), 179–187.

Eitzen, D. S., and Sage, G. H. (1996). *Sociology of North American Sport.* Dubuque: Wm. C. Brown.

Evans, V. (1978). "A Study of Perceptions Held by High School Athletes Toward Coaches." *International Review of Sport Sociology,* 13, 47–53.

Franklin, J. H. (1994). *From Slavery to Freedom.* New York: McGraw-Hill.

George, N. (1992). *Elevating the Game: Black Men and Basketball.* New York: HarperCollins.

Hoose, P. (1989). *Necessities: Racial Barriers in American Sports.* New York: Random House.

Jones, B., Leonard, W., Schmitt, R., Smith, D., and Tolone, W. (1987). "A Log-Linear Analysis of Stacking in College Football." *Social Science Quarterly,* (March), 70–83.

Lederman. D. (1990). "Athletes in Division I Found Graduating at Higher Rate Than Other Students." *The Chronicle of Higher Education,* July 5.

Leonard II, W. M. (1993). *A Sociological Perspective of Sport.* New York: Macmillan Publishers.

Lombardo, B. (1978). "The Harlem Globetrotters and the Perception of the Black Stereotype." *The Physical Educator,* 35(2), 60–63.

McMartin, J., and Klay, J. (1983). "Some Perceptions of the Student Athlete." *Perceptual and Motor Skills,* 57(3), 687–690.

McPherson, B., Curtis, J., and Loy, J. (1989). *The Social Significance of Sport.* Champaign: Human Kinetics.

NCAA Report. (1996). *1996 NCAA Division I Graduation-Rates Report.* Overland, Kans.: The National Collegiate Athletic Association.

NCAA Report (1989). *The Status of Minority Participation in Intercollegiate Sports.* Washington, DC: American Institute of Research.

Nixon, H. L. (1982). "The Athlete as Scholar in College: An Exploratory Test of Four Models." In *Studies in the Sociology of Sport,* edited by A. Dunleavy, A. Miracle, and C. Rees. Fort Worth: Texas Christian University Press, 239–256.

Oliver, W. (1994). *The Violent Social World of Black Men.* New York: Lexington Books: New York.

Sailes, G. A. (1996). "An Examination of Basketball Performance Orientations Among African American Males." *Journal of African American Men,* 1(4), 37–46.

———. (1993a). "An Investigation of Academic Accountability Among College Student Athletes." *Academic Athletic Journal,* Spring, 27–39.

———. (1993b). "An Investigation of Campus Typecasts: The Myth of Black Athletic Superiority and the Dumb Jock Stereotype." *Sport Sociology Journal,* 10, 88–97.

————. (1991). "The Myth of Black Sports Supremacy." *Journal of Black Studies,* 21(4), 480–487.

————. (1987). "A Socioeconomic Explanation of Black Sports Participation Patterns." *The Western Journal of Black Studies,* 11(4), 164–167.

————. (1984). "Sport Socialization Comparisons among Black and White Adult Male Athletes and Nonathletes." Doctoral Dissertation, University of Minnesota.

Schneider, J., and Eitzen, S. (1986). "Racial Segregation by Professional Football Positions, 1960–1985." *Sociology and Social Research,* 70, 259–262.

Sokolove, M. (1988). "Are Blacks Better Athletes Than Whites?" *Inquirer: The Philadelphia Inquirer Magazine* (April 24), 16–40.

Steele, Shelby. (1990). *The Content of Our Character.* New York: St. Martin's Press.

13

Stacking in Major League Baseball

Earl Smith and C. Keith Harrison

> *A primary function of sociologists is to search out the determinants and consequences of diverse forms of social behavior.*
> —Robert K. Merton

> *The most important person on the team, in any one game, is the pitcher.*
> —Robert Adair

Many of the concerns in America today focus on the issue of equal access to the opportunity structure that exists in our society. These concerns, then, drive the debates about who gets what in America. To be sure, the tumultuous debates surrounding Affirmative Action in the mid-1990s are rooted within the demise of many of the traditional resources that used to accrue to hard-working people. The main resource we include here is life-long career advancement employment.

It is a well-known fact that today many Americans starting their careers will not be in the same career across ten to fifteen years. These career changes will occur at least twice, and possibly four times in the life course. To be successful, then, regardless of the venture—business, nursing, aircraft repair, or university-level teaching—you need the opportunity to break into the ranks of these established professions. Opportunity is the critical index that informs the discussion herein. This need for opportunities is no less true for the sporting enterprise in general and for the national pastime, baseball, in particular. To be sure, we are reminded that while baseball has the longest running professional sports league in America, it also has the longest history of racial discrimination in team sports (Smith, 1996).

Over the course of several years, a number of important empirical studies have demonstrated the continued existence of problems that some athletes have when trying to break into the games they want to play. Some of the most important literature addresses the problems encountered when stacking or positional segregation is allowed to persist in major league baseball (MLB).

This article is an analysis of stacking in MLB. In conducting the analysis, we reviewed several of the most important stacking studies to date and herein offer an analysis of their findings. What we attempt to do is address a long overdue subject: How can an institution like MLB openly depart from patterns of a multicultural civilized democracy, call itself America's game—but still allow position segregation—and other invidious distinctions to persist? An example of this is the legal scholar Professor Ken Shropshire (The Wharton School), who has shared with us a most fascinating article on the Philadelphia Phillies (Hayes, 1996). According to the analysis by Hayes, the Phillies had no African American players on their active 25-man roster. According to club president, Mr. Bill Giles, "it is our intention to get some African Americans who can play. But you can't do it just by snapping your fingers." What makes this story fascinating is that it confirms our suspicion about the deep-seated prejudice and racism in baseball, and especially that which continues to play itself out through stacking.

Review of the Literature

The literature on baseball is rich (Goldstein, 1995). It chronicles the game, players, and even the many towns and cities where MLB games are played. It is, to be sure, a literature about America (see Giamatti, 1989).

In 1967 Aaron Rosenblatt published his article entitled "Negroes in Baseball: The Failure of Success," which appeared in the popular discussion journal *Trans-Action*. In summarizing what Rosenblatt discusses in the paper, we should note that he starts his essay, documenting the time frame from 1953 to 1965, by looking at the historical importance of the entry of Jackie Robinson into MLB. Rosenblatt also notes that token integration was the order of the day. He then shows that the mere presence of African American players did not necessarily ensure that they would have access to all playing positions. He even asserts that African

American players had to be better, and had to possess superior skills both offensively and defensively to those of white players if they were to win a position on the team. Several key findings include that, for the entire 13-year period of the research, African American batters had a superior batting average over their white counterparts. Furthermore, during the period of the research there were less than 30 African American pitchers and for the same period, no African American managers, one coach and one umpire. Rosenblatt concludes his work this way: "The distribution of both player and nonplayer positions [in] baseball hierarchy is different for the two races. Discrimination appears to operate for managerial jobs on the field and in the front office as well as for player positions below the star level." For such an early paper, Rosenblatt's findings are very incisive. He certainly got to the point, and even today he continues to be cited by scholars (Brooks and Althouse, 1993).

Another paper, more in line with the traditional empirical research found in the social sciences than the Rosenblatt paper, is John Loy and Joseph F. McElvogue's 1970 research entitled, "Racial Segregation in American Sport."

Using a standard definition of *centrality*, Loy and Elvogue attempt to test Blalock's proposition that baseball is free of racial discrimination (Blalock, 1967). While the authors agree with Blalock that a critical examination of sport is necessary in enhancing the development of sociological theory, they find that "Blalock was...perhaps naïve in assuming that professional baseball is an occupation which is remarkably free of racial discrimination" (p. 6).

Loy and Elvogue also found that only a small portion of African Americans occupy central positions, on either the defense or offense. From there the authors raised several interesting questions, one of which was: Does this finding (relationship between race and position) indicate the presence of racial segregation? They do not fully answer the question, but rather speculate that there are many forms of discrimination, other than segregation (p. 15).

In what is essentially an update of the 1970 paper, Loy teamed with Curtis and in 1978 published "Race/Ethnicity and Relative Centrality of Playing Positions in Team Sports." In summary, Curtis and Loy reviewed nine stacking studies in MLB. The major research question was draped around similar questions being asked of corporate America— that is, if high status/high reward positions apply to baseball. They found that stacking exists, but were unsure as to why, feeling that "there have been few direct tests of interpretations" (p. 310).

In 1986 a seminal paper appeared by Marshall Medoff. Medoff's paper, entitled "Positional Segregation and the Economic Hypothesis," set in motion a round of debates on the topic that continue until today.

According to Medoff, the training and development costs are a primary locus of *causation* when players decide to challenge for specific positions. For Medoff, certain sports and positions require expensive development costs, along with extensive/expensive training. To clarify his perspective on the question, Medoff offers three hypotheses for positional segregation. These are: (1) biological, (2) psychological, and (3) sociological. The most plausible explanation for Medoff is number three or what he describes as the *economic* hypothesis. African American baseball players are not economically able to afford the costs associated with the game. He concludes by noting that at the same time, he also sees a modest increase in African American income and, moreover, a decrease in prejudice and outright discrimination on the part of both white management and the players themselves against African American players (p. 302). These two factors, says Medoff, account for the increase of African Americans at central positions.

In the paper by Norris Johnson entitled, "A Methodology for Studying Stacking in Football and Baseball" (1988) we see an attempt at methodological qualification in the research on stacking. The Johnson study found that stacking exists in baseball because coaches try to match athletes with positions assumed to require particular personal and physical characteristics. What has to be remembered here is that Johnson is reporting on *assumed* personal and physical characteristics.

As mentioned above, the Medoff article elicited a wave of responses. Marc Lavoie—"The 'Economic' Hypothesis of Positional Segregation"— says, flatly, that Medoff was wrong (1989). According to Lavoie, African American athletes do not choose to play noncentral positions as Medoff claims. They are forced to assume these positions if they want to play the game. Discrimination leads to truncated distributions, and barriers against minorities are greatest where assessment is subjective.

In a paper wherein Smith was senior author, Smith and Seff published "Race, Position Segregation, and Salary Equity in Professional Baseball" (1990). Using data for all players, including salary data, the authors computed the relationship between salary and productivity. They concluded that African American players have to be superior to white players if they expect to play on a regular basis. Smith and Seff also found the existence of stacking and also found that African American players were not considered for positions that have traditionally been described as the "outcome/control" positions, traditionally reserved for white players.

In 1991 Professor John Phillips published "The Integration of Central Positions in Baseball: The Case of the Black Shortstop." In this research Phillips disaggregated the central positions of third base, first base, second base, and shortstop. This disaggregation was done to disentangle the more important central positions from the less central positions (e.g., first base). Based on a collection of several years of data by position and race/ethnicity, Phillips concluded that by the mid-1980s African Americans began assuming the field at the position of shortstop. On the basis of this finding, he feels this shows a decrease of racial discrimination in professional baseball. Near the end of his research (p. 162) Phillips concludes that he is unsure why stacking exists but that it is still evident.

In a very interesting paper entitled "In Search of an Alternative Explanation of Stacking in Baseball: The Uncertainty Hypothesis," Lavoie and Leonard (1994) see the problem of stacking linked to the inability of assessment of a ballplayer's abilities at a given position. The authors put it this way (p. 141): "stacking is due to a form of racial discrimination. The more difficult it is to accurately and objectively measure performance, the higher the probability that subjective and less relevant factors will be taken into account when hiring or promotion decisions are made." In their analysis Lavoie and Leonard follow closely the logic of Blalock (1967), who insisted that the easier it was to assess individual performance, the less discrimination we would see by employers. And, while their "uncertainty hypothesis" cannot fully explain stacking at least for some parts of the hypothesis and especially that which attempts to explain performance differentials, it moves us closer to an explanation that advances our thinking on the subject.

Although this review of the stacking literature is not encyclopedic, collectively the papers reviewed represent a good portion of the research on stacking. To be sure, this research has informed our work presented here. The above represents the core of the stacking literature that has survived over time.

Stacking and Its Attendant Problems

Before beginning this section of the article, it should prove helpful to acknowledge how stacking is defined herein. While stacking is often studied in the context of centrality and dominance, in this paper stacking is defined as:

The placement of African American baseball players at specific playing positions, and not others. Stacking is to mean that African American baseball players are relegated to playing positions based on race/ethnicity and not on the basis of their playing abilities. Furthermore, African American baseball players are positioned on the field in such a way so that they, more so than white players, have less of a chance to play a leading, determining role in the outcome of the contest. Thus, stacking is a discriminatory practice, set in place to keep the number of African Americans on the team low. The concomitant effect of this long-standing practice is that African American players have less of a chance to assume leadership positions as coaches and managers when their playing careers are over.

Furthermore, to augment this definition we can ask if stacking is any different than other processes such as those addressed by urban sociologists since the end of World War II. Specifically, we are referring to the issue of housing. The problems at one end of the continuum are viewed as "white flight" and at the other end as "piling up"—both of which are very similar to our current knowledge about stacking. "Piling up" is an extremely relevant concept for understanding stacking. In their successful book, *The Negro Population in Chicago*, published by the University of Chicago Press, Otis and Beverly Duncan hit upon an issue that is beneficial herein. The formation of urban ghettos took shape along specific, distinct dimensions. That is to say, their formation did not just happen. Kusmer (1979), Osofsky (1968), Frey (1979), Degraff (1970), Kushner (1979), and Du Bois (1899) have all demonstrated the existence of severe racial antagonisms in housing, stemming from the turn of the century through our time. As well, some of the authors point to the post-World War II African American south to north migration trek as being a critical factor in the establishment of the northern urban ghetto (Duncan and Duncan, 1957).

As more and more African Americans moved north, whites fled to, among other places, suburban enclaves (Frey, 1979). As the northern ghetto solidified, bringing about the demise of the once racially mixed neighborhood, the expansion of the ghetto ceased: the line had been completely drawn across geographical and racial boundaries.

Housing, decent housing, was difficult, to say the least, for African American families to achieve. This is especially true of the Levittown variety that has received attention in the now famous nostalgic memoirs of the 1940s, 1950s, and the 1960s (Halberstam, 1993). Individuals and families were forced to subdivide their living space, thus making ghettoization a living reality for the majority of northern urban African Americans (Bianchi, Farley, and Spain, 1982).

Urban ghetto population densities created the *piling up* phenomenon that the Duncans researched. It is the contention that piling up and stacking are similar phenomena never linked before, for the simple reason that for the most part academics don't cross disciplinary lines. The first author is trained in the areas of urban sociology and anthropology. In the late 1960s and early 1970s a major focus of social science research was on the new social movements of African Americans, all over the U.S., claiming their rights to equal housing and citizenship (Cose, 1993).

To be sure, it is the special language and methodologies we use to explain our research and findings that distinguish us from other academics. Therefore, sport scholars not trained in urban research would not find the piling up phenomenon of use to their work. This is the point being made here, that the language we use to describe and explain our work is so very important; language is everything.

The twenty-five-year review of stacking research (Leonard and Smith, 1997) reveals the similarities of stacking to piling up. This is evident—from the baseball front office, to the coaching and manager ranks, to the playing field—that African Americans in baseball have been discriminated against—that is, piled up—even to the point of total exclusion during the heyday of the Negro leagues (Sammons, 1994). Does the sophisticated language found in the stacking research best explain this phenomenon? We believe it needs considerable help. To adequately convey the overall conclusions found in stacking research requires that these be embedded within the more explicit sociological research findings that explain racial stereotyping and the persistence of discrimination in American society.

Remember, African Americans, unlike any other group in American society, did not choose to be segregated and discriminated against from the time they arrived on these shores hundreds of years ago. The critical race theory scholar Professor Kimberly Crenshaw (1995: 103–22) put this best: "Black people do not create their oppressive worlds moment to moment but rather are coerced into living in worlds created and maintained by others; moreover, the...source of this coercion is...racism."

This insight is important. From the early research by Loy and Elvogue (1970) to the most recent research by Lavoie and Leonard (1994) we find that what is being discussed—even if some of these discussions are more implicit than explicit—is racial discrimination and segregation. It might help to define both terms to make sure that their true meanings are being adequately communicated.

Discrimination

Dr. Robert K. Merton (Columbia University Emeritus Professor) addressed the issue of discrimination years ago (1976), and it is fruitful to make reference to his analysis.

According to Professor Merton, discrimination needs to be carefully addressed, for invoking that none of the great documents of the U.S.—The Preamble of the Constitution, Declaration of Independence, as well as the Bill of Rights—explicitly state that all humans are created equal in capacity or endowment.

That the great pugilist Joe Louis is superior, not equal, to other bruisers, is patently clear; that Einstein is superior to all other thinkers is patently clear. What, in fact, the American creed does say is made abundantly clear by Professor Merton (1976, p. 190): "Instead the creed asserts the indefeasible principles of human right to full equity—the right of equitable access to justice, freedom, and opportunity, irrespective of race or religion or ethnic origin."

According to Professor Merton, all that is necessary, in a democracy like our own, is the opportunity, the opportunity to succeed. This feature of Merton's argument is also, I believe, the essence of the arguments articulated by Professor Edwards in his book entitled *Sociology of Sport* (1973, p. 205). There he notes that stacking "refers to the practice of stacking black athletes in certain positions on athletic teams while denying them access to others." Edwards continues, "thus, where leadership and outcome control role responsibilities are institutionally attached to a particular sports position, one should expect to find blacks being excluded from that position" (1973, pp. 209–10).

Edwards concludes his analysis by noting that "control in sports [have] fixed zones of role responsibility" and, further, thus excluded African American players from leadership positions both on and off the playing field. This is especially evident to the astute observer when looking at the makeup of coaches and managers at all levels of sports.

Segregation

Segregation is not supposed to be present in modern America (Cose, 1993). Yet it is. In his dynamic little book entitled *Take Time for Paradise: Americans and Their Games*, the late baseball commissioner and former president of Yale University A. Bartlett Giamatti put it this way (1989, p. 13): "It has long been my conviction that we can learn far more about the conditions and values of a society by contemplating how it chooses to play, to use its free time, to take its leisure, than by examining how it goes about its work." Remembering that the late commissioner was also a poet, it would be wise to add here that work and leisure need not necessarily be separated out as competing entities. In a healthy economy and society they go together. Further, we need to continue to recognize the interconnections between sport and society, with sport having been defined as a microcosm of society (Frey and Eitzen, 1991).

Focus of This Research

This article sets for its task a review and analysis of stacking in MLB. MLB is viewed here as a strategic research site (see Merton, 1987). To be sure, MLB can be viewed as a strategic site for empirical reasons, especially since there is such a long tradition of baseball research.

When we couch research concerns in the language of the day, it becomes hard to ascertain just what we mean, especially after twenty-five years of language use. The prevailing sentiment in the late 1960s up through the mid-1970s as far as race relations went (meaning black/white relations) was that African Americans wanted to integrate with their white neighbors, co-workers, and fellow citizens.

While the issue is more complicated than that, this assessment may simply be just plain wrong. Hochschild's (1995) magisterial study of African American and white perspectives on the "American dream" points in the opposite direction. According to her research, what she found was that *most* African Americans and whites resist segregation and for the most part have similar values. The differences that do exist are more along social class lines than racial ones.

Data and Methodology

The data for the study are taken from the 1986 MLB season. The data were derived from *Sports Illustrated*, the *Sporting News Official Baseball Register*, and *Topps Baseball Cards*. The objectives sought were to identify all players by ethnicity, their position, and their game statistics.

In describing the sample, it should be noted that the majority of the players are white (67.3%), approximately one-fourth are African American (21.5%), and eleven (11%) percent are Hispanic. One player is Asian.

The median salaries for white players, African Americans, and Hispanics are (1) all players: $286,667; (2) white: $275,000; (3) African American: $315,000; and (4) Hispanics: $195,000.

The statistical procedure used was multivariate analysis and was limited to the African American and white players only. The data analysis consists of Pearson correlation coefficients, cross tabulations, and multiple regression.

Table 1 shows both the number and percentage of ballplayers by race and position occupancy. These data are instructive: undoubtedly there is a large discrepancy between where African American players are positioned and where white players are positioned. The deeper insight taken from the table shows no support for the Medoff (1986) hypothesis, stating that upward mobility by African Americans would eliminate position segregation. Table 1 is a clear illustration of position segregation in MLB.

Tables 2 and 3 show the correlation analysis—separately run on white and African American players—indicating that salary is moderate to strongly related to the measures of skill. The relationships are in the expected direction.

Table 4 is a cross tabulation of infield/outfield positions by race. The highly significant chi-square (46.89 with 1 degree of freedom; $p<.000$) strongly supports the hypothesis that racial segregation in MLB is related to centrality. The overrepresentation of white players at the central positions, as shown in Table 4, supports this assertion.

Table 5 show the results of the regression analysis. The R-square for the for the model is .37, thus indicating that 37 percent of the variation in salary is being explained. The major finding here is that a player's skill level (e.g., hits, at bats, home runs, etc.) is what affects a player's salary.

Discussion and Conclusion

> *Professional sports seem to have finally reached the stage where stacking or positional segregation has become a non-issue.*
> —Lapchick (1996)

Although the phenomenon of stacking is now well documented, the social, economic, and even psychological mechanisms that underlie it

TABLE 1
Race and Position Occupancy in Major League Baseball, 1986 (N=1014)

Position	American League		National League		Both Leagues	
	Wh	Bl	Wh	Bl	Wh	Bl
Pitcher	99	8	103	4	202	12
	(50.5%)	(12%)	(54.4%)	(7.4%)	(52.4%)	(9.8%)
Catcher	27	0	21	0	48	0
	(13.7%)	(0%)	(11.1%)	(0%)	(12.4%)	(0%)
Shortstop	10	3	5	7	15	10
	(5.1%)	(4%)	(2.6%)	(12.9%)	(3.8%)	(8.1%)
1st Base	11	5	13	2	24	7
	(5.6%)	(7%)	(6.8%)	(3.7%)	(6.2%)	(5.7%)
2nd Base	6	10	11	2	17	12
	(3.0%)	(14.7%)	(5.8%)	(3.7%)	(4.4%)	(9.8%)
3rd Base	19	2	10	4	29	6
	(10%)	(2.3%)	(5.2%)	(7.4%)	(7.5%)	(4.9%)
Outfield	24	40	26	35	50	75
	(12%)	(58.8%)	(13.7%)	(64.8%)	(12.9%)	(61.4%)
N=	196	68	189	54	385	122

Note: Designated hitters are excluded from the analysis.

TABLE 2
Person Correlation Coefficients for Salary, Position, and Measures of Skill for White Ball Players

	Salary	Position	At Bat	Bat Avg.	Runs	Hits	Home Runs	RBI
Salary	1.000							
	.000							
Position	.034	1.000	.664	.000				
At Bats	.572	.065	1.000					
	.000	.378	.000					
Bat	.174	−.083	.355	1.000				
Avg.	.018	.264	.000	.000				
Runs	.518	−.051	.870	.378	1.000			
	.000	.493	.000	.000	.000			
Hits	.570	.028	.933	.429	.930	1.000		
	.000	.705	.000	.000	.000	.000		
Home	.479	−.074	.620	.140	.709	.623	1.000	
Runs	.000	.322	.000	.060	.000	.000	.000	
RBI	.512	−.039	.826	.310	.868	.867	.838	1.000
	.000	.603	.000	.000	.000	.000	.000	.000

Note: Table entries are Pearson Correlation Coefficients and Significance Levels.

TABLE 3

Person Correlation Coefficients for Salary, Position, and Measures
of Skill for African American Players

	Salary	Position	At Bat	Bat Avg.	Runs	Hits	Home Runs	RBI
Salary	1.000							
	.000							
Position	.008	1.000						
	.926	.000						
At Bats	.535	−.005	1.000					
	.000	.954	.000					
Bat	.163	.014	.126	1.000				
Avg.	.084	.877	.185	.000				
Runs	.514	−.120	.786	.239	1.000			
	.000	.213	.000	.011	.000			
Hits	.524	.003	.865	.288	.816	1.000		
	.000	.975	.000	.011	.000	.000		
Home	.502	−.151	.503	.179	.668	.585	1.000	
Runs	.000	.121	.000	.060	.000	.000	.000	
RBI	.588	−.026	.742	.211	.801	.814	.844	1.000
	.000	.785	.000	.026	.000	.000	.000	.000

Note: Table entries are Pearson Correlation Coefficients and Significance Levels.

are only now being understood. Based on the aforementioned analysis, it can be stated that even today—well into the 1990s—position segregation exists in MLB.

It is a rather commonplace belief among sport scholars that African American athletes at the high school level are often "stacked" once they graduate and head for the university (Hoose, 1989). This is especially true in football, but takes place in baseball as well. The impact of this insight is twofold: (1) many aspiring athletes never make the grade, and (2) the way that athletes are stirred to other positions makes it very difficult to conduct research on the movement of high school athletes who play certain positions in team sports and are then moved once they head for college (Davis 1995: 659–60). This problem grows as we get closer to the professional team sports.

If stacking (discrimination) no longer exists, as some sport sociologists (Coakley, 1994) and others contend (Center for Sport and Society, 1995) then, *why*:

• Is there a dearth of African Americans in MLB?
• Are there so few African American pitchers?

TABLE 4
Cross Tabulation of Race by Position

Position	White	Black	Total
Infield	335	47	382
Outfield	50	75	125

Note: Chi-Square = 46.89 (df = 1), p < .000

TABLE 5
Regression of Baseball Players' Salaries on Race, Position,
Measures of Skill and the Interaction of Race and Position,
and the Interaction of Race and Home Runs

Independent Variables	Standardized Regression Coefficients	T-Values
Race	−.045	−0.483
Position	.019	0.290
At Bats	.222	1.85*
Hits	.237	1.90*
Home Runs	.187	2.65**
Race* Position	.020	0.298
Race* Home Runs	.076	0.916

* Indicates .10 Significance Level
** Indicates .05 Significance Level

• Are there so few African American catchers?
• Are there so few African American shortstops?

Many of these questions have no immediate or clearly discernible answers. Other questions raised throughout this article are very clear: the continuation of patterns of stacking leads to the lack of full opportunities during their playing career. For ex-African American baseball players it curtails their ability to contend for positions of leadership after their playing days are over. Listen to the baseball Hall of Fame player Joe Morgan (cited in Shropshire, 1996a):

> You have to realize, when you're a professional athlete one of the problems with a professional athlete is that you think that your career is going to go on forever. And a lot of people do not start to think about what they're going to do after the game. And when you have the players making the amount of money they are making today, they are not really concerned with having a job in baseball after it's done. And I think therein lies part of the problem. (p. 459)

This research has demonstrated the continued existence of stacking in MLB. It has been demonstrated that stacking is the overall result of thinking about the playing abilities of African American players and the over-reliance on the negative social stereotype in forming opinions regarding where African American players should play.

There is no clearer indication of this thinking than in the research by Coach Terry Smith (1992). He found, through interviews with minor league coaches and scouts, that they routinely relied on their unfounded subjective views for player placement:

> Stereotyping was found to exist in virtually every explanation for stacking given by players, coaches and administrators.... There were numerous physiological stereotypes such as the reference made about African Americans possessing "natural talent."...One coach said, if you see a greyhound [African American] over here, and a sheepdog [White] over there...you need somebody on the club to get down and dirty like the sheepdog, but you need the guys like the greyhound to roam the outfield.... Not all stereotypes addressed physical attributes; there were many stereotypes concerning the mental capabilities of African Americans compared to Whites. Many Whites were likely to give a similar response to this White player's when comparing the two races: White people seem to be more intelligent and know more about their roles for positions that they play on a team.... They [White pitchers] possess a cool presence on the mound—the ability to deal with adversity.

The Smith study helps to close the explanation gap that has existed for too long in the considerable line of empirical research on stacking. Although conducting a different type of analysis, Leonard and Smith (1997) arrive at similar conclusions, as does Smith (1992). As we are aware from the nonsport literature (Terkel, 1994) these negative attitudes must be eradicated before full participation can be achieved throughout our society.

In a paper (Smith, 1996) that hinted at the possibility of "reverse stacking," a concept that needs much further research, Smith briefly explored some of the other avenues of employment for African Americans and discovered some data of interest:

> The data in the table entitled "Managerial and Professional Occupations Held by Women, African Americans, and Latinos, 1994" tells a very big story. Among the positions classified as "executive/administrative" African Americans hold seven percent (7%). The ten year change is 38%, thus telling us that across the decade African Americans made a jump of some 31%. In the category of "teachers, college, and university" African Americans hold 5% of the positions and the ten year change is six percent (6%). Scanning the list, you can see that African Americans do not make up fifteen percent (15%) of any category, excepting that of social workers where they are twenty-four percent (24%).

The argument was that there are definitely similarities between other occupations and sports as the quotation makes clear. The category of "social workers" represents the outfield, as this profession deals primarily with the dispossessed of our society. Earlier, the disciplinary linkages were established with the sociological research on housing.

The stacking data for the thirty-five-year period in Leonard and Smith (1997), for example, indicates that African Americans made some gains, but not significant ones, in playing positions. The data indicate that African Americans are still primarily located in noncentral positions. The importance of this finding is that it is in central positions where more responsibility and decision-making takes place and where a player has a greater influence on the ability of the team to reach their designated goals.

In our assessment, what remains in the research on stacking is: (1) further discussion that looks seriously at the full meaning of both segregation and discrimination in our society, not just on the playing fields, and (2) the mapping of strategies to dismantle stacking, once and for all. This sounds similar to a line of logic put forward by Harvard sociologist William Wilson. It is impossible today to ignore what he calls the "accumulation of disadvantages that stems from racial restrictions" (Wilson, 1996). The starting line is not the same nor is the playing field level. Wilson adds clarity to this assessment when he argues that the accumulation of disadvantages must be taken into account in any research that examines race/ethnic differences in America.

To do away with, forever, the insidious forms of racial discrimination and segregation that still impact what Americans can and cannot do across society, including social relationships inside baseball, is a very desirable goal.

References

Adair, Robert. (1990). *The Physics of Baseball.* New York: Harper & Row.

Bianchi, Suzanne, Farley, Reynolds, and Spain, Daphne. 1982. "Racial Inequalities in Housing." *Demography*, 19:37–51.

Blalock, H. (1967). *Toward a Theory of Minority-Group Relations.* New York: John Wiley.

Brooks, Dana, and Althouse, Ronald (Ed.). (1993). *Racism in College Athletics: The African American Athlete's Experience.* Morgantown, Virginia: Fitness Information Technology, Inc.

Charnofsky, Harold. (1968). "Baseball Player Self-Conception Versus the Popular Image." *International Review of Sport Sociology*, 3: 44–46.

Coakley, Jay J. (1994). *Sport In Society: Issues and Controversies.* Boston: Mosby.

Cose, Ellis. (1993). *The Rage of the Privileged Class: Why Are Middle-Class Blacks Angry? Why Should America Care?* New York: Harper Collins.

Crenshaw, Kimberly W. (1995). "Race, Reform, and Retrenchment." In Kimberly Crenshaw, N. Gotanda, Gary Peller, and Kendall Thomas (Eds.), *Critical Race Theory* (pp. 103–122). New York: New Press.

Curtis, James, and Loy, John. (1978), "Race/Ethnicity and Relative Centrality of Playing Positions in Team Sports." *Exercise and Sport Sciences Review*, 6: 285–313.

Davis, Timothy. (1995). "The Myth of the Superspade: The Persistence of Racism in College Athletics." *Fordham Urban Law Journal*, 22: 615–98.

———. (1996). "African-American Student-Athletes: Marginalizing the NCAA Regulatory Structure?" *Marquette Sports Law Journal*, 6: 199–227.

Degraff, Lawrence. (1970). "The City of Black Angeles: Emergence of the Los Angeles Ghetto." *Pacific Historical Review*, 39: 323–352.

Du Bois, William Edward. ([1899] 1995). *The Philadelphia Negro*. New Introduction by Elijah Anderson. Philadelphia: University of Pennsylvania Press.

Duncan, Otis, and Duncan, Beverly. (1957). *The Negro Population in Chicago*. Chicago: University of Chicago Press.

Early, Gerald. (1994). "The Black Intellectual and the Sport of Prizefighting." In *The Culture of Bruising* (pp. 5–45). Hopewell, NJ: The Ecco Press.

Edwards, Harry. (1973). *Sociology of Sport*. Homewood, IL: Dorsey Press.

———. (1994). "Playoffs and Payoffs: The African-American Athlete as an Institutional Resource." In *The State of Black America-1994*, Billy Tidwell (Ed.) (pp. 85–111). Washington, DC: National Urban League.

Farley, Reynolds, and Frey, W. (1994). "Changes in the Segregation of Whites from Blacks." *American Sociological Review*, 59: 23–45.

Feagin, Joe. (1989). "The Continuing Significance of Race: Antiblack Discrimination in Public Places." *American Sociological Review*, 56: 101–16.

Frey, James, and Eitzen, D. S. (1991). "Sport and Society." *Annual Review of Sociology*, 17: 503–22.

Frey, William. 1979. "Central City White Flight." *American Sociological Review*, 44: 425–448.

Gendzel, Glen. (1995). "Competitive Boosterism: How Milwaukee Lost the Braves." *Business History Review*, 69, 4:530–66.

Giamatti, A. Bartlett. (1989). *Take Time for Paradise: Americans and Their Games*. New York: Simon and Schuster.

Goldstein, Warren. (1995). *Playing for Keeps: A History of Baseball*. New York: Cornell University Press.

Halberstam, David. 1993. *The Fifties*. New York: Villard Books.

Hayes, Marcus. (1996). "Pale By Comparison." *Sport* (July 18): 80–83.

Hochschild, Jennifer L. (1995). *Facing up to the American Dream: Race, Class, and the Soul of the Nation*. Princeton, NJ: Princeton University Press.

Hoose, Philip. 1989. *Necessities: Racial Barriers in American Sports*. New York: Random House.

Johnson, Norris. (1988). "A Methodology for Studying Stacking in Football and Baseball: A Preliminary Note." *Sociology of Sport Journal*, 5: 270–77.

Kushner, James, (1979). "Apartheid in America: An Historical and Legal Analysis of Contemporary Racial Residential Segregation in the United States." *Harvard Law Journal*, 22: 547–560.

Kusmer, Kenneth. (1979). *A Ghetto Takes Shape*. Urbana: University of Illinois Press.

Lapchick, Richard. (1996). *1995 Racial Report Card*. Boston: Northwestern University Center for the Study of Sport in Society.

———. (1995). *1995 Racial Report Card*. Boston: Northwestern University Center for the Study of Sport in Society.

Lavoie, Marc. (1989). "The Economic Hypothesis of Positional Segregation: Some Further Comments." *Sociology of Sport Journal*, 6:163–66.

Lavoie, Marc, and Leonard, Wilbert M. II. (1994). "The Search for an Alternative Explanation of Stacking in Baseball." *Sociology of Sport Journal*, 11: 140–54.

Lemert, Charles (Ed.). (1993). *Social Theory*. Boulder, CO: Westview Press.

Leonard, Wilbert M. II (1978). "Stacking in Collegiate Basketball: A Neglected Analysis." *Sociology of Sport Journal* 7: 294–301.

———. (1988). "Performance Characteristics of White, Black and Hispanic Major League Baseball Players: 1955–1984." *Journal of Sport and Social Issues*, 12: 31–43.

———. (1993). *A Sociological Perspective of Sport*. 4th edition. New York: Macmillan.

———. (1995). "Prepared Comments at the Symposium on Sports Reform, Notre Dame University." *College and University Law*, 22: 88–95.

Leonard, Wilbert M., and Smith, Earl. (1997). "Twenty-Five Years of Stacking Research in Major League Baseball: A Theoretical Assessment." *Sociological Focus*.

Loy, John, and Elvogue, Joseph. (1970). "Racial Segregation in American Sport." *International Review of Sport Sociology*, 5: 5–24.

MacAloon, John. (1987). "An Observer's View of Sport Sociology." *Sociology of Sport Journal*, 4: 103–15.

McPherson, B. (1975). "The Segregation by Playing Position Hypothesis in Sport: An Alternative Explanation." *Social Science Quarterly*, 55: 960–66.

Massey, Douglas, and Denton, N. (1993). *American Apartheid: Segregation and the Making of the Underclass*. Cambridge, MA: Harvard University.

Medoff, Marshall. (1986). "Positional Segregation and the Economic Hypothesis." *Sociology of Sport Journal*, 3: 297–304.

Melnick, Merrill, and Loy, John. (1996). "The Effects of Formal Structure on Leadership Recruitment." *International Review for Sociology of Sport*, 31: 91–104.

Merton, Robert K. (1976). *Sociological Ambivalence and Other Essays*. New York: The Free Press.

———. (1972). "Insiders and Outsiders: A Chapter in the Sociology of Knowledge." *American Journal of Sociology*, 78: 7–47.

———. (1987). "Three Fragments from a Sociologist's Notebooks: Establishing the Phenomenon, Specified Ignorance, and Strategic Research Materials." *Annual Review of Sociology*, 13: 1–28.

Nelson, Mariah Burton. (1994). *The Stronger Women Get, The More Men Love Football*. New York: Harcourt Brace.

Osofsky, Gilbert. 1968. *Harlem: The Making of a Ghetto*. New York: Harper and Row.

Phillips, John. (1983). "Race and Career Opportunities in Major League Baseball: 1960–1980." *Journal of Sport and Social Issues*, 7: 1–17.

———. (1991). "The Integration of Central Positions in Baseball: The Black Shortstop." *Sociology of Sport Journal*, 8: 163–67.

Rees, C. Roger, and Miracle, Andrew (Ed.). (1986). *Sport and Social Theory*. Champaign, IL: Human Kinetics Press.

Rimer, Edward. (1996). "Discrimination in Major League Baseball." *Journal of Sport and Social Issues*, 20: 115–33.

Sammons, Jeffrey T. (1994). "Race and Sport: A Critical Historical Examination." *Journal of Sport History*, 21: 203–78.

Shropshire, Kenneth. (1996a). "Merit, Ol' Boy Networks, and the Black-Bottomed Pyramid." *Hastings Law Journal*, 47: 455–72.

———. (1996b). *In Black and White: Race and Sports in America*. New York: New York University Press.

Smith, Earl. (1981). "An Analysis of the Social Stereotype with Special Reference to Afro-Americans." *Humboldt Journal of Social Relations*, 8: 61–82.
————. (1995). "The Self-Fulfilling Prophecy: Genetically Superior African American Athletes." *Humboldt Journal of Social Relations*, 21: 139–63.
————. (1996). "Stacking and Reverse Stacking in American Team Sports," Paper Read at the Symposium on Race & Sport, Washington State University, April 28.
Smith, Earl, and Seff, M. (1990). "Race, Position Segregation and Salary Equity in Professional Baseball." *Journal of Sport and Social Issues*, 13: 92–110.
Smith, Rodney. (1996). "When Ignorance is Not Bliss: In Search of Racial and Gender Equity in Intercollegiate Athletics." *Missouri Law Review*, 61: 329–92.
Smith, Tracy. 1992. "Explanations for Patterns of Racial Segregation in Professional Baseball." Master's Thesis. Miami University, Oxford, Ohio.
Terkel, Studs. (1994). *Race: How Blacks and Whites Think and Feel about the American Obsession*. New York: Anchor Books.
Weiner, R. (1995). "Stanford Coach Was Ready for Call." *New York Times*, October 14.
Wilson, William J. (1991). "Studying Inner-City Social Dislocations: The Challenge of Public Agenda Research." (1990, Presidential Address, American Sociological Association.) *American Sociological Review*, 56: 1–14.
————. (1996). "Class Consciousness." Review of *Class, Race, and Affirmative Action* by Richard Kahlenberg. *New York Times Book Review*, July 14.

14

African American Male Head Coaches: In the "Red Zone," But Can They Score?

Dana D. Brooks, Ronald Althouse, and Delano Tucker

The role of high school and college coaches has been afforded significant visibility and prominence within American Society (Sage, 1980). The coach is often viewed as a "father-figure" or "mother-figure," and mentor, teacher, academic advisor, or friend by the many student athletes who play for them. According to Coakley (1994), coaching has emerged as a specialized, technical profession with an emphasis on team supervision and maintaining a winning athletic record. George Sage (1980), a highly respected sports sociologist, wrote that the role of the coach has become more powerful and his/her authority is being accepted by the public. Yet coaching remains an honorable profession, and many young athletes pursue academic careers with the aspiration of becoming a college coach.

Employment data tend to be encouraging. According to a 1994 NCAA report, the NCAA employed 11,991 full-time coaches and 8,936 part-time coaches in 1991–92. These data represented a 26.8 percent increase in the number of coaches employed since 1986 (Benson, 1994). The report further concluded that the largest number of coaches (Division I) were found in basketball (2,037) and football (2,388). Student-athlete participation data are just as impressive. Football had the highest number of student athlete participation in 1991–92 (45,579), while women's basketball was supported by 808 institutions.

Wouldn't it seem reasonable that increases of coaching employment opportunities (NCAA Division I-A) and increased student participation numbers by African American athletes (15,119 in 1994) (1994 NCAA Division I Graduation Rate Report) should result in hiring of more African American head coaches? Unfortunately, the data showed that African Americans have been underutilized in the various NCAA coaching and administrative ranks. While there are special concerns about women, particularly opportunities for African American women, the opportunity for African American men to enter NCAA coaching ranks or to achieve parity within the athletic department has hardly improved, and at best improved only slightly. There is not much evidence of overcoming the unconscious racism over the past fifty years. *Black Issues in Higher Education* (Farrell, 1994) reported that from 1991 to 1993, there were 1,109 new head coaches (excluding historically black colleges), yet African Americans represented only 143 (12.9 percent) of the new head coaches (Farrell, 1994). Similarly, between 1991 to 1994 the number of new assistant coaches increased by 2,394 but only 213 were new African American assistant coaches (9%).

Where are the African American Coaches? The Numbers Game

Only recently (about 1986–1987), in response to a growing clamor about racism in collegiate sport, sport organizations and their assemblies, including the NCAA and the Black Coaches Association (BCA), began to systematically collect and analyze employment data relative to African American coaching career mobility patterns. Reporting in the mid-1980s in the *Chronicle of Higher Education*, Farrell (1987) found the following surprising NCAA data: (1) only two athletic directors in the 105 Division 1-A institutions were African American, (2) three Division 1-A head football coaches were African American, and (3) about 25 of the head basketball coaches at the 273 predominantly white institutions (Division I) were African American. NCAA data published in 1988 confirmed that African Americans held 4.6% of the full-time men's head coaching positions at NCAA member institutions and 4.8% of full-time head coaching positions of women's teams (NCAA Council Subcommittee, 1988). The report was particularly alarming because not much hope was expressed that the situation was going to improve in the near future.

But African Americans were coaching. By 1986 the NCAA did recognize some progress in the number of African American head basketball coaches. Notable coaches included: Walt Hazard, UCLA; Tony Yates, Cincinnati; George Raveling, Iowa; Larry Farmer, Weber State; Nolan Richardson, Arkansas; David Gaines, San Diego State; John Chaney, Temple; Clem Haskins, Western Kentucky; Bob Le Grand,

University of Texas-Arlington; Wilkes Rittle, University of Illinois-Chicago; John Thompson, Georgetown University (*Ebony,* 1982, 1986).

Unlike college basketball, college football has been less receptive to hiring African American head football coaches. In 1987 there were three African American head football coaches (Division l-A): Francis Peay, Northwestern University; Wayne Nunnely, University of Nevada at Las Vegas; and Cleve Bryant, Ohio University (Farrell, 1987b). A few years later, Richard Lapchick (1991), noted scholar and advocate for the African American student athletes, reported there were only two African American head football coaches in 1991. The decline continued, and in 1992 the number of African American head football coaches among the 105 Division l-A teams was reduced to zero (*Chronicle of Higher Education,* 1992). The absence of African American head college coaches did not go unrecognized.

In 1994, the BCA (organized in 1987 to address specific concerns plaguing African American coaches and athletic directors at all levels) charged that major college football has the "worst record in hiring minority coaches" (*NCAA News,* 1994a, p.16). During the 1994–95 academic year, the BCA planned to investigate the head football coaching hiring decisions at the following institutions: Colorado, Stanford, Ohio University, the University of Richmond, University of Mississippi, University of Oklahoma, Oklahoma State University, University of Akron, Iowa State University, and Louisiana State University.

Sport science literature in popular magazines and newspapers consistently pointed to the lack of parity of African Americans in NCAA coaching and other leadership positions. For example, Brown (1992) found that of the 298 NCAA Division I institutions, minorities were underrepresented in coaching (8%) in Division I football. Yet minority head coaches were "best" represented in men's basketball (19.3%). Historically, the percentage of men's teams with African American head basketball coaches rose from none in 1970 to 5.4% in 1980 and 8.4% by 1985 (Berghorn, Yetman, & Hanna, 1988). By contrast, in 1970, only 14% of NCAA Division I schools had at least one African American assistant coach. The percentage of African American assistants increased from 41% in 1975 to 47% in 1980 to 57% in 1985 (Berghorn, Yetman, and Hanna, 1988). The rise in African American assistant coaches may be a result of an increase in the number of African Americans participating in college sports or African American assistant coaches needed to recruit African American players. Wulf (1987) believed that it is generally acknowledged that one of the major tasks of the African

American assistant coaches was to recruit African American players. Unfortunately, many of these positions are viewed as dead-end jobs with no chance for promotion (Dent, 1987).

Responding to external challenges as well as internal pressures to address the lack of African American head coaches, the NCAA formed the Special Subcommittee to Review Minority Opportunities in Intercollegiate Athletics in 1987. The primary "charge" to this committee was to address issues of opportunities for African Americans in college athletics with a special focus on coaching and administrative positions. Between November 20, 1987, and October 7, 1990, about three years, it held no fewer than sixteen meetings. As a result of having some of its recommendations approved, the NCAA: (1) established the NCAA ethnic minority enhancement program, (2) reviewed and endorsed the NCAA affirmative action plan, and (3) conducted a survey to examine the current circumstances regarding minority participation in administrative and coaching positions in the NCAA. One significant outcome of the subcommittee's work was the appointment of a permanent NCAA committee, the Minority Opportunities and Interest Committee, to address issues identified by the subcommittee (NCAA Council Subcommittee, 1991).

In an effort to identify current employment opportunities, the Minority Opportunities and Interest Committee conducted a four-year study of member institutions. In 1993–94, it reported that African Americans made up 12.9% of the 2,321 revenue sports coaches, and realized a 1.1% increase from 1992–93 (*NCAA News*, 1994b). On the other hand, the report concluded that the number of minorities working in athletic administration has changed very little since 1990. Summary African American coaching data supported their conclusion: black head coaches at Division I level in 1990–91 comprised 6.1%; 1991–92, 7.2%; 1992–93, 8.7%; and 1993–94, 9.71%.

Football Coaching Opportunities or Dead End?

Clearly, the number of African American head coaches, especially in football, continues to lag behind. In 1975, Willie Jeffries became the first African American head football coach hired at a major white institution (Wichita State) (*Jet*, 1979). Twenty years later, in 1995, three African Americans were hired in Division l-A, bringing the total to six African American coaches in this division in 1995: North Texas, Matt Simon; Oklahoma State, Bob Simmons; Stanford, Tyrone Willingham;

Louisville, Ron Cooper; Temple, Ron Dickerson; and Wake Forest, Jim Caldwell (Campbell, 1995). Writing in *Sports Illustrated* (1990), William Reed merely expressed resignation when he wrote, "There is the persistent notion that football is less a black coach's sport than basketball is" (p. 138). Reed (1990) was pessimistic about the future status of African American head football coaches in 1990, particularly with regard to the few African Americans holding positions of offensive or defensive coordinator. Many regard coaching experience at the coordinator level as a prerequisite to attaining a head football coach position. Recent information in the *Black Coaches' Association Journal* (April 1996) provided an overview of the status of African Americans coaching revenue sports and administrative positions (see Table 1).

Summarizing the state of affairs of African American head football coaching in America, Rudy Washington, executive director of the Black Coaches' Association, said, "If you look at the whole scope of things, we've only come a little way. There is not a level playing field by any

TABLE 1
Are We Making Progress?

As of January 1, 1996 (NCAA Division I, including historically black colleges and universities):

Sport	Number of Coaches
Men's Basketball	69
Women's Basketball	37
*Football	7
Chief Executive Officers	26
Athletic Directors	18
Senior Women's Administrator	26
Faculty Athletics Representatives	29
Commissioner	2
Associate Commissioner	1
Assistant Commissioner	1
Other Staff	14
Interns	8
Administrative Assistants	8

Note: *(Division I-A only)
Source: "Are We Making Progress?" *BAC Journal,* April 1996.

stretch of the imagination" (Farrell, 1995, p. 32). Charles Whitcomb, faculty athletics representative at San Jose State University and chairman of the NCAA Minorities Opportunities and Interest Committee, sent a strong message that we must remain vigilant and committed to recruit more African American head coaches to assure leadership positions. "We have to keep the flame lit and try to bring about more diversity" (Farrell, 1995, p. 32).

The lack of head coaching employment opportunities is significant since a little more than one-quarter of all NCAA student athletes are African American (*The Chronicle of Higher Education*, 1994). Some African American coaches and scholars believe the dearth of head coaches is a result of racism and discrimination on the part of college athletic directors.

What are the Causes?

Cleve Bryant (former head coach at Ohio University) said, "The deck is stacked against you. You are going to have to have a Superman 'S' on your chest" (*Daily News*, 1992, p. 82). Dickerson (past president of the Black Coaches Association) said, "Big bucks still control college athletics" (*Daily News*, 1992, p. 82). Alex Wood (former black assistant coach at the University of Miami) said, "For a black to become a head coach is like playing the lottery" (*Daily News*, 1992, p. 82). John Chaney (basketball coach at Temple University) was quoted as saying, "The problem in hiring black coaches and administrators lies not with all NCAA institutions, nor with the 290 institutions in Division I, but with 50 or 60 institutions with highly visible athletic programs" (Farrell, 1987a, p. 42). Chaney further stated that "These institutions are the ones guilty of playing musical chairs and continuing to hire the same people for jobs and denying access to minorities" (Farrell, 1987a, p. 42). Derrick Bell (1992) reminds us that modern discrimination is not practiced indiscriminately. "Whites, ready and willing to applaud, even idolize black athletes and entertainers, refuse to hire, or balk at working with, blacks" (p. 6). To Bell (1992) race does matter in American society. Counterbalanced to this position, Dinesh D'Souza (1995) wrote in his book *The End of Racism*:

> The main contemporary obstacle facing African Americans is neither white racism, as many liberals claim, nor black genetic deficiency, as Charles Murray and others reply. Rather it involves destructive and pathological cultural patterns of behavior: excessive reliance on government, conspiratorial paranoia about rac-

ism, a resistance to academic achievement as "acting white," a celebration of the animal and outlaw as authentically black, and the normalization of illegitimacy and dependency. These group patterns arose as a response to past oppression, but they are now dysfunctional and must be modified. (1995, 24)

The author concluded that racism is hardly the most serious problem facing African Americans today. The argument is hard to defend given the recent poverty statistics. Poverty data reported that the unemployment rate of African American college students is 4.4% (3.0% for whites). Equally disturbing, the percent of African Americans completing four or more years of college is 11% (24.6% for whites), and the median income of African American families is $18,660 ($32,368 for whites). Finally, data reported that 48% of prison inmates are African American (*The Journal of Blacks in Higher Education,* 1993–1994). The data suggested a measure of racial inequality in America.

Coaching Career Models: The Impact of Stacking, Personal Attributes, and Structural Barriers

The sport sociology literature clearly revealed that coaching in college sports is primarily a white domain. The absence of African Americans in NCAA Division I programs in the head coaching position, especially football and other nonrevenue sports, may be related to stacking (Brooks and Althouse, 1993; Chu and Segrave, 1981; Curtis and Loy, 1978; Eitzen and Tessendorf, 1978; Eitzen and Yetman, 1977). Stacking refers to situations in which African Americans are relegated to specific team positions (such as wide receiver and defensive back) and excluded from competing for others (quarterback). It is evident that the stereotype hypothesis (belief that African Americans lack the leadership ability to occupy coaching positions) is one of the most widely accepted explanations for stacking in college sport (Edwards, 1973; Eitzen and David, 1975; Eitzen and Yetman, 1977). College football is a highly structured and complex organization. To date, few researchers have studied the hiring practices of NCAA Division I football coaches. In an attempt to map coaching career patterns, Anderson (1993) traced college career head coaching mobility and reached the following conclusion, "Becoming an assistant coach often is a prerequisite to becoming a coordinator and becoming a coordinator is a prerequisite to becoming a head coach and becoming a head football coach is frequently a prerequisite to becoming an athletic director" (p. 63). This model appears to be linear, simplistic, and built on previous coaching experience. Nonetheless, the author concluded that race functions to keep African Americans from entering the pool from which head coaches are selected. It was interesting to read that the findings from this study further supported the existing *centrality* sport literature tying previous playing position, race, and access to head coaching positions. Anderson's research (1993) revealed that white assistant coaches were twice as likely to have played the quarterback position in college.

Anderson's study lends support to Latimer and Mathes's (1985) finding that African American coaches tended to have played and coached peripheral positions (i.e., running backs, wide receivers) at a higher rate than their white counterparts. In effect, the centrality argument claims that central/leadership positions beget leadership positions, with whites more likely to occupy central positions.

In an attempt to identify other variables impacting coaching career patterns, Banks (1979) and Grenfell and Freischlag (1989) studied the relationship between coaching career success and career paths by identifying the relationship between personal attributes (knowledge of the game, communication skills, personality, and recruiting skills) and job responsibilities of coaches. Unfortunately, the personal attribute arguments could not explain that the majority of the African American coaches perceived they had the necessary personal attributes to become head coach, yet remained an assistant coach (Brooks, Althouse, King, and Brown, 1989). Brooks and Althouse (1993) concluded that none of the positions articulated in the literature could fully explain the coaching mobility paths followed by coaches. It is true that coaches' careers are truly unique to that individual. Brooks et al., (1989) reached the conclusion that focus must be given to integrate micro- and macro-level variables in order to understand the recruitment and upward mobility of African American coaches.

In an attempt to further analyze coaching career mobility, Brooks and Althouse (1993) identified factors that may explain the absence of African Americans in head coaching positions in college athletics. Factors such as race, previous athletic participation, the impact of structural barriers (conference affiliation, type of institution), and success of the program and career mobility pattern were identified as possible variables influencing coaching mobility patterns at the college level. It is apparent that structural barriers and persistent discrimination patterns, "old boy" network, and media publicity may affect coaching career mobility patterns of African American coaches. A cadre of African American legal scholars provides some additional insights into understanding the African American college coaching experience. Davis (1994) and Shropshire

(1996) wrote about the persistent and prevalent existence of racism in college athletics. The author believed the inequality of access for African Americans to college coaching demonstrates the racial stereotype, "The black athlete is inferior to the white athlete regarding intellectual and leadership abilities" (Davis, 1994, p. 657). Both Davis (1994) and Shropshire (1996) agree that the NCAA must develop long-term solutions to address the subtle forms of racism, including the underutilization of African Americans in head coaching positions.

The purpose of this article was to continue investigating the political economy of intercollegiate athletics related to the African American male head coaching experience. The authors were interested in identifying structural and macro-level variables impacting African American hiring decisions at the NCAA Division 1 level. The researchers were especially interested in identifying coaching career mobility patterns and perceived barriers to African American coaching success in the sport of NCAA Division I college football.

Getting the Evidence

Subjects

Three 1995–96 African American head football coaches NCAA Division I (Tyrone Willingham, Louisville [currently Stanford]; Jim Caldwell, Wake Forest; Alex Wood, James Madison) and one member of the Black Coaches Association's Board of Directors (Desmond Robinson, Assistant Football Coach, West Virginia University) were requested to participate in a twenty- to thirty-minute telephone interview during the summer of 1996. All interviews were tape recorded.

After reviewing the literature (Banks, 1979; Brooks and Althouse, 1993; Brooks et al. 1989; Ferrell, 1987a and b; Frieschlag and Jacob, 1988; Latimer and Mathes, 1985; Sage, 1980), the researchers developed the following interview questions:

- *Demographic Questions:*
  Current position, years in current position, previous coaching experience, highlights of coaching career, education and playing experience.

- *Interview Questions:*
  1. Over the past three years, have you hired or replaced assistant coaches? If yes, how many?

2. Do you have specific roles and responsibilities for the assistant coaches that you hired? Have these responsibilities changed over time or with different combinations of assistants?

3. How many African American assistant coaches do you have on your staff? How many African American assistant coaches are paid or volunteer?

4. What do you expect from African American assistant coaches? What do they have to do to be successful for your program?

5. What makes a great assistant coach?

6. It has been said that African American assistant coaches legitimize their specific sport programs in the African American community. How would you react to this statement? Would your athletic program be credible without at least an African American assistant coach on your staff?

7. What do you consider to be your strongest coaching attributes during your early career as head coach? Mid-career? Late career?

8. Throughout your career as a head coach, has your relationship with your assistant coach(es) changed? Early career? Mid-career? Late career?

9. Looking back, what got you your first head coaching position?

10. In the near future what *barriers* do African American (men) coaches face at the college level?

11. What actions or strategies should college administrators initiate to address the barriers that you identified (facing African American men) to coaching?

12. What impact, if any, will Title IX have on African American (males) coaching career mobility paths?

The following interview questions were developed for African American assistant coaches:

1. How many African American assistant coaches are on staff or in programs with you?

2. What are your specific roles and responsibilities as assistant coach?

3. Do assistant coaches today need specific ties to certain communities (i.e., New York, Baltimore, Detroit, Chicago) to assist with recruiting assignments?

4. It has been said that African American assistant coaches legitimize their specific sport programs in the African American community. How would you react to this statement?

5. How long can a person afford to be an assistant? Do you think every assistant wants to be or figures he can become a head coach? Do expectations change over career? Early? Mid? Late?
6. What makes a great assistant coach?
7. How do you, as assistant coach, contribute to the overall coaching staff? How much do you expect to gain? How do you opt or attempt to get experience/coaching credentials?
8. In the near future what barriers face African American (men) coaches at the college level?
9. What actions or strategies should college administrators initiate to address the barriers that you identified (facing African American men) to coaching?
10. What impact, if any, will Title IX have on African American (male and female) coaching career mobility paths? What is your reaction to current Title IX regulations on your campus?
11. What advice would you offer young African American (men) seeking jobs as college coaches?

Discussion

The African American head football coaches interviewed were hired within the past three years and are in the process of developing their football programs and evaluating staff performances.

Review of the literature and interview sessions suggested that coaching careers follow numerous pathways and were very much unique to each individual coach. Brooks et al. (1989) interviewed members of the board of directors of the Black Coaches Association in an attempt to map coaching career models of African American assistant coaches. The researchers were able to label four coaching career paths: (1) Blalack's talent model, (2) personal attribute model (coach mobility tied to selected attributes), (3) internal mobility career model (mobility tied to professional networks and decision making), and (4) stem and branch structural model (coaching mobility tied to success of program). The focus of this research was to tie together coaches' personal relations with occupational mobility.

For purposes of this article researchers focused on the career path(s) of selected African American head football coaches utilizing the personal attributes path and the internal mobility coaching career path model.

Personal Attributes of Coaches

The personal attribute model identified by Brooks et al. (1989) and Grenfell and Freischlag (1989) suggested that coaches gain upward mobility to the head coaching ranks as they acquire the attributes necessary to function as a head coach. Coaching interviews conducted for this article tend to support the existence of this model.

African American head football coaches identified specific personal attributes they utilized in selecting assistant coaches. The authors were surprised to learn that personal attributes such as understanding of the coaching profession were not previously identified in the literature. Coach Willingham stated, "I think there are a lot of people who would love to dabble in coaching, believing it is something anyone can do, but it's like any other profession, there is a certain skill that you have to have acquired to really be proficient at it." Other coaching skills identified by Willingham included ability to communicate with young people, positive attitude-positive people, educators, and teachers. Coach Willingham believes his strongest attributes are his ability to concentrate and focus. These same attributes characterized him as a football player at Michigan State University.

Coach Alex Wood utilizes the following attributes when selecting an assistant coach, "I'm looking for good men—good solid, moral, morally upstanding men who love to work with kids. The first and foremost— looking for guys who aspire to be role models, want to be role models and good teachers, and good spirituality about them." For Coach Wood, these attributes are of primary importance and coaching comes second.

Coach Wood identified "persistence, perseverance" and the ability to be mobile as the attributes that he used to achieve his goal of becoming a head coach. He stated that you have to go where the jobs are and you have to be patient. In our interview with Coach Wood, he expressed a love for coaching and working with young athletes that echoed throughout the interview session. "All I want to do is work with kids and coach people like I was coached when I was coming up."

In summary, the head football coaches were able to identify personal attributes that they looked for in hiring assistant coaches. These findings tend to support previous research (Banks, 1979; Freischlag and Jacob, 1988; Grenfell and Freischlag, 1989). Coaches believe that selected personal attributes are directly associated with coaching success.

The reader should be cautioned that the personal attribute coaching career model does not fully explain head coaching success. Brooks et al. (1989) found that variables such as "ability to 'fit-in' the situation" and "compatibility with the athletic director" were additional factors in becoming a head coach.

It became very apparent throughout the interview session that it was important for the head coaches to gain valuable coaching experience throughout their career. The job responsibilities of the coaches included: (1) graduate assistant, (2) offensive coordinator/ defensive coordinator, (3) recruiting, and (4) coaching experience on the offensive and defensive side of the ball.

Internal Coaching Career Mobility Patterns

Coaching mobility may depend on recruiting network ties and communication lines with individuals in decision-making positions (i.e., athletic directors, presidents) (Brooks and Althouse, 1993; Brooks and Althouse, in press). Coaching mobility may be tied to other variables such as success of the head coach, prestige of the institution, and type of institution (public or private).

The African American assistant and head coaches interviewed tended to follow the regional nature of college coaching career mobility. The coaches often changed coaching assignments (four or five times) prior to becoming a head coach. The coaches demonstrated significant ties to their alma mater, by first being employed by their alma mater as graduate assistants or assistant coaches.

Highlighting this point, Stanford University's head football coach, with seventeen years coaching experience, began as a graduate assistant at Michigan State University. After four months he moved to a full-time job at Central Michigan University. After a brief stay, he returned to Michigan State as a full-time coach. Additional career changes took Coach Willingham to North Carolina State University, Rice University, Stanford University, the NFL, and back to Stanford University as head football coach.

Head Coach Alex Wood of James Madison University followed a similar coaching career path, holding numerous assistant head coaching positions throughout the country. He initially played football at the University of Iowa, became a graduate assistant coach at Iowa in 1978, and after graduating from college, he held an entry level coaching position at Kent State University coaching tight ends and wide receivers (1979). Followed by coaching on defense at Southern Illinois (1981), Coach Wood became the defensive coordinator at HBCU Southern

University (1982). After leaving Southern, he went to Wyoming (1985–86) where he coached on the offense side of the ball to "gain more experience and prepare myself for the position that I presently hold" (Head Football Coach, James Madison University). Additional coaching employment opportunities took him to Washington State University for two years with the responsibility of recruiting coordinator. From Washington State he went to the University of Miami (running back coach) for four years, and from Miami he went to Wake Forest University (1993–94) where he became the offensive coordinator for two years, and is now in his second year as the head coach at James Madison University.

Jim Caldwell, head football coach, Wake Forest University, began his coaching career as a graduate assistant at the University of Iowa. Jim's coaching career path was as follows: Southern Illinois University (secondary coach and defensive coordinator), Northwestern University (secondary coach under Dennis Green), University of Colorado (quarterback coach and receivers under Bill McCartney), University of Louisville (secondary coach under Howard Snellenberger), and Penn State University (under Joe Paterno for seven years coaching wide receivers and quarterbacks).

When selecting an assistant coach, Coach Caldwell looks for individuals who are loyal, dedicated to improving themselves, and who have the ability to communicate with players. Coach Caldwell believes his strongest personal assets are his organizational, leadership, and communication skills. He also stated that it is important to be marketable, have technical knowledge about x's and o's, and the desire to improve oneself.

An analysis of the coaches' career paths revealed some very enlightening information. First, coaches realized the importance of networking and its relationship with career development. Coaches were able to gain employment at a variety of very prestigious Division I institutions (i.e., Michigan State, Washington State, Wake Forest, Miami, North Carolina) prior to becoming head football coach at their current institutions. The ability to serve as an assistant coach under the direction of successful head coaches such as Darrell Rogers, Dennis Green, Billy McCartney, Joe Paterno, and Duffy Daugherty had a positive impact on their coaching mobility success. It does appear that being associated with a "big time" athletic program and nationally recognized head coach did increase the coaches' chances of becoming a head football coach. The assistant coaches were themselves labeled as successful coaches by their peers in the profession.

In summary, throughout their coaching careers the African American coaches did expand personal acquaintances with other head coaches and assistant coaches. In an attempt to build the pool of potential future African American head coaches, the coaches hired African American assistant coaches to fill a variety of coaching responsibilities. The role of graduate assistant continues to be the first level of entry into the coaching ranks. Any legislation aimed at reducing the number of graduate assistants will have a negative impact of expanding the potential pool of African American coaches (Farrell, 1993b). Marian Washington, past president of the Black Coaches Association, reported that the graduate position has been one major avenue to assist black coaches to gain entrance into the athletic arena (Farrell, 1993b). It is an obvious fact that serving as a graduate assistant coach serves a vital link in providing the novice coach with valuable experiences. According to Jim Caldwell, the graduate assistant position, "Allows individuals to serve an apprenticeship in preparation to become a college football coach" (Farrell, 1993b, p. 42). In addition to the graduate assistant role, the offensive/defensive coordinator position is all-critical to achieving head coaching success. It appears that occupying the role of offensive or defensive coordinator is a control "node" point in becoming a head coach in NCAA Division I football. The coordinators have major leadership responsibilities with the organization, and these roles are central to the success of the program. Efforts must be expanded to move African American assistant coaches into these positions.

None of the coaching models presented to date clearly explains head coaching mobility success. Football is a very complex organization employing a large staff of assistant coaches, athletic trainers, team physicians, recruiting specialists, academic support staff, and business office. Coaching careers within a complex organization such as football is going to differ significantly from careers followed by basketball, baseball, or track, and field head and assistant coaches. An alternative coaching career model must be developed that continues to integrate macro- and micro-level variability.

Conclusion

In summary, over the past five years African Americans have achieved a level of success in being assistant basketball coaches and head basketball coaches. Unfortunately, NCAA Division I football has been slow in hiring African Americans as head coaches. Other nonrevenue sports such as baseball, swimming, golf, wrestling, volleyball, and gymnastics have also witnessed the underutilization of African American head coaches. NCAA Division I football, which represents a multimillion dollar industry, is labeled by some researchers as a "cartel," and has been requested to address its hiring practices and to take corrective action. The NCAA and the Black Coaches Association have been vigilant in monitoring the hiring practices of member institutions. An interview with assistant football coach Desmond Robinson, West Virginia University, and Coach Alex Wood, both of whom are board members of the Black Coaches' Association and original members, reminded us, the purpose of the organization was to organize African American coaches—men and women—in all sports from college to high school, and to intervene whenever the organization can to provide African Americans in positions of authority, and to make sure there was fair treatment across the board. The Black Coaches' Association continues to be an advocate for minority hiring practices within the NCAA and high schools, and will play a pivotal role in assisting African American coaching mobility.

The interview sessions and the literature revealed that African American football head coaching success is tied to professional network contact, previous playing and coaching experience, and affiliation with "big time" football programs. It also became apparent that coaching mobility is associated with previous experience as an offensive and defensive coordinator. It is therefore unlikely that we should expect to see additional African American head football coaches unless they get this coaching experience. Similarly, Anderson (1993) concluded that race does function to keep African Americans out of these positions.

Turning our attention to the role of the historically black colleges and universities (HBCUs), the authors believe they share some of the burden to help increase the number of African American head coaches not only on their own campus but also on the predominantly white campuses as well. The Black Coaches' Association is undertaking more positive efforts to include the HBCUs in its attempts to increase opportunities for African American coaches (Farrell, 1993). Marian Washington (1992 BCA president) is given credit for mending fences with the HBCU coaches. Fence-mending is needed according to Ken Free, former commissioner of the Mid-Eastern Athletic Conference, because, "There is some concern that an organization representing black coaches should include head coaches at HBCUs" (Ferrell, 1993, p. 13). It was agreed that African American coaches located at black institutions do represent a pool of knowledge and information that would assist this mission of the Black Coaches' Association. Marian Washington pledged that under her administration more effort will be offered to include historical black colleges in planning and decision-making processes.

For those administrators truly interested in hiring more African American coaches, we draw attention to the proactive initiatives at Temple University. Temple University has been very successful in its efforts to identify and hire African American men and women head coaches. In 1993, Temple had the following head coaches on staff: Ron Dickerson–football; John Chaney–basketball; Nikki Franks–fencing, and Tina Sloan Green–lacrosse. Temple president Peter J. Liacouras said, "Race has nothing to do with it. Temple has picked the right people who have varying degrees of success and the coaches who are African American had to be successful. Of course, we have a commitment to opening up opportunities for people who are highly skilled, and for some blacks it is an opportunity to realize their full potential" (Farrell, 1993a, p. 29).

Temple University seems to be successful in hiring African American head coaches because central administration and the athletic director are committed to diversifying its coaching ranks, and Temple has a long distinguished history of providing opportunities to minorities through its outreach mission.

College administrators are requested to establish "affirmative action," "proactive recruiting" programs to attract and hire African American males to various head coaching positions, especially football (Brooks and Althouse, 1993; Shropshire, 1996). All efforts must be taken to break down the "old boy" subculture and "old-boy" hiring network (Boeck and Shuster, 1991; Sperber, 1990). Sperber's (1990) image of the coach subculture is one of white middle-aged males. Unfortunately, according to Sperber, coaches and athletic directors perpetuate their subculture by hiring their duplicates. This condition is important since the turnover rate of Division 1-A football coaches remains an average of 2.8 years (Sperber, 1990). Coaches do leave their positions for a variety of reasons (financial, family, new job offer). However, many of these coaches rotate from Division I institutions to the next, resulting in few actual vacancies being filled by novice or less experienced coaches including African American coaches.

Looking toward the future, the coaches were optimistic about coaching opportunities for African American men. However, they all realize that NCAA legislation (any attempt to reduce the number of graduate assistants), Title IX and gender equity, and the "big-business" aspect of

NCAA Division I football will impact future hiring opportunities. Coach Caldwell echoed, "I am optimistic in terms of what's been happening with our profession.... I think in 1992 when there weren't any African American head coaches [football] in Division I, and now we are increasing the number steadily."

Assistant football coach Desmond Robinson is under the opinion that having a positive attitude and the belief that you will achieve are keys to coaching success. He concluded that the biggest barrier to achieving a head coaching position is yourself and not race.

The coaches did admit there is pressure to win, produce revenue, and put a quality "product" on the field. The football organization supports 85 scholarship players, a large secretarial staff, a recruiting staff, equipment staff, and various other support individuals (i.e., ground crew). Therefore, the head coach's knowledge and skills must go beyond "technical" knowledge about the game of football. It is important for potential African American head coaches to recognize and prepare themselves for this aspect of their coaching responsibilities.

Finally, Title IX and gender equity are already having an impact on male coaching careers. It is the sense of the coaches that all legislation should be about enhancing opportunity and not denying opportunity. It is important for college athletic programs to reward talent (men and women). At the same time, it is important to realize that the men's revenue sport programs are the primary fund raisers in Division I athletics. There is general support for the concept and principles of Title IX and gender equity. Yet there is some fear that funding may not be available to support the current levels of men's and women's athletic programs. Reduced funding may result in cuts to coaching staffs, reduction in the number of graduate assistants or the elimination of some men's athletic programs. There are real concerns and issues that must be addressed individually on each campus.

To paraphrase Dr. Martin Luther King, Jr., the African American coaches have a dream that they will not be judged by the color of their skin but by the content of their character.

There has been some progress made in the hiring of African Americans to head coaching positions. The social justice in football is on the opponents 10-yard line (in the red zone). Scoring means eradicating all forms of injustice existing in the NCAA structure and reaffirming its commitment to a diversified coaching staff.

According to Anderson (1993), vertical mobility of African American athletes to a position of dominance (coaching and administration) remains constricted. Institutional racism remains and appears to have a possible impact on athletic coaching career mobility especially in the sport of NCAA Division 1-A football.

References

Anderson, D. (1993, April). "Cultural Diversity on Campus: A Look at Intercollegiate Football Coaches." *Journal of Sport and Social Issues,* 17(1): 61–46.

BAC Journal. (1996). "Are We Making Progress?" Vol. 3, No. 1 (April): 7.

Banks, O. (1979). "How Black Coaches View Entering the Job Market at Major Colleges. *Journal of Physical Education and Recreation,* 50: 62.

Bell, D. (1992). *Faces at the Bottom of the Well: The Permanence of Racism.* New York, NY: Basic Books.

Benson, M. T. (1994). The Sports and Recreational Programs of the Nation's Universities and Colleges, Report #8, 1957–1992. The National Collegiate Athletic Association, Overland, KS.

Berghom, F., Yetman, N., and Hanna, W. (1988). "Racial Participation and Integration in Men's and Women's Intercollegiate Basketball: Continuity and Change, 1958–1989." *Sociology of Sport Journal,* 5: 107–124.

Boeck, G., and Shuster, R. (1991, March 19). "College 'Old Boy Network' Hard to Crack." *USA Today,* 11A.

Brooks, D., and Althouse, R. (1993). "Racial Imbalance in Coaching and Managerial Positions." In D. Brooks and R. Althouse, *Racism in College Athletics: The African American Athlete's Experience,* pp. 101–142. Morgantown, WV: Fitness Information Technology.

———. (In press). "The African American Coaching Experience: A Case of Social Injustice?" *Trends and Issues Affecting Ethnic Minority Populations in Health, Physical Education, Recreation and Dance.* Reston, VA: AAHPERD.

Brooks, D., Althouse, R., King, V., and Brown, R. (1989). "Opportunities for Coaching Achievement and the Black Experience. Have We Put Marginality into the System?" Proceedings of the 32nd Annual ICHPER Conference, 246–254.

Brown, B. (1992, September 25). "Study: Minorities Missing from Top Jobs at Colleges." *USA Today,* 7C.

Campbell, R.M. (1995, October 9). "Five New Division I Football Coaches Unbeaten So Far." *The NCAA News,* 32(35), 10.

Chronicle of Higher Education. (1994). "The Proportion of Black People among Sports Administrators at Member Institutions of the National Collegiate Athletic Association has Changed Little Over the Past Four Years, According to a Study by a Panel of the Association." (September 14): 62.

——— (1992). "And Then There Were None." (January 29): A36.

Chu, D. B., and Segrave, J. O. (1981). "Leadership and Ethnic Stratification in Basketball." *Journal of Sport and Social Issues,* 5(1): 15–32.

Coakley, J. J. (1994). *Sport In Society: Issues and Controversies,* 5th edition. Philadelphia: Mosby-Year Book, Inc.

Curtis, J. E., and Loy, J.W. (1978). "Race/Ethnicity and Relative Centrality of Playing Positions in Team Sports." *Exercise and Sport Science Review,* 6: 285–313.

Daily News. (1992). "Bottom Line is 0-for-106: Colleges Come Up Empty." (August 28): 82.

D'Souza, D. (1995). *The End of Racism: Principles for a Multiracial Society.* New York: The Free Press.

Davis, T. (1994, Winter). "Intercollegiate Athletics: Competing Models and Conflicting Realities." *Rutgers Law Journal,* 25(2): 269–327.

Dent, D. (1987). "Black Coaches Remain Scarce in College Ranks." *Black Enterprise,* 18(5): 34.

Ebony. (1986). "A Boom in Black Coaches." (April): 59–62.

———. (1982). "Black Head Coaches: Taking Charge on Major Campuses." (May): 57–62.

Edwards, H. (1973). *Sociology of Sport.* Chicago, Illinois: Daisy Press.

Eitzen, D. S., and David, C. S. (1975). "The Segregation of Blacks by Playing Positions in Football: Accident or Design?" *Social Science Quarterly,* 55: 948–59.

Eitzen, D. S., and Tessendorf, I. (1978). "Racial Segregation by Position in Sports: The Special Care of Basketball." *Review of Sport & Leisure,* 3(1): 109–128.

Eitzen, D.S., and Yetman, N. R. (1977). "Immune from Racism." *Civil Rights Digest,* 9, 3d3.

Ferrell, C. S. (1987a, May 6). "Scarcity of Blacks in Top Jobs in College Sports Prompts Founding of Group to Monitor Hiring." *The Chronicle of Higher Education,* 40–42.

———. (1987b, September 23). "NCAA Effort to Spur Black-Coach Hiring Gets Mixed Reviews. *The Chronicle of Higher Education,* A39, A40.

———. (1992, August 13). "Black Coaches Association to Mend Fences with Historically Black Colleges." *Black Issues In Higher Education,* 9,13.

———. (1993a, January 14). "Temple Sets Precedent in Hiring of Black Coaches." *Black Issues in Higher Education,* 9, 29–31.

———. (1993b, July 15). "College Football to Fight for Graduate Assistant Positions: Proposal Would Ensure Minority Participation in Coaching Pipeline." *Black Issues in Higher Education,* 10, 40–43.

———. (1994, September 22). "NCAA: Blacks Make the Plays But Call Few of the Shots." *Black Issues in Higher Education,* 11: 34–36.

———. (1995, September 7). "Progress Yes, But...." *Black Issues in Higher Education,* 12: 32–34.

Frieschlag, J., and Jacob, R. (1988). "Developmental Factors among College Men Basketball Coaches." *Journal of Applied Research In Coaching and Athletics,* 3(2): 87–93.

Grenfell, C., and Freischlag, J. (1989). "Developmental Pathways of Men's and Women's College Basketball Coaches." Unpublished paper presented at the MHPERD Convention, Boston, MA, April, 1989.

Jet. (1979). "NCAA's First Black Head Football Coach is Ready to Tackle the Pressure." (March 22): 48.

Journal of Blacks in Higher Education. (1993–1994). "Vital Signs: Statistics that Suggest a Measure of Racial Inequality," Volume 2 (Winter): 38.

Lapchick, R. (1989, Spring). "Future of Black Student: Ethical Issues of the 1990's." *Educational Record,* 32–35.

Lapchick, R. (1991). *Five Minutes to Midnight-Race and Sport in the 1990's.* New York: Madison Books.

Latimer, S., and Mathes, S. (1985). "Black College Football Coaches Social, Educational, Athletic and Career Pattern Characteristics." *Journal of Sport Behavior,* 8(3): 149–162.

National Collegiate Athletic Association (1994). NCAA Divisional Graduate-Rates Report. Overland, Kansas, June.

NCAA Council Subcommittee (1991). Final report of the NCAA Council Subcommittee to review minority opportunities in intercollegiate athletics. Opryland Hotel, Nashville, Tennessee, January 5–6.

NCAA Council Subcommittee (1988). Summary of the survey of NCAA member institutes and conferences on minority representation: Report to the NCAA council subcommittee to review minority opportunities in intercollegiate athletics. Mission, Kansas, August.

NCAA News (1994a). "BCA to Analyze Hiring Practices at 10 Universities." Vol. 31, No. 45 (December 14): 16.

NCAA News (1994b). "Minority Members in Athletic Administration Unchanged." Vol. 31, No. 30 (August 17): 5, 13.

Reed, W. (1990, November 26). "Equality Begins at Home: It's Time to Give Black Football Coaches a Chance." *Sports Illustrated*, 73(22): 138.

Sage, G. (1980). "Sociology of Physical Educator/Coaches: Personal Attributes Controversy." *Research Quarterly for Exercise and Sport*, 51 (1): 110–121.

Shropshire, K. L. (1996, January). "Merit, Ol' Boy Networks and the Black Bottomed Pyramid." *Hastings Law Journal*, 47(2): 455–472.

Sperber, M. (1990). *College Sports Inc.: The Athletic Department vs. The University*. New York: Henry Holt and Company.

Wulf, S. (1987). "Opportunity Knocks (NCAA to Work for Black Coaches)." *Sports Illustrated*, 5.

VI

Professional Sports:
Chasing the Dream

15

Race, Sport, and Future Orientation

Othello Harris

One of the most important beliefs in America is that personal striving results in upward mobility; it is the essence of the American dream. But American society, like other human societies, is characterized by stratification—that is, "differential access to whatever is of value in the society at a given point and over time, primarily because of social, not biopsychological variables" (Rossides, 1976:15). Whether this inequality is explained in functionalist terms (i.e., social inequality ensures that the most important societal positions are filled by the most qualified persons), from a Marxian perspective (i.e., social stratification is the result of different groups' relationship to the means of production), or some other perspective (e.g., the Weberian view that stratification is the result of the interaction of class, status, and power), the issue of stratification is one of the central, enduring themes of sociology (Giddens, 1991).

While most Americans recognize a class system in the United States (as indicated by the common use of such terms as "the upper-middle class," "the lower class," etc.) many still consider American society to be an open one. For the ambitious, prepared, and skilled, there are avenues to improve class standing. One need look no further than the Horatio Alger novels for examples of how hard work and virtue allow talented people to rise from humble beginnings to success. Sports are presumed to be one path to success.

The conventional view of sports suggests several ways in which sports involvement can lead to personal success and upward mobility. First, athletic participation may contribute to the development of abilities, attitudes, and behavior patterns that are valued in the occupational world (e.g., leadership skills). Second, athletic participation may allow one

241

to earn an athletic scholarship, which may lead to the attainment of academic degrees or the acquisition of marketable skills. Third, athletic participation may be a route to occupational sponsorship—i.e., athletes may benefit from nonathletic jobs as a result of their visibility from and association with sports. Fourth, athletic participation may lead to a career in professional sports (Loy, 1968).

A number of studies have found support for the idea that sports are a vehicle of social mobility. Loy (1972) found that former university athletes experienced a high degree of social mobility when their occupational status scores were compared to their fathers'. (Loy, however, used no comparison group—he did not compare fathers' and sons' scores for the general student population at the university.) In a more recent study, Eisen and Turner (1992) reported that former Olympians exhibited an impressive rise in socioeconomic standing relative to their parents and the public. Most subjects in their study found that Olympic participation facilitated occupational attainment.

Haerle (1975: 375) argues that sports ability and participation "may compensate for the possible handicap of social class and may overcome the negative educational consequences of lower social status." Athletics, that is, may draw some academically marginal young people into the educational mainstream. Indeed, several studies have shown educational aspirations to be enhanced by participation in sports, especially among those who would, by family background, seem to be least disposed to college (Rehberg and Schafer, 1968; Schafer and Rehberg, 1970; Spreitzer and Pugh, 1973; Otto and Alwin, 1977; and Bend and Petrie, 1978).

However, much of the more recent research on sports and social mobility questions the role of sports in social advancement (Greendorfer, 1987), especially as it concerns upward mobility for African American males (Leonard, 1997; Edwards, 1984; Curry and Jiobu, 1984). Wells and Picou (1980) argue that many of the benefits typically associated with sports participation (e.g., higher educational aspirations and higher g.p.a.s) accrue to Caucasian males only. Gaston (1984) states that popular culture and organized sports contribute to the destruction of African American males. The media participate in the production and maintenance of African American males' fantasies of participating in professional sport while contributing nothing to their interest in other, perhaps more achievable, professions.

Sport may well be a visible mobility channel for African American youth. Snyder and Spreitzer (1983) suggest that sport is an activity on which many young black males focus their energy and future aspirations. It is one of the few occupational systems that offers a substantial number of success models for African Americans. Although African Americans are approximately 14 percent of the U.S. population (U.S. Bureau of the Census, 1995) they are approximately 24 percent, 60 percent and 80 percent of the professional baseball, football, and basketball players, respectively (Coakley, 1996). This "black dominance" in the three major professional sports—baseball, football, and basketball—has led to a number of explanations for this phenomenon. Among these are: (1) genetic or physiological explanations—African Americans have certain innate physical characteristics that make them better suited for sports (Kane, 1971); (2) psychological explanations (e.g., African Americans have a greater ability to relax under pressure) (Kane, 1971); (3) historical-genetic explanations—African Americans were bred for activities that require physical abilities as a result of slavery where only the fittest survived (Kane, 1971); and (4) sociological explanations—sport is one of the few institutions open to African Americans for achievement.

The sociological explanation, according to Edwards (1979) accounts for the channeling of millions of African Americans into athletic career aspirations. The high visibility of African American athletes and the low visibility of other successful African Americans (such as African American executives and other professionals) in American society accentuates the restricted focus of African American youth on sports (Lapchick, 1984).

McPherson (1971) says sports offer actual opportunities for upward mobility to only a minority of African Americans. And, this upward mobility is of short duration followed, typically, by a return to the athlete's original class position. Edwards (1976) sees sports as an impediment to achievement in other areas by African Americans—it stifles the pursuit of rational alternatives by African Americans. Scott (1971), whose position is similar to Edwards's, reports that for every African American person taken from the ghetto by an athletic scholarship, hundreds of lower-class youths have wasted their lives futilely preparing to be sports stars. Whether one accepts the sport-impedes-mobility or the sport-enhances-mobility thesis (Braddock, 1980), the literature suggests that sport is an attractive career goal to many young African American males.

This research examines African American and Caucasian high school basketball players' perceptions of sports as an avenue of social mobility.

It also investigates the effect of school type—public or private—for evidence of a conditional relationship between race and sport orientation.

Variables and Measurement in the Sample

The data for this study were collected from two male high school summer basketball leagues in Washington, D.C. These leagues attract the top area teams. All coaches in these leagues were contacted and informed about the survey. A total of 23 teams—all of the teams in both leagues—agreed to participate in the study. The teams included both public and private schools. Data were obtained from 19 of the teams. The return rate was 64.3%.

The sample consists of 187 basketball players in grades nine through twelve. One hundred sixteen (63.4%) were African American and 59 (32.2%) were Caucasian. Twelve (6.4%) were "other." (Because of the small number of cases and the variation in this category, they were not analyzed.) Eight (4.6%) were 9th graders; 25 (14.5%) were 10th graders; 59 (34.1%) were 11th graders; and 81 (46.8%) were 12th graders. Both structured and open-ended questions were used to investigate the self-images, aspirations, and family background of the students. All students who participated did so voluntarily and were assured of anonymity.

In this study two types of measures were used: single items and a Guttman-type scale. Guttman scaling assumes a priori ordering of the items; knowing one's total score should allow us to predict his responses to each individual item (Guy et al., 1987). The items used for this scale fit the assumption of a cumulative continuum making Guttman scale a practical choice. The coefficient of reproducibility and the coefficient of scalability were calculated. They are reported in the text following the scale items.

The literature suggests that African Americans may place a disproportionate emphasis on sport as an avenue of mobility and success. The issue, from the standpoint of this research, is whether perception of sport as a success route contributes to African American motivation for participation in sport. Specific research questions include the following:

- Is sport seen as the best route to success for African Americans?
- Are African Americans more likely to perceive basketball as a means to a college education?
- Are African Americans more likely to expect to become professional athletes?

- Are African Americans more likely to be motivated to play by these considerations?

Sport as a Mobility Route for African Americans

The following question was used to determine whether students in the study perceived sport as being especially strategic for the mobility and success of African Americans:

Some people feel that, for African Americans, sports are the best route to success; the best way out of poverty and despair. How do you feel about this idea?

Strongly agree   ❏   Disagree   ❏
Agree   ❏   Strongly disagree ❏

Reasons for Playing Basketball

Student-athletes' motivations were explored with the item below, which was designed to represent a range of possible reasons for involvement in basketball:

Would you say that a big reason you play basketball is that:

	Very true	Pretty true	Not very true	Not at all true
I enjoy it.	❏	❏	❏	❏
I hope to get a college scholarship.	❏	❏	❏	❏
I get a chance to show my talents.	❏	❏	❏	❏
I learn to work towards team goals.	❏	❏	❏	❏
I plan to play basketball in college.	❏	❏	❏	❏
I learn to control my emotions.	❏	❏	❏	❏
I get to release my frustrations.	❏	❏	❏	❏

The Pro-Future Scale

Three items were selected to measure student-athletes' aspirations toward a professional sports career. These items were combined to create a pro-future scale. The following three items were selected: 1. "Would you like to become a professional athlete someday? [ ] No [ ] Yes"; 2. "(If yes): How much would you like to be a professional athlete? [ ] Very much [ ] Pretty much [ ] Somewhat"; and 3. "What do you think your chances are of becoming a professional athlete? [ ] Very good [ ] Pretty good [ ] Not very good."

These items were dichotomized with yes = 1, no = 0 for question 1. For question 2, very much = 1, all other responses = 0. And for question 3, very good = 1, all other responses = 0. Scores were then added across items that produced a Guttman scale with scores ranging from 0 to 3. Twenty-six percent of the respondents scored 0, 29% scored 1, 38% scored 2, and 7% scored 3 on the scale. The coefficient of reproducibility is 92%; the coefficient of scalability is 75%.

Background Characteristics

This section deals with the relationships among some of the background characteristics of the athletes and the major variables central to this research. The concern here was to describe the sample in some detail, to indicate how African American and Caucasian student-athletes differ with regard to some basic demographic factors, and to identify some of the important features of the public-private school context conditional variable. Table 1 presents percentage differences by race for three family background variables and five measures of racial composition of different aspects of the students' lives.

A slightly higher percentage of African Americans than Caucasians (67.2% to 59.3%) attend public schools. As Table 1 shows, the data on family background suggest that African Americans are more likely to come from less privileged settings. They are much more likely to live in a father-absent household, and are less likely to have mothers or fathers with formal education beyond a high school diploma. This race difference is especially pronounced among those in public schools. The private school context appears to include students from higher status backgrounds. Race differences among these students are significantly different only on their father's education. Here nearly all (96%) of the Caucasian students have fathers with some college training while about two-thirds (65%) of the African Americans have fathers with some college training.

The data on racial composition suggest African Americans and Caucasians live in quite different social worlds. Very few Caucasians live in mostly black neighborhoods, attend mostly black schools, or have

TABLE 1
Race by Selected Family and Integration Control Variables

	ALL			
	Percent		N	
	White	Black	White	Black
Father Absence	10	46	(55)	(93)
Mother's ED(>HS)	75	52	(59)	(109)
Father's ED(>HS)	86	52	(59)	(109)

	PUBLIC				PRIVATE			
	Percent		N		Percent		N	
	White	Black	White	Black	White	Black	White	Black
Father Absence	9	56	(32)	(63)	9	27	(23)	(30)
Mother's ED(>HS)	71	39	(35)	(71)	79	71	(24)	(38)
Father's ED(>HS)	80	44	(35)	(71)	96	65	(24)	(37)

	ALL			
	Percent		N	
	White	Black	White	Black
MOSTLY OR ALL BLACK NEIGHBORHOOD	3	71	(59)	(116)
HIGH SCHOOL	2	46	(59)	(116)
TEACHERS	2	35	(59)	(116)
COACHES	5	50	(59)	(116)
TEAM	29	80	(59)	(115)

	PUBLIC				PRIVATE			
	Percent		N		Percent		N	
	White	Black	White	Black	White	Black	White	Black
MOSTLY OR ALL BLACK NEIGHBORHOOD	3	74	(35)	(78)	4	63	(24)	(38)
HIGH SCHOOL	3	64	(35)	(78)	0	8	(24)	(38)
TEACHERS	3	49	(35)	(78)	0	0	(24)	(38)
COACHES	3	64	(35)	(78)	8	21	(24)	(38)
TEAM	23	82	(35)	(77)	37	76	(24)	(38)

African American teachers or coaches. The Caucasian students do report more contact with African Americans as members of basketball teams, where nearly 30% report most of the members of their high school team are African American.

The responses of the African American students suggest much more variation in the racial composition of their social worlds. Most African American students are members of largely African American basketball teams and come from mostly black neighborhoods, although fewer African Americans report having mainly African American coaches or attending a mostly black high school (50% and 46%, respectively). Finally, most African American students report having predominantly Caucasian teachers. Only 35% of the African American students say their teachers are mostly or all African American.

These composition differences, like the family background differences, are greatest in the public school context. Public school Caucasians have little exposure to predominantly black worlds, except on the basketball team, and public school African Americans are most likely to live in black worlds.

In the private context, more complex patterns appear, especially for the African American students. Private school Caucasians are much like public school Caucasians with exposure to African Americans limited to the basketball team. Private school African Americans are markedly different from Caucasians only on the neighborhood and basketball team members measures; they are more likely to come from neighborhoods and play for teams that are mostly or all black. Looking at public and private school African Americans, it is clear that private school African Americans are less likely to attend mostly black schools, and have teachers and coaches of their racial group. Thus, private schools draw African American students from mostly black neighborhoods but create a higher exposure to Caucasian students, teachers, and coaches.

Data Analysis Strategy

The format of data presentation is percentage distributions of questionnaire item responses by race, with a summary statistic, Pearson r, that indicates the strength and significance of any differences. After comparing African Americans and Caucasians in the total sample, the sample was stratified by type of school and investigated, again for race differences. That is, we asked, "Are the differences or lack thereof conditional by school context?" The study also examined school context differences after stratifying by race to see if there are significant differences within a race group by school context. This produced the following comparisons: (1) African American/Caucasian comparisons for the entire sample; (2) African American/Caucasian comparisons for public schools and for private schools; and (3) public/private school comparisons for African Americans and for Caucasians.

Other Independent Variables

Following the investigation of school context differences, a set of independent variables—family factors—were introduced (i.e., father's absence, father's education, and mother's education); their effects on the dependent variables were assessed. At this stage partial r's were selected for the summary statistic. The tables are stratified by type of school, and by family variables.

Findings

As Table 2 indicates, the majority of African Americans and Caucasians believe that sport is the best mobility route for African Americans. There is no statistically significant race difference in perceptions of sport as a mobility channel for African Americans. (However, African Americans were more likely to have stronger opinions about the mobility issue, pro or con, than Caucasians.)

TABLE 2
Beliefs about Sport as the Best Mobility Route for Blacks by Race

	Race	
	White	Black
	%	%
Response Categories	(N)	(N)
Strongly Disagree	3.4	10.4
	(2)	(12)
Disagree	34.5	27.0
	(20)	(31)
Agree	50.0	40.9
	(29)	(47)
Strongly Agree	12.1	21.7
	(7)	(25)

$r = .02$, N.S.

TABLE 3
Reasons for Playing Basketball: Percent Responding "Very True"

Reasons for Playing	% (N)
Enjoy	88.6 (155)
Team	56.6 (99)
Scholarship	50.6 (88)
Talent	45.1 (79)
College	44.3 (77)
Control	24.1 (42)
Release	20.6 (36)

If sport is viewed as an avenue of mobility for African Americans, are there race differences in the reasons athletes give for playing basketball? Are African Americans more likely than Caucasians to play basketball for instrumental reasons—for reasons that suggest future involvement in sport at a higher level?

Table 3 shows the reasons the students give for playing basketball. (Note: this table is organized by the proportion saying a particular reason is "very true.") Before examining African American/Caucasian differences, it should be noted that the top two reasons are personal enjoyment and working toward team goals. At least two of the next three reasons are instrumental (implying a future in basketball, at least at the college level): hopes of getting a scholarship, plans to play basketball in college, and display of basketball talents. The least endorsed reasons concern control of emotions and release of frustrations.

As Table 4 indicates, African Americans are more likely than Caucasians to say it is very true that being a member of the basketball team helps them learn to work toward team goals, by a difference of 64% to 25%. African Americans were also more certain (a) that one of the reasons for playing basketball was to earn a college scholarship (65% to 41%); (b) that getting a chance to show talents was a reason for

TABLE 4
Reasons for Playing Basketball by Race

	Enjoy		Team		Scholarship	
	White % (N)	Black % (N)	White % (N)	Black % (N)	White % (N)	Black % (N)
Response Categories						
Not true at all	0.0 (0)	0.7 (1)	13.6 (8)	7.0 (8)	3.4 (2)	1.7 (2)
Not very true	0.0 (0)	2.6 (3)	32.2 (19)	9.6 (11)	1.7 (1)	3.4 (4)
Pretty true	6.8 (4)	10.3 (12)	28.8 (17)	20.0 (23)	54.2 (32)	30.2 (35)
Very true	93.2 (55)	86.2 (100)	25.4 (15)	63.5 (73)	40.7 (24)	64.7 (75)
	$r = -.12$		$r = .18**$		$r = .35***$	

Talent Control				College Release			
	White % (N)	Black % (N)	White % (N)	Black % (N)	White % (N)	Black % (N)	White % (N)	Black % (N)
Not true at all	3.4 (2)	1.7 (2)	15.3 (9)	6.1 (7)	13.8 (8)	7.8 (9)	25.4 (15)	27.6 (32)
Not very true	11.9 (7)	6.9 (8)	28.8 (17)	13.9 (16)	34.5 (20)	20.7 (24)	33.9 (20)	32.8 (38)
Pretty true	54.2 (32)	38.8 (45)	30.5 (18)	26.1 (30)	36.2 (21)	43.1 (50)	18.6 (11)	19.8 (23)
Very true	30.5 (18)	52.6 (61)	25.4 (15)	53.9 (62)	15.5 (9)	28.4 (33)	22.0 (13)	19.8 (23)
	$r = .20**$		$r = .29***$		$r = .20**$		$r = -.02$	

Note: **p < .01; ***p < .001.

playing basketball (53% to 31%); (c) about plans to play basketball in college (54% to 25%); and (d) that basketball involvement helps them to control emotions (28% to 16%). All the above relationships are statistically significant beyond the .01 level. In sum, African Americans are more likely to report playing basketball for reasons that clearly involve an anticipated future in basketball. These reasons indicate instrumental concerns—African Americans more than Caucasians play because they hope to get a college scholarship, they plan to play basketball in college, and they get a chance to show their talent. Caucasians were slightly more likely than African Americans to endorse enjoyment as a reason for playing basketball.

It has been found that the majority of African Americans and Caucasians see sport as the best route to social mobility for African Americans, and that African American and Caucasian student-athletes have different motives for playing basketball. Do African Americans have different future orientations toward sport than Caucasians? Are African American high school basketball players more likely than Caucasian high school basketball players to see professional basketball in their future?

Table 5 shows African Americans were more likely than Caucasians to score high on the pro-future scale. Eleven percent of African Americans and 2% of Caucasians scored at the highest level on the index, while 23% of African Americans and 34% of Caucasians scored at the lowest level. Furthermore, slightly more than half the African Americans (54%) had scores in the upper half of the pro-future scale, while more than two-thirds (68%) of the Caucasians had scores in the lower half. The Pearson r for the relationship is .20, and it is statistically significant beyond the .01 level.

To summarize, we found no race difference in perceptions about sport as a mobility route for African Americans; African Americans

TABLE 5
Pro-Future Scale by Race

		Race	
		White	Black
		%	%
Response	Categories	(N)	(N)
Low	0.	33.9	23.2
		(20)	(26)
	1.	33.9	23.2
		(20)	(26)
	2.	30.5	42.9
		(18)	(48)
High	3.	1.7	10.7
		(1)	(12)
			r = .20**

Note: **p < .01

and Caucasians have different motives for playing basketball (African Americans are more likely to play for nearly all of the reasons investigated); and, as individuals, African Americans are more oriented toward a future in sport. Do these findings hold, however, by school context? As stated earlier, private school and public school black students come from different social worlds. Public school students tend to come from families that are less well off, economically. It is possible that, for them, sport is an especially attractive career goal.

School Context

Rather than present detailed percentage tables for all of the items by the two school contexts, Table 6 summarizes the findings by reporting the r's for black/Caucasian differences. It also includes a column reporting whether the public or private context, within race groups, is where there is the highest endorsement for an item. Table 6 compares African Americans in private schools to African Americans in public schools, and Caucasians in private schools to Caucasians in public schools. Instead of reporting r's for the public/private comparison within race groups, Table 6 indicates by the abbreviation of PUB or PRV where one school context is markedly higher than the other at the .05 level in the comparisons.

TABLE 6

Race Differences in Orientations toward Basketball: Black/White Differences within School Contexts and School Context Differences within Race Groups

| | Black/White Differences | | | Pub/Prv Differences | |
Orientations	All	Public	Private	Whites	Blacks
Mobility	.02	.07	−.07		
Enjoy	−.12	−.13	−.12		
Team	.18**	.17*	.18		
Scholarship	.35***	.38***	.28*		
Talent	.20**	.27**	.04		PUB
College	.29***	.37***	.13		PUB
Control	.20**	.27***	.07		PUB
Release	−.02	−.02	−.02		
Pro-future	.20**	.21*	.15		PUB

Note: *p < .05; **p < .01; ***p < .001.

Table 6 has five columns. The first reports the r's for the African American/Caucasian differences already observed and reported. The next two columns report the r's for African American/Caucasian differences separately for public and private school contexts. The last two columns indicate whether there is a marked difference within the race groups for the two school contexts.

As Table 6 indicates, there is no school context effect on the question of mobility. In both contexts African Americans and Caucasians have similar views of sport as a mobility channel for African Americans.

Examining the student-athletes' motives for playing basketball, with the exception of playing to get a college scholarship, the finding that African Americans have different reasons for playing than Caucasians is true mainly in the public school context. African Americans are more likely to report they play basketball because they hope to get a college scholarship in both the public and private school context. However, in public schools they are more likely than Caucasians to say they: (1) plan to play in college, (2) play to show their talent, (3) play to control their emotions, and (4) play because they learn to work toward team goals. It is also only in public schools that the findings indicate a significant race difference in orientations toward a professional future in sport. Turning to the public/private difference within race groups, there are no differences at all for Caucasians. But for African Americans, those in public schools are distinctive on three of the seven items and in their future orientations; they play basketball to show their talent, because they plan to play in college, and because it helps them to control their emotions. That is, African Americans in public schools are not only different from Caucasians on motives for playing basketball and their future orientations, they are also different from private school African Americans in these areas.

Family Factors

Race differences were revealed in several of the above motives, especially for African Americans in public schools. Are the race differences linked to family background factors? As indicated in the overview section, African Americans are more likely than Caucasians to come from father-absent and lower SES families. A concern is whether or not these differences are important in illuminating the patterns of African American distinctiveness in orientations toward sport.

Table 7 presents the Pearson r's for all of the variables examined in this chapter and the partial r's when controlling for the following fam-

TABLE 7
Race Differences (Pearson's r's) in Orientations toward Basketball
by School Context: Controlling for Family Factors (Partial r's)

Orientations	School Context	r	Family Factors		
	PUBLIC		FA	FED	MED
Mobility		.07	.03	.07	.06
Enjoy		−.13	−.05	−.09	−.08
Team		.17*	.12	.12	.14
Scholarship		.38***	.26**	.34***	.37***
Talent		.27**	.19*	.23**	.25***
College		.37***	.26**	.33***	.37***
Control		.27**	.19*	.23***	.23**
Release		−.02	−.02	−.02	−.00
Pro-future		.21*	.09	.20*	.20*
	PRIVATE				
Mobility		−.07	−.12	−.05	−.06
Enjoy		−.12	−.16	−.07	−.12
Team		.18	.14	.14	.19
Scholarship		.28*	.28*	.20	.29*
Talent		.04	.04	.02	.04
College		.13	.15	.12	.13
Control		.07	.06	.09	.07
Release		−.02	.00	−.01	−.02
Pro-future		.15	.18	.03	.16

Note: *p < .05; **p < .01 ; ***p < .001.

ily factors: father-absence, father's education and mother's education. Most of the differences between African Americans and Caucasians appear in the public school context. The partial r's for the three family factors suggest a pattern similar to the previous one. These control variables have altered the relationships between the independent and dependent variables only slightly, in most cases, and certainly not enough to revise the findings on African American distinctiveness. The differences found between African Americans and Caucasians do not appear to be due to differences in family background.

A similar pattern is found when examining the private school context. Stratifying by family factors results in little change in the relationships. These findings suggest that family background has little or no effect on the distinctiveness orientations of Caucasian and African American student-athletes toward playing basketball.

To summarize, the majority of African Americans and Caucasians see sport as the best mobility route for African Americans, regardless of the type of school they attend. African American and Caucasian student-athletes have different motives for playing basketball. African Americans, especially public school African Americans, play for instrumental and future oriented reasons. Family background factors do not explain the differences in the orientations of African American and Caucasian student-athletes toward playing basketball.

Conclusions

The findings of this investigation indicate that race differences exist in the future orientation of African American and Caucasian student-athletes. There are race differences in the reasons they play basketball; African Americans more frequently expect a payoff in terms of a college scholarship or a professional career. This study also indicates that student-athletes view sport as a route to social mobility for African Americans. While this finding is interesting, what is striking is that both African American and Caucasian student-athletes perceive sport to be the *best* means to attaining social mobility for African Americans. Sport is expected to be a more reliable path to a better future for African Americans than education, the acquisition of vocational skills, the development of entrepreneurial skills, and so forth. This finding may be due, in part, to the high visibility of professional athletes (and other entertainers) as examples of success, while other successful African Americans are less visible—if not invisible—(Edwards, 1979) and to the perception that sport is an institution relatively open to African Americans at a time when there are barriers to achievement in other societal institutions (Harris and Hunt, 1982).

While the hypothesis about perceived barriers to achievement in nonentertainment endeavors may help to explain the channeling of African Americans into sport from the perspective of African American males, it is important to note that African American males are not the only ones who believe that black males' fortunes lie in sport. Their Caucasian peers are as likely to see sport as the most likely path to upward mobility for African Americans.[1] To what do we attribute this finding?

As most Americans, and especially nonminorities, see America as having a relatively open opportunity structure where attributes such as talent, motivation, education, and aspiration lead to success, it is unlikely that the Caucasian student-athletes perceive societal barriers to African Americans achieving success through conventional means. Perhaps they believe that African Americans are advantaged when it comes to athletic skills (e.g., they are better suited for certain sporting activities) but are disadvantaged in other skill areas. Or maybe the Caucasian student-athletes view sport as a gateway to prosperity for African Americans because they believe African Americans are content to cast their lot with the sporting institution. The important point here is that sport is perceived to be the way to a better life for African American males by themselves and others. Perhaps the argument that African American males self-select themselves into a narrow range of occupational areas needs to be reexamined, not only as a result of the perceptions of their Caucasian peers, but also for insight into the perceptions and influence of significant others inside and outside the black community.

The interest in the effects of sport on African American youth emanates from the ongoing intellectual and political debate over the impact of sport on African American mobility. Does sport, as a vehicle for motivating young African Americans and feeding them into academic programs and future occupations, enhance mobility? Or does it, for the most part, drain African American talent and attention away from more realistic opportunity structures, and thus impede mobility? Is the cultural celebration of African American athletes, on balance, positive or negative for the black community?

I have suggested above that African American student-athletes are more future oriented about sport because of perceived barriers to achievement in other institutions, and expectations of success in the sporting arena. This would seem to indicate that African American student-athletes attempt to bypass conventional paths to mobility and see their futures linked to careers in sport. However, it may be, instead, that African American student-athletes hold traditional views of social mobility—that education is the means to advance one's position. And it is possible that for them the way to obtain a college education is through sport participation. Private school African Americans in this study would, especially, seem to exhibit this pattern. While they are less likely than public school African Americans to aspire to a career in professional sport, they are as likely to play basketball in hopes of being awarded a scholarship. Sport, then, may be viewed as a means to achieving the American dream through conventional means; it provides a bridge to the larger opportunity structure.

This study indicates sport is viewed by some as a "passport to the good life" (Edwards, 1979) for African American males. It does not examine whether sport enhances or impedes social mobility for African American youth. Perhaps future research will examine: the extent to which it contributes to academic and future occupational achievement (it certainly provides needed scholarships); whether it is a misguided priority among African American youth; and whether the emphasis on sport leaves African American student-athletes without skills needed for success.

Notes

I would like to thank Larry L. Hunt, Janet Hunt, John Pease, and the late Morris Rosenberg for their helpful comments on earlier drafts of this article. I am also grateful to the editor of *JAAM* for valuable suggestions and insightful comments. An earlier version of this paper was presented at the 1990 North Central Sociological Association meetings in Louisville, Kentucky.

1. The idea that sport is a means to a better life for African Americans is not confined to high school student-athletes. The Miller Lite Report on American Attitudes toward Sports (Miller Brewing Co., Milwaukee, Wisconsin, 1983), in a study of adults, also found that the majority of African Americans and Caucasians thought sport offered more opportunities for the social advancement of African Americans than other fields.

References

Bend, Emil, and Petrie, Brian M. (1978). "Sport Participation, Scholastic Success, and Social Mobility." *Exercise and Sport Sciences Reviews*, 5: 1–44.

Blackwell, James E. (1975). *The Black Community: Diversity and Unity.* New York: Dodd, Mead and Co.

Boyle, Robert. (1963). *Sport: Mirror of American Life.* Boston: Little, Brown and Co.

Braddock, Jomills H. (1980). "Race, Sports, and Social Mobility: A Critical Review." *Sociological Symposium*, 30 (Spring): 18–38.

Coakley, Jay J. (1996). *Sport in Society.* St. Louis: Mosby.

Curry, Timothy J., and Jiobu, Robert M. (1984). *Sports: A Social Perspective.* Englewood Cliffs, NJ: Prentice-Hall.

Edwards, Harry. (1976). "Change and Crisis in Modern Sport." *Black Scholar* 8(2): 60–65.

———. (1979). "Sport Within the Veil: The Triumphs, Tragedies and Challenges of Afro-American Involvement." *The Annals of the American Academy of Political and Social Science*, 445 (September): 116–27.

———. (1984). "The Collegiate Athletic Arms Race: Origins and Implications of the 'Rule 48' Controversy." *Journal of Sport and Social Issues*, 8 (Winter/Spring): 4–22.

Eisen, George, and Turner, Diana. (1992). "Myth and Reality: Social Mobility of the American Olympic Athletes." *International Review for the Sociology of Sport*, 27(2): 165–73.

Gaston, John C. (1984). "The Destruction of the Young Black Male: The Impact of Popular Culture and Organized Sports." *Journal of Black Studies*, 16(4): 369–84.

Giddens, Anthony. (1991). *Introduction to Sociology*. New York: W.W. Norton & Company.

Greendorfer, Susan. (1987). "Psycho-social Correlates of Organized Physical Activity." *Journal of Physical Education, Health, Recreation and Dance* (September): 59–64.

Guy, Rebecca F., Edgley, Charles E., Arafat, Ibtihaj, and Allen, Donald E. (1987). *Social Research Methods: Puzzles and Solutions*. Boston: Allyn and Bacon.

Haerle, Rudolph K. (1975). "Education, Athletic Scholarships, and the Occupational Career of the Professional Athlete." *Sociology of Work and Occupations*, 2 (November): 373–403.

Harris, Othello, and Hunt, Larry L. (1982). "Race and Sports: Some Implications of Athletics for Black and White Youth." *Journal Behavioral and Social Sciences*, 28 (Fall): 95–106.

Kane, Martin. (1971). "An Assessment of 'Black is Best.'" *Sports Illustrated* 34 (Jan. 18): 72–83.

Lapchick, Richard. (1984). *Broken Promise*. New York: St. Martin's Press.

Leonard, Wilbert M. II (1997). *A Sociological Perspective of Sport*, 5th ed. Boston: Allyn and Bacon.

Loy, John W. (1968) "The Study of Sport and Social Mobility. " In G. S. Kenyon (Ed.) *Aspects of Contemporary Sport Sociology*, (pp. 101–33). Chicago: The Athletic Institute.

———. (1972). "Social Origins and Occupational Mobility of a Selected Sample of American Athletes." *International Review of Sport Sociology*, 7:5–23.

———. (1976). "The Black Athlete: An Overview and Analysis." In Daniel M. Landers (Ed.), *Social Problems in Athletics*, (pp. 122–50). Urbana: University of Illinois Press.

McPherson, Barry D. (1971). "Minority Group Socialization: An Alternative Explanation for the Segregation by Playing Position Hypothesis." International Symposium on the Sociology of Sport, Waterloo.

Otto, Luther B., and Duane F. Alwin. (1977). "Athletics, Aspirations, and Attainments." *Sociology of Education*, 42 (April): 102–13.

Rehberg, Richard A., and Walter E. Schafer. (1968). "Participation in Interscholastic Athletics and College Expectations." *American Journal of Sociology*, 73 (May): 732–40.

Rosenberg, Morris, and Roberta G. Simmons. (1972). *Black and White Self-Esteem: The Urban School Child*. Rose Monograph Series. Washington, D.C.: American Sociological Association.

Rossides, Daniel W. (1976). *The American Class System*. Boston: Houghton, Mifflin.

Schafer, Walter E., and Rehberg, Richard A. (1970). "Athletic Participation, College Aspirations and College Encouragement." *Pacific Sociological Review* 13 (Summer): 182–86.

Scott, Jack. (1971). *The Athletic Revolution*. New York: Free Press.

Snyder, Eldon E., and Spreitzer, Elmer A. (1983). *Social Aspects of Sport*, 2nd ed. Englewood Cliffs, NJ: Prentice-Hall.

Spreitzer, Elmer A., and Pugh, Meredith. (1973). "Interscholastic Athletics and Educational Expectations." *Sociology of Education*, 46 (Spring): 171–82.

U.S. Bureau of the Census. (1988). *Statistical Abstract of the United States: 1988.* Washington, D.C.: U.S. Government Printing Office.
Wells, Richard H., and Picou, J. Steven. (1980). "Socialization for Educational Achievement." *Journal of Sport Behavior*, 3 (3): 119–28.

16

A Comparison of Professional Sports Career Aspirations Among College Athletes

Gary A. Sailes

The glorification of professional athletes and professional sports in the United States appears to have a powerful effect on American youth, often creating unrealistic expectations about their chances of signing a professional sports contract (Coakley, 1993; Leonard, 1993). Moreover, the chance of a college athlete ever signing a professional sports contract is less than 1% while the average career of the professional athlete is less than four years. By the time professional athletes reach the end of their sports careers, most other individuals may be just starting their careers (Coakley, 1993; Leonard, 1993).

African American males are more likely to have African American professional athletes as role models than their white counterparts. Edwards (1973) and Sailes (1984, 1987) have argued that holding professional athletes as role models has contributed, in part, to the disproportionate representation of African American athletes in the three major professional sports (i.e., football, basketball, and baseball). The high number of successful African-American professional athletes has fueled young athletes' hopes of playing professional sports. Consequently, many African-American males have relied on sports for status and prestige more frequently than their white counterparts. It has been argued that this pattern is a response to institutional racism against African Americans that has limited employment opportunities in other segments of American society (Edwards, 1973; Harris, 1993; Sailes, 1987, 1993). Moreover, success in sports has been a means for African American males to generate self-esteem and self-empowerment (Majors, 1990).

Despite the odds against it, members of the lower or working class are more likely to view sport as a vehicle for social and economic mobility (Oliver, 1980). Perceptions that few opportunities exist through traditional channels have contributed to the development and experiences of this compensatory value system (Rehberg and Cohen, 1975; Sailes, 1987). The majority of African American scholarship student athletes come from lower socioeconomic backgrounds (Coakley, 1993); therefore, it is reasonable to assume that race and class are variable, which influence the sport socialization and value development of African American males. Such socialization and value orientation encourage sport participation for reasons of social status and prestige (Majors, 1990; Sailes, 1984).

Rehberg and Cohen (1975) argue that the singular focus of sports participation to obtain professional sports status has overshadowed the desire for academic achievement, leading to poor academic achievement and low graduation rates. Sailes (1993) cites obsessive coaches and the business mentality of college athletic departments as important factors causing the lack of academic achievement among college student athletes. Telander (1989, 1990a, 1990b, 1992) has noted that Division I college athletics serve as a farm system for professional sports and argues that student athletes should be allowed to pursue professional sports without jeopardizing their college eligibility. College athletics likely serve as the focal point for professional sports recruitment.

By contrast, among high school student athletes, sports contribute to physical, social, and educational development (Harris, 1993; Sabo, 1988). Coakley (1993) and Leonard (1993) found that student athletes performed at higher levels in the classroom than their nonathlete peers. In addition, it was found that high school student athletes believed that participation in high school athletics could possibly deliver educational, social, and life-skill benefits and opportunities that would facilitate the transition to purposeful productivity and full employment later on (Harris, 1993; Oliver, 1980). Moreover, high school athletes had higher aspirations to attend college, and parents took a greater interest in their offspring's socialization, when they were involved in high school sports. The desire to play professional sports was positive because it required participation in the college sports system which exposed the student-athlete to a higher level of scholarship and required academic eligibility (McElroy, 1981). With these considerations in mind, the present study sought to identify those male student athletes most likely to aspire to participate in professional football or basketball.

Method

Participants

Questionnaires were forwarded to athletic academic advisors at 50 NCAA Division I institutions. The advisors were asked to administer the questionnaire to male student athletes participating in basketball and football. A total of 390 student athletes responded to the questionnaire (basketball, $n = 170$; football, $n = 210$). The participants were grouped according to their status on the following variables: family income, race, year in school, grade point average (GPA), and having received an honor for athletic achievement (see Table 1). The return rates for Hispanic ($n = 8$), Pacific Islander ($n = 0$), and Native American ($n = 2$) student athletes were too small to consider for this investigation. The return rates for African American ($n = 217$) and Caucasian ($n = 163$) participants were adequate to conduct a statistical analysis.

Instrumentation and Data Collection

A review of the literature failed to identify an instrument that met the specific needs of this particular investigation; therefore, an instrument was developed to address the questions of interest. The result was a 12-item questionnaire that was forwarded to members of the National Association of Academic Advisors for Athletics (N4A) who were employed at NCAA Division I institutions. A total of 50 schools were randomly selected from the N4A directory. Thirty-one schools responded for a return rate of 62%. It was felt this high return rate would eliminate any subsequent bias which might have existed with a lower return rate. Advisors were instructed to administer the instrument to the student athletes they counseled. Participants were asked to complete the instrument when they showed up for advisement and were informed that their participation was voluntary. At no time was identifying information about the school or participants requested by or provided to the researcher.

Results

The data revealed that approximately half the sample (52%) planned to pursue a career in professional sports after college. Moreover, 95% of respondents chose to attend their college to increase their chances of being drafted into professional football or basketball. However, once on campus, only 44% of the sample felt attending that specific college would increase their chances of being drafted. Half of respondents felt their chances of being drafted were very good. Eighty-three percent indicated they would enter the professional sports draft before graduation if they were drafted early. Only 27% indicated they would return to school at some time in the future to complete their degree if they were drafted before graduation.

Analysis of variance (ANOVA) was used to examine significant differences between groups. The Tukey HSD procedure was employed to locate significant differences on multiple variables within the variable groups labeled *Year in School* and *Family Income*. It was hypothesized that student athletes who received athletic achievement honors or awards would have the best chances of entering professional sports and therefore would have higher aspirations to play professional sports. However, there was no significant difference in the professional sports aspirations of outstanding athletes ($M = 15.4$, $SD = 2.97$) and those student athletes who were not honored for athletic achievement ($M = 15.1$, $SD = 3.20$), $F = 1.16$, $p = .603$. It was also hypothesized that student athletes with the highest professional sports aspirations would not be as serious about their academics and would have lower GPAs than those with lower aspirations. However, this investigation did not reveal a statistically significant difference between student athletes who had an A or B GPA ($M = 12.9$, $SD = 3.92$) and student athletes whose GPA was a C or below ($M = 13.6$, $SD = 3.45$), $F = 1.29$, $p = 1.30$.

Significant differences in professional sports aspirations among student athletes by race, family income, and by year in school were observed. Means and standard deviations are presented in Table 1. African American student athletes had significantly higher professional sports aspirations than their white counter-parts, $F = 1.84$, $p < .001$. Surprisingly, upper-income student athletes had significantly higher professional sports orientations than middle- and lower-income student athletes, $F = 5.90$, $p = .003$. This finding is in direct contrast to what had been hypothesized. Finally, freshmen, junior, and fifth-year senior student-athletes had significantly higher professional sports aspirations than sophomores and seniors, $F = 24.40$, $p < .001$.

Discussion

While the data from this study are preliminary, they provide some insight into the pervasiveness of professional sports aspirations among a

TABLE 1
Comparison of Group Means

Variable	n	X	SD	F	p
Family income					
Upper income	27	15.7	4.18	5.90	.003
Middle income	299	13.2	3.42		
Lower income	54	13.2	3.65		
Race					
African-American	217	13.8	3.94	1.84	.000
Caucasian	163	12.9	2.90		
Year in school					
Freshman	144	14.3	2.80	24.40	.000
Sophomore	72	12.1	2.95		
Junior	82	15.2	2.58		
Senior	64	10.6	3.94		
Fifth year	18	13.5	5.65		
Grade point average					
A or B	81	12.9	3.92	1.29	1.30
C or below	299	13.6	3.45		
Honors					
Yes	45	15.4	2.97	1.16	603
No	335	15.1	3.20		

segment of male student athletes participating in NCAA Division I basketball and football. It was not surprising to find that African American student athletes had significantly higher aspirations toward professional sports than their white counterparts. In examining the participation percentages of African Americans and whites in professional basketball and football, the over-representation of African American professional athletes and their subsequent visibility may encourage African American youth to fantasize more about the possibilities of their participation. Edwards (1973) suggested that perceived institutional racism and discrimination in American society disproportionately channeled African Americans into the areas of entertainment and spores. Moreover, Lapchick (1988) reported that an African American family is seven times more likely to push a male youth into sports than a white family.

Oliver (1980) found that lower-income student athletes were more likely to have higher aspirations than their middle- and upper-income counterparts. Thus, it was surprising to find in the present study that upper-income student athletes had higher aspirations regarding professional sports than middle- and lower-income student athletes. The fact that this investigation had larger African American participation numbers than Caucasians might account for the higher aspirations among the participants from a higher-income background. Table 1 indicates that the largest group was middle-income. It is likely that the number of African Americans is higher in that group. It is possible that undisclosed race dynamics within groups confounded the data and actually supported the contention that race was a factor in professional sports aspiration. Further study is needed to determine the validity of this contention.

It was interesting to note that student athletes who did not distinguish themselves athletically had approximately the same aspirations to play professional sports as those student athletes who did distinguish themselves with athletic honors. Student athletes with little or no chance of playing professional sports—based on the assumption of a positive correlation between athletic honors and professional potential—held the same aspirations as those student athletes who had the most viable chance of playing professional sport. It is reasonable to assume that the appeal of professional sports is very powerful; consequently, the self-evaluation of less successful student athletes is neither realistic nor carefully considered.

Previous research suggests that athletes who trained hardest in order to enter the professional sports draft would be most likely to ignore their academic studies (Harris, 1993; McElroy, 1981; Rehberg & Cohen, 1975). Sailes (1993) asserted that elite student athletes were required to maintain academic eligibility in order to compete to gain exposure to professional sports talent scouts. He found that elite student athletes did little more than major in eligibility. That is, they did not study to receive grades higher than those required to maintain their athletic eligibility, at least a C average. Thus, it was hypothesized that student athletes aspiring to play professional sports would earn lower grades than those not having like aspirations. The results of this investigation failed to support that hypothesis; student athlete performance in the classroom was not related to level of professional sports aspiration. It appears that student athletes earning good grades had aspirations to play professional sports similar to those of their counterparts earning lower grades.

Freshmen, juniors, and fifth-year seniors held higher aspirations to play professional sports in comparison to sophomores and seniors. Follow-up interviews with student athletes at a large midwestern university produced the following analysis. Freshmen student athletes entered college with high aspirations to play professional sports. It is likely they considered their first year on campus as the beginning of the professional sports process. By their sophomore year, still relegated to the practice or reserve squad, the futility of their situation began to appear and their aspiration to play professional sports began to diminish. How ever, it is likely that they started getting more playing time, and established a greater understanding of the dynamics of their sport— possibly becoming starters by their junior year—that would explain an increase in professional sports aspiration during that period. By their senior year, lower aspirations might be the result of the realization of their lesser playing ability compared to the elite class of more talented teammates. Finally, fifth-year seniors' increased professional sports aspiration could emanate from the realization that their talents were commensurate with professional sports opportunities outside the United States or that their skills might provide the opportunity for temporary employment with a professional team during their summer training camp. This scenario is only hypothetical, and it is only one of many plausible explanations to determine the reasons for the differences year in school generated.

Conclusion

While this investigation is far from conclusive, it does illuminate some possibilities regarding the professional sports aspirations among a sample group of college student athletes. Just as the pervasiveness of professional sports cannot be denied, its impact on American youth and our intercollegiate athletes cannot be ignored. The lure of professional sports can have serious consequences for contemporary student athletes who tend to put "all of their eggs into one basket." Currently, approximately one fourth of NBA athletes and one third of NFL athletes have completed their college degrees (Coakley, 1993). When their careers are over in three to four years, many professional athletes will likely have few marketable skills and will be disenfranchised and unemployable in mainstream society. They will exist on the periphery of employment opportunities, unable to compete with their counterparts who have degrees. The attraction of professional sports should be kept in proper perspective. Student athletes should be encouraged to pursue their college degrees and develop marketable skills regardless of their ability. They should be informed that less than 1% of college student athletes ever play professional sports and that the average professional sports career lasts only four years.

Student athletes who distinguish themselves athletically should not be discouraged from pursuing professional athletics after college. If any group of aspiring athletes has the greatest potential for signing a professional sports contract, it is this group. However, they should be counseled to complete the degree to counter the hardships that might occur due to career-ending injuries. In addition, regardless of their athletic talent, there are many athletes with equal or more ability. The competition for few positions in professional sport makes having alternative plans very important and crucial to future success in the job market.

The average career of the typical professional athlete is only four years. The typical professional athlete is 25 years old when his professional sports career ends. However, his youth, inexperience, and lack of practical work experience will place him at the bottom in the group of new entrants into the work force. Today's athletic academic advisor would be well advised to inform his or her male student athletes that common sense dictates a more sober approach when considering post-college careers. One cannot continue to put all of one's eggs in a single basket when dealing with an industry that is as business-oriented as professional sports and treats its employees as replaceable parts. Advisors should also assist and encourage student athletes to explore ways in which skills developed in athletics transfer to other work settings. Doing so helps student athletes to prepare for post-athletic life while valuing and respecting the importance of their athletic experiences and aspirations. Maintaining minimum eligibility standards and majoring in eligibility to get a shot at professional sports simply is not smart. Specific goal setting and counseling led by common sense are the best guarantees for today's college student athlete to be successful in a highly competitive and technically oriented job market.

References

Coakley, J. (1993). *Sport in Society: Issues and Controversies.* St. Louis: Mosby Publishers

Edwards, H. (1973). *Sociology of Sport.* Homewood, IL: Dorsey Press.

Harris, L. (1993). *The 1993 Lou Harris Study on High School Athletics.* Boston: Northeastern University Center for the Study of Sport in Society.

Lapchick, R. (1988, November). *Race and Sport in American Culture.* Paper presented at the annual meeting of the North American Society for the Sociology of Sport, Boston.

Leonard, W. (1993). *A Sociological Perspective of Sport.* New York: Macmillan Publishers.

Majors, R. (1990). Cool Pose: Black Masculinity and Sports. In *Sport, Men and the Gender Order: Critical Feminist Perspectives*, edited by M. Messner and D. Sabo. Champaign, Ill.: Human Kinetics, 109–114.

McElroy, M. (1981). "A Comparison of Sport and Nonsport Occupational Aspirations Among Disadvantaged Youth." *Journal of Sport Psychology,* 3(1), 58–68.

Oliver, M. (1980). "Race, Class, and the Family's Orientation to Mobility through Sport." *Sociological Symposium,* 2, 62–85.

Rehberg, R., and Cohen, M. (1975). "Athletes and Scholars: An Analysis of the Compositional Characteristics and Images of These Two Youth Cultures and Categories." *International Review of Sport Sociology,* 10, 91–106.

Sabo, D. (1988). *Report on Minority Sports Participation.* New York: Women's Sports Foundation.

Sailes, G. (1993). "An Investigation of Academic Accountability Among College Student-Athletes." *Academic Atlantic Journal,* Spring, 27–39.

———. (1987). "A Socio-economic Explanation of Black Sports Participation Patterns." *Western Journal of Black Studies,* 11, 164–167.

———. (1984). *Sport Socialization Comparisons Among Black and White Adult Male Athletes and Nonathletes.* Unpublished doctoral dissertation, University of Minnesota, Minneapolis.

Telander, R. (1992, May 4). "Youth has been Served: The NFL has been Tapping Underclassmen, and the Results have been Mostly for the Good." *Sports Illustrated,* 76, 78.

———. (1990a, April 23). "Their Moment has Come: Letting College Juniors into the NFL Draft was Overdue. *Sports Illustrated,* 72, 96.

———. (1990b, November 12). "Relaxing the Ties that Bind: At Last, Collegians May be able to Test the Pro Waters." *Sports Illustrated,* 73, 94.

———. (1989, October 2). "Something Must Be Done." *Sports Illustrated,* 71, 92–113.

Contributors

Ronald Althouse currently teaches in the School of Physical Education at West Virginia University, Morgantown.

Vernon L. Andrews is currently an assistant professor conducting research at the University of Canterbury in Christchurch, New Zealand.

Dana D. Brooks currently serves as dean of the School of Physical Education at West Virginia University, Morgantown.

Mikaela Dufur is a doctoral student in the Department of Sociology at The Ohio State University.

Vinay Harpalani is a student at the University of Delaware, studying integrative human sciences.

Othello Harris is with the Departments of Physical Education, Health and Sport Studies, and Black World Studies at Miami University.

C. Keith Harrison is assistant professor of kinesiology, sport, and physical education at Washington State University.

Billy Hawkins is a faculty member in the Department of Physical Education at the University of Georgia, Athens.

David W. Hunter is chair of the Department of Health, Physical Education, and Recreation and director of the exercise physiology laboratory at Hampton University.

Richard Majors is deputy editor and founder of the Journal of African American Men. He is the co-editor of *The American Black Male: His Present Status and Future.*

Gary A. Sailes teaches in the Department of Kinesiology at Indiana University, Bloomington, and is editor of the *Journal of African American Men.*

Earl Smith is Debbie and Mike Rubin Professor of American Ethnic Studies, Professor of Sociology, and director of American Ethnic Studies at Wake Forest University.

Delano Tucker currently teaches in the Department of Physical Education at Wayne State University, Detroit.

Christopher P. Uchachz is a member of the Department of Kinesiology at the University of Illinois, Urbana-Champaign.